Rhetorical Philosophy and Theory
Series Editor, David Blakesley

Defining Reality

Defining Reality

Definitions and the Politics of Meaning

Edward Schiappa

Southern Illinois University Press
Carbondale and Edwardsville

Library of Congress Cataloging-in-Publication Data

Schiappa, Edward, 1954–
    Defining reality : definitions and the politics of meaning / Edward Schiappa.
        p. cm. — (Rhetorical philosophy and theory)
    Includes bibliographical references and index.
    1. Definition (Logic). I. Title. II. Series.
    BC199.D4 S38 2003
    160—dc21
    ISBN 0-8093-2500-4 (alk. paper)
    ISBN 0-8093-2501-2 (pbk. : alk. paper)   2002008489

The paper used in this publication meets the minimum requirements of
American National Standard for Information Sciences—Permanence
of Paper for Printed Library Materials, ANSI Z39.48-1992. ♾

For Liz and Lauren

Contents

Preface

Is Pluto really a planet? Are people who strap explosives to themselves suicide bombers, terrorists, martyrs, or freedom fighters? Was former president Bill Clinton lying when he claimed he did not have "sexual relations" with Monica Lewinsky? The preceding questions obviously involve disputes over definitions. Even though the first question is concerned with a definitional controversy among scientists and the second and third among politicians and lawyers, I argue in this book that the process of answering such questions is quite similar. Instead of posing the questions in the time-honored manner of "What is X?" (in these cases, "What is a planet?," "What is a terrorist?," or "What are sexual relations?"), I suggest that we reformulate the matter as "How *ought* we use the word X?" given our particular reasons for defining X. Specifically, I advocate that we think of one appropriate form of definition as "X counts as Y in context C."

Although much of this book concerns how we talk about particular definitions, it is more broadly about what I call *definitive discourse*—discourse that defines, whether in an explicit discourse *about* a definition, discourse that argues *from* a particular definition, or discourse that stipulates a view of reality via an argument *by* definition. The book collects my longstanding efforts to understand definitive discourse. It represents a synthesis of the theories that describe all discourse as suasive, as well as analyses of illustrative case studies compiled over the years—beginning in the Reagan era and ending with a Supreme Court decision announced in the spring of 2001. By the end of the book, I hope to encourage the reader to consider the possibility that in an important sense, almost *all* discourse is definitive discourse. That is, all discourse contributes to what can be described loosely as the social construction of reality.

But what does "social constructionism" mean? As Ian Hacking's useful book *The Social Construction of What?* illustrates, that label has been stretched in so many directions that it is important to identify the point of using such a label. All that I contend in this book is that definitions, because they are linguistic propositions, unavoidably depend on social interaction. Definitions can be usefully thought of as human-made "ideas" we have about the "objects" of our world that we share for various social purposes (Hacking 1999, 22). To use John Searle's distinction (1969), definitions are institutional, not brute, facts. Although the arguments developed in this book require a version of social constructionism to get off the ground, the various debates concerning realism do not have to be resolved once and for all prior to the claims I want to make about definitional disputes. Just about everyone would agree with what Searle describes as the first premise of realism, that is, the belief that "reality" exists independently of our representations of it (1995, 150). I take this to mean merely that there is an extra-human world that would continue to exist even if all humans perished overnight. But that is about as far as I am willing to go with Searle's account. Where we part company is when we start to talk about language and its "relationship" to the extra-human world. On such matters, I want to stress the contingency of our language use and argue that no definition is inevitable. Those commitments led me to write this book in the key of Thomas S. Kuhn and Richard Rorty, and that is enough for most folks to classify me as a social constructionist (cf. Hacking 1999, 99).

To return, momentarily, to Searle's distinction between institutional and brute facts, I am aware of those who argue that his distinction is important. Facts concerning what counts as a "strike" or "ball" in baseball, or what counts as "money" or "marriage," obviously depend on human-made institutions and would not exist without them, while facts about "giraffes" or "water" are supposedly "brute" facts because they are about things we believe would exist even if all humans vanished. I think the analysis of definitions is a useful way to explore and to begin to deconstruct the institutional/brute fact distinction because it quickly becomes apparent than no matter *what* we are trying to define, our definitions are linguistic propositions and as such are unavoidably historically situated and dependent upon social interaction if they are to be entitled to any standing at all. The beliefs that inform definitions are human beliefs that are always subject to revision, whether the definition is one advanced by a philosopher, a scientist, an attorney, a legislator, a political activist, or anyone else.

There are, as Rorty points out, "millions of ways of describing the piece of space time occupied by what we call a giraffe." Our descriptions or definitions of a giraffe are precisely that—ours—and would not be the same as, say, "a language-using ant or amoeba, or a space voyager." We define and describe as we do "because of our needs and interests," not because there is some correct way that the giraffe "really is" (1999, xxvi). I share Rorty's belief that we can do without the metaphysical view of the world that underlies Searle's notion of brute facts and related notions like "natural kinds." Indeed, much of this book is devoted to exploring the implications of the anti-essentialism and anti-representationalism that characterizes contemporary pragmatism.

Finally, a few comments are in order about the limitations of this project. Recognition of the key role that definitions play in argumentative disputes can be traced back to *stasis* theory of the ancient Greeks (Dieter 1994). Despite my fondness for classical Greek thought, I decided that it was neither necessary nor particularly helpful to limit my analysis to the sort of approach stasis theory advocates. I hope that fans of stasis theory will forgive this omission in return for a promise that this is an issue to which I plan to return.

This book draws from a diverse body of literature for its arguments—from philosophy to classical philology, from constitutional law to cognitive psychology. In venturing into so broad an intellectual terrain, I am quite certain that in the pages that follow I stumble from time to time. Also, there was no practical way to integrate everything I want to say about definitions with the burgeoning scholarly literature on category formation, classification, and concepts (see, for example, Bowker and Star 1999; Fodor 1998; Johnstone 1978; Lakoff 1987; Senft 2000). Although I obviously draw from philosophical writings concerning language and definitions, my interests are quite different from those of most contemporary analytic philosophers. It would take a book many times the length of this one to engage all the possible interlocutors interested in the nuanced debates over the precise logical status of definitional statements or over which qualified version of realism is best (see, for example, Hacking 1999; Fetzer, Shatz, and Schlesinger 1991; Matthews 1998). I also have made no effort to integrate all of the potentially relevant work of various continental postmodern philosophers, especially Foucault, though I try to provide a few nods in the appropriate direction. My only excuse for this omission is that I have not yet found a good way to integrate my own political and humanistic leanings with such writings. I am, at least, not alone on this matter (Fraser 1989, Best and Kellner 1991). Obvi-

ously, it is not surprising in a book that argues language is never neutral that my own political preferences will become evident to the reader.

Despite these potential limitations, it is my hope that I have produced
an argument worthy of consideration about how those of us engaged
in definitional controversies might do so more productively. If anyone
reading this book is more conservative than I, both politically and theoretically, and can write a good defense of a realist approach to definitions, I invite her or him to do so as a useful counterpart to this book.

Acknowledgments

My interest in definitions began when I was a novice high school debater grappling with the possible meanings of the national debate topic. For those unfamiliar with competitive interscholastic debate, the team affirming the resolution is expected to provide an interpretation that is "topical"; that is, the debaters cannot talk about matters wholly irrelevant to the resolution but must advance a case that "fits" or "falls under" the scope of the resolution. How does one defend or attack the idea that the affirming team has a "topical" case? Through the strategic use of definitions, sometimes aided by a creative approach to grammar. Accordingly, years later when I was a college debater and the national topic involved a federal "land use" policy, debaters from around the nation found ways to advocate everything from bail bond reform to legalizing marijuana to protecting the ozone layer. Much of what I now believe about definitions and the process of defining was shaped by the twenty-plus years I spent as a debater or debate coach, so to all my friends and foes from my debate days, I offer my thanks for the frustration and the fun.

Many people have assisted me in the process of writing this book. Sincere thanks go to representatives of the National Wildlife Association and the Environmental Protection Agency for their help with my research on wetlands and to attorney Louis Sirkin for agreeing to be interviewed about the Mapplethorpe obscenity trial. I am deeply appreciative to all my colleagues here at the University of Minnesota for their support and friendship. Portions of this book were written while I taught at Purdue University. I am thankful for the supportive colleagues I found there, and in particular I want to thank Paaige Turner and Robin Clair for their consistent enthusiasm for this project over the years. Special thanks go to Omar Swartz and Bob Hinrichs for the research assistance. Many thanks also go to Peter B. Gregg for preparing the index. I thank all the various audiences who have responded to presentations based on this project throughout much of the 1990s, and a special thanks go to Karlyn Kohrs Campbell, Alan G. Gross, Robert L. Scott, Douglas N. Walton, and David Zarefsky for providing feedback to the penultimate draft of this book.

Portions of this book have appeared previously. A part of chapter 3 first appeared as "Arguing about Definitions" in *Argumentation* 7 (1993): 403–17. An earlier version of chapter 5 appeared as "Toward a Pragmatic Approach to Definition: 'Wetlands' and the Politics of Meaning" in *Environmental Pragmatism,* edited by Andrew Light and Eric Katz (London: Routledge, 1996), 209–30. An earlier version of chapter 6 appeared as "Analyzing Argumentative Discourse from a Rhetorical Perspective: Defining 'Person' and 'Human Life' in Constitutional Disputes over Abortion" in *Argumentation* 14 (2000): 315–32. Chapter 9 is derived largely, with some revision, from "The Rhetoric of Nukespeak," *Communication Monographs* 56 (1989): 253–72. Finally, the analysis of *PGA Tour, Inc. v. Martin* in chapter 10 first appeared in "What Is Golf?: Pragmatic Essentializing and Definitional Argument in *PGA Tour, Inc. v. Martin," Argumentation and Advocacy* 38 (2001): 18–27, and is used with the permission of the American Forensic Association. Thanks to the National Communication Association, the American Forensic Association, Routledge, and Kluwer Academic Publishers.

I wish to thank Dean Steven Rosenstone at the University of Minnesota for awarding me the Paul W. Frenzel Chair of Liberal Arts. Without the time afforded by this chair, this book might never have seen the light of day. Finally, thanks go to my family for the love, support, and patience that we writers all need and sometimes deserve, but for which we rarely do enough to show our appreciation.

Part One

Introductory Matters

1
Definitions Matter

Definitions Constitute Rhetorically Induced Social Knowledge

The primary thesis of this book is that definitional disputes should be treated less as philosophical or scientific questions of "is" and more as sociopolitical and pragmatic questions of "ought." I am not advocating the abandonment of the legitimate factual or empirical matters that acts of defining involve, but I am advocating greater emphasis on the ethical and normative ramifications of the act of defining. It is my belief that many important problems that people face in a variety of roles—as citizens, family members, employees and employers, scholars, among others—might be faced more squarely and productively if they approached definition as constituting rhetorically induced social knowledge. Definitions put into practice a special sort of social knowledge—a shared understanding among people about themselves, the objects of their world, and how they ought to use language. Such social knowledge typically takes the form of an explicit and often "authoritative" articulation of what particular words mean and how they should be used to refer to reality. Describing definitions as "rhetorically induced" calls attention to the persuasive processes that definitions inevitably involve. Not all definitions are accepted and used. A major tenet of this book is that the difference between those definitions that are accepted and used and those that are not is a matter of persuasion; hence, many arguments concerning definitions are open to rhetorical analysis (Chesebro 1985).

Precisely what I mean by "rhetorical analysis" will become clear as the book progresses, but two points of explanation may be helpful at the outset. First, rhetorical analysis typically focuses on persuasion conducted through symbolic means. The word "rhetoric" comes from the Greek *rhêtorikê*, which originally referred to the art or skill of a *rhêtôr*— an experienced public speaker. Believing that such skills could be analyzed and better understood, Aristotle defined rhetoric as "an ability, in each [particular] case, to see the available means of persuasion" (Kennedy 1991, 36). Today the term rhetoric is used to designate two different sorts of practices: specific acts of persuasion, such as a public oration, as well as the analysis of such acts. As historian and rhetorical critic David Zarefsky puts it, "Rhetoric may be taken to be the study of the process of public persuasion. It is the study of how symbols influence people" (1986, 5). In the context of this book, rhetoric is meant in this second sense, although the persuasive processes that definitions involve take place in private as well as public settings. A rhetorical analysis of definition, then, investigates how people persuade other people to adopt and use certain definitions to the exclusion of others.

Second, a rhetorical analysis is not at odds with a philosophical analysis. In fact, rhetorical analysis is an important part of what has been described as a return to "practical philosophy." Stephen Toulmin has offered an eloquent argument for a return to practical philosophy that engages contemporary social concerns. Specifically, he suggests that the line between politics and philosophy is no longer helpful in an age when "matters of practice" are literally "matters of life and death" (1988, 343). Part of Toulmin's turn to practical philosophy is motivated by a rejection of the Platonic goal of absolute certainty resulting from "geometrical" reasoning and by his belief that philosophers need to return to the study of persuasive argumentation (1958). Toulmin notes that contemporary philosophers "are increasingly drawn into public debates about environmental policy, medical ethics, judicial practice, or nuclear politics. . . . These practical debates are no longer 'applied philosophy': they are philosophy itself" (1988, 345).

Accordingly, in this book I set forth a series of theoretical propositions about language, meaning, definition, and reality, illustrated with a series of case studies. I have done so in the belief that certain ideas that often are dubbed "philosophical" have important consequences for how we live our lives. Although the link between philosophizing—talking about topics such as "meaning" and "truth"—and the pragmatic question of how we ought to live is as old as Socrates (if not older), we typically proceed as if the link is only relevant to a very few special people, such as Gandhi, Marx, or Martin Luther King. As Toulmin implies, some topics addressed by professional philosophers are relevant to all of us. We all think and act with a set of beliefs about what the world is like, what is ethical, and how language works. In this sense, we are all guided by assumptions that one potentially can articulate and examine. This book is motivated, in part, by the belief that it is time to take many important ideas that are well known among professional philosophers of language in order to identify those that can inform and enhance the discussion of pressing definitional issues. As Toulmin puts it, "[I]t is time for philosophers to come out of their self-imposed isolation and reenter the collective world of practical life and shared human problems" (1988, 352).

"Definitional Ruptures" Deserve Investigation

The study of definition has a long and distinguished past. For readers interested in the history of the many attempts to describe and define "definition," I recommend Richard Robinson's concise book *Definition* (1950). I do not intend to chart that complicated history or to provide a comprehensive account of previous philosophical investigations into such matters as meaning and reference, although I selectively draw from such literature where it is relevant. For the purposes of this book, the prototypical formal definition is a standard dictionary definition. Other typical examples are legal definitions, such as those found in *Black's Law Dictionary*, which culls definitions from statutes and court rulings, or definitions set forth in scholarly publications. Ostensive definitions, discussed later in this book, are *informal* definitions that involve little more than pointing to something and labeling it.

Definitions are traditionally regarded as involving strictly factual propositions. It used to be quite common to believe that questions of fact are very different from questions of value. The separation of fact and value has relied on various metaphysical distinctions, such as the theory that facts involve objective reality and values reflect subjective human preferences. Most philosophers have abandoned many of the metaphysical distinctions used to separate facts and values, but most people, including highly trained scholars, continue to assume that matters involving "is" and "ought" are so distinct that they require very different ways of thinking and arguing about them. My objective in this book is to show that definitions can be understood more productively as involving claims of "ought" rather than "is" and then to demonstrate that a pragmatic approach to definition further bridges the gap between facts and values. Before arguing these points, however, a firmer grasp of how definitional disputes are usually understood is needed.

Definitions typically are treated as reporting one of two kinds of fact. What often have been called "real" definitions are attempts to describe what something "really is." When someone asks what piety is, or "What is piety?," that person typically wants to know more about the phenomenon to which people are referring when they say "piety." Indeed, most questions of the form "What is X?" are asking not "How do we use the word X?" but instead are asking what X *is* in reality.[1] This sort of definitional fact can be called a *fact of essence.*

The earliest recorded examples of questions involving facts of essence, at least in Western history, are described in the fourth-century BCE writings of Plato and Xenophon. Both sources tell us that Socrates used to pose the question *ti esti*—What is it?—with respect to a variety of topics. Many of the early Platonic dialogues are organized around questions of the form "What is X?" The dialogue *Gorgias* begins by asking "What is rhetoric?"; *Euthyphro* asks "What is piety?"; *Theaetetus* asks "What is knowledge?"; and so forth. In each instance, Plato is not asking simply how people use the term X; he wants to know what X *really is*—what its "essence" or true nature is. Plato believed that one did not really know what something is unless one could give a *logos* or account of it. So when Socrates' line of questioning led persons into contradicting themselves, as often happened in Plato's dialogues, the implication is that those people did not know the true account or correct definition of X.

Occasionally, Plato portrayed Socrates as providing an authoritative account of various "things." In the dialogue *Gorgias,* for example, Socrates does, in fact, give a working definition of "rhetoric." Similarly, Xenophon's account in *Memorabilia* of Socrates' discussions involving "What is X?" questions implies that Socrates sometimes offered answers of his own (§4.6 in Marchant 1923, 332–47). For the purposes of this book, anytime someone posits a question of the form "What is X?" or attempts to offer a definition based on what he or she believes X really or truly is, the result is an effort toward a fact of essence, or what also is called a "real" definition.

The second kind of definitional fact can be described as a *fact of usage.* When someone asks what a particular word means, typically she or he is asking how people use the word. This sort of definition is called a lexical definition, and it is the sort of definition found in a dictionary.

As many philosophers have pointed out, when someone asks what a word means, we answer using other words. We rarely answer by pointing to the object or event to which the word refers; instead, we usually define one word by suggesting other words that can be used more or less interchangeably with the word being defined. How people actually use a word is, in principle, an empirical question. For example, if someone asks, "What does 'bachelor' mean?," one might answer, "An unmarried man." It is demonstrably false to say that most people use the word "bachelor" to describe a particular color, while it is demonstrably true that people use the word to describe some unmarried men. Dictionaries purport to record the most common way words are used; thus, what a given word means is a question of fact, in this case a fact of usage.

Most people, when they talk about definitions, do not automatically think about the difference between facts of essence and facts of usage; they assume the two amount to the same thing. That is, people use "bachelor" to describe unmarried men because, after all, that is what bachelors really are, right? I will call the often unspoken and unexamined belief that definitions unproblematically refer both to the *nature of X* and to *how the word X is used* the "natural attitude" toward definition. I borrow the phrase "natural attitude" from Alfred Schutz and Thomas Luckmann, who describe the natural attitude as the belief that the objects of our world (including language) are simply "there" and can be taken for granted. Schutz and Luckmann believe that the natural attitude is the ordinary state of affairs in human existence. Likewise, I believe that normally we take the status of definitions for granted. As philosopher Douglas N. Walton observes, "[P]opular opinions tend to take certain assumptions about definitions for granted, without reflecting on them too deeply. It is taken for granted that words, especially scientific terms and terms used in legal statutes and government regulations, have an objective meaning." Accordingly, "[I]t is often assumed that when there are verbal disputes about the definitions of words, that such disputes are relatively trivial, and can easily be resolved" (2001, 122). Except for periods of what I call *definitional ruptures,* we normally get by just fine assuming that definitions are "out there," specifically in dictionaries, and that dictionaries are reliable guides to the nature of the things they define.

Before I argue what I think is faulty about treating definitions as propositions of fact, it may be useful to identify some of the implications of the concepts discussed so far. First of all, although the natural attitude elides the distinction between facts of essence and facts of usage, the two sorts of facts are derived from incompatible theories of definition. For example, Plato believed that most people of his time were ignorant about the true nature of reality. In his famous *Republic,* he describes people as living their lives in caves, thinking that the shadows on the wall are "real." It is the philosopher's task, Plato believed, to pull people out of the cave and force them to see things the way they really are. For Plato, then, common usage of word X was in no way a reliable guide to the true nature of X. Similarly, anyone who seriously believes that he or she can provide a real definition has no need of a lexical definition. If you know what X really is, then it does not matter what other people say it is.

If, on the other hand, one consciously accepts a lexical approach to definition, then someone's claim that the dominant usage of a word is not what it "really" means will fall on deaf ears. That is, if you believe that the meaning of a word X is what the dictionary tells you it is, then someone claiming that the dictionary is wrong and that she or he knows what X really is will probably sound somewhat strange.

Even though the natural attitude combines two incompatible theories of definition, most of the time we never notice the incompatibility. The reason is that we rarely experience definitional ruptures. At most, we have a temporary definitional "gap": we hear an unfamiliar word, we look it up in a dictionary, and that settles the matter. We assume that we are now clued into both how the word X is used and what sort of thing or event X is. Or, let us say we hear a familiar word used in an unfamiliar way. A friend of mine refers to a haircut as a "shingle." Is such a usage correct? Does my friend really know what in the world a shingle *is?* Again we might consult some sort of definitional authority to settle the matter. It turns out that a dictionary indicates that "shingle" can mean either an item used in building construction or a close-cropped haircut. So I conclude that my friend is *using* the word correctly (if arcanely) and indeed knows what a shingle *is.*

The difference between a definitional gap and a definitional rupture can be described as follows: A gap can be resolved without the process of defining itself becoming an issue; not so with a rupture. Up to this point, the definitional disputes I have been describing have been fairly simple and straightforward. Those involved in a definitional gap have been portrayed as having a simple and obvious recourse—that of consulting a dictionary. That this is the way we settle the vast majority of our questions and disputes over definitions probably needs no proof other than reference to the reader's own experience.

But it is easy to imagine situations in which someone might challenge the definition found in a dictionary. Let us say that I hear my students referring to a song they obviously are enjoying, and they say, "That song is really *bad.*" I object to their use of the word "bad" by pointing to the dictionary definition of "bad" and arguing that they obviously are not using the word correctly. My students are likely to point out to me that what *they* mean by "bad" in this context may not be what the dictionary defines as "bad" but that they understand each other and agree on its usage. They may even try to explain their usage such that I figure out that when they say "bad," they mean "good." Even this rather hackneyed example is sufficient to point out that resolving certain kinds of definitional disputes, which I call ruptures, requires that we address the issue of how words are defined. The students reject the definition found in the dictionary as irrelevant to their usage. The natural attitude has been disrupted because the assumption that dominant usage as recorded in dictionaries corresponds to what things *are* has been called into question in such a way that the participants in the conversation have to reconcile the difference. They might do so by employing a fact of essence: "That is not what bad *is.*" Or they may do so by claiming a fact of usage: "That is not how we use 'bad'." In either case, the taken-for-granted status of dictionary definitions has been challenged, and the participants are required to employ a theory of definition, self-consciously or not, to close the rupture.

Rather than rely on an example that some might dismiss as merely slang, consider a definitional dispute in a scholarly setting. Some years ago, a noted scholar in communication studies suggested that the word "argument" should be defined in a broad way in college argumentation classes. Not long after, another scholar claimed that the first scholar had failed to distinguish between two senses of "argument," $argument_1$ as a discrete product of discourse ("She wrote an airtight argument") and $argument_2$ as an interactive process ("We had a fierce argument that lasted for hours"). Since that time, other argumentation scholars have suggested other definitions of "argument," including an $argument_0$ and an $argument_3$. These scholars, if asked, no doubt would suggest that standard dictionary definitions of the word "argument" are irrelevant. The natural attitude is ruptured as soon as these scholars defend their respective definitions as better than the alternatives based on one of the two kinds of facts identified previously: they either argue that, as experts, they have superior knowledge of what an argument really *is* (a fact of essence), or they argue that the word "argument" is used differently by experts and teachers of argument than it is by average language users (a fact of usage).

I hope that the reader will grant, at least for the moment, that these two examples of definitional ruptures are fairly typical of what happens when a group of language users reject a standard definition. The reasons given for dismissing, say, a dictionary definition can be grouped as appeals to facts of essence or facts of usage; in the vast majority of cases, they fall into one of those two categories. Even the argument that a dictionary is simply "outdated" is incomplete unless followed by the claim that, hence, the dictionary "doesn't know what X *is*" or "doesn't know how people are using the word *now.*"

I believe that definitional ruptures are widespread and that the traditional conceptual tools for dealing with them are unproductive and incomplete. Controversies over sexism, art and obscenity, "life" and "death," abortion, and sexual harassment, just to name a few, can be understood, in part, as definitional ruptures that can be "mended" more democratically and more productively by augmenting the "factual" approach to definition with a more pragmatic approach. In later sections, I argue that real definitions (facts of essence) are unproductive and that claims about facts of usage are better understood as value (ought) propositions than as fact (is) propositions. The usefulness of such a perspective will have to be judged by the reader. At the very least, even if my claims are rejected, I hope that our understanding of the conundrums of shared meaning will be enhanced by a reappraisal of the ways and means of definition.

2
Language and Definitions:
How We Make Sense of Reality

> The fact is that for many years after starting to talk a child learns new words at the rate of more than 10 per day! Yet little is known about how children do it. Certainly they do not do it by memorizing dictionary entries. (Miller and Gildea 1987, 94)

To understand how definitions function, it is useful to begin with an overview about how we acquire linguistic skills. Specifically, how do we acquire specific word meanings? How do children learn to use a language? There is widespread agreement that children's ability to acquire a dynamic vocabulary and the basic grammatical structure of their language is remarkable, but there is disagreement about how, precisely, children accomplish such tasks. So-called nativists, inspired initially by the groundbreaking work of Noam Chomsky, believe that language is an innate skill in human beings (1965, 1968). Chomsky has proposed a theoretical construct he calls a *language acquisition device* (LAD) that provides all of us with the biological ability to acquire and use language. The task of linguistic studies is to specify the structure and workings of the LAD. Although the specific language one learns to speak (Chinese or German, for example) may depend on one's upbringing, all languages share a "universal grammar" (UG) that is similar at the level of "deep structure." To draw on an oft-cited metaphor from computer science, all humans have similar "hardware" (the LAD), but because the linguistic "input" or "data" differs from culture to culture, the "output" by individual language users (spoken or written sentences) also will differ. The more we understand about what features all languages have in common (UG), the more can be inferred about the LAD (Crain and Lillo-Martin 1999).

In the age-old dispute about whether human action is a product of biological nature or environmental nurture, the nativist approach emphasizes nature. By contrast, behaviorist approaches to language acquisition emphasize nurture. Verbal behavior is seen as simply one of many forms of behavior that must be learned (Skinner 1957). Language acquisition is not an innate ability but is the result of being encouraged (reinforced) or discouraged (punished) to behave in particular ways. Except for inheriting the physical ability to speak, biology has little to do with language acquisition. Furthermore, behaviorists consider the notions of an unseen LAD and a hypothesized UG highly dubious. Instead, they prefer to focus on how specific groups of language users teach their young to construct sentences, to use new words, and to perform other forms of verbal behavior.

Although both sides have their advocates, it is doubtful that many contemporary linguists would agree with either a purely nativist or a purely behaviorist account of the origins of language acquisition. Cognitivists, for example, accept the importance of one's learning environment but do not view children as passive recipients of external stimuli. Rather, children learn certain skills that they turn around and use to manipulate and to learn about their environment. Furthermore, cognitivists tend to emphasize that children acquire language in recognizable stages that correspond to their overall cognitive development. For example, "[O]ne reason infants do not begin to learn words until the end of their first year is that they do not develop the requisite cognitive abilities until this time," abilities such as adequate memory and attention (Merriman, Schuster, and Hager 1991, 288). It is also hypothesized that children generally do not learn words that refer to objects until they are at a stage at which they understand that objects continue to exist even when they are out of sight (Corrigan 1978). Recognition of "object permanence" is developed during the sensorimotor stage, as described by Piaget. The so-called strict cognition-first viewpoint insists that a child first must develop the need for a word "in his own thinking" and then sets about acquiring appropriate linguistic tools (MacNamara 1972, 5; Nelson 1974). Recent research, however, suggests that there is a complex interaction between language acquisition and cognitive development; sometimes cognitive development precedes linguistic abilities, while other times differences in linguistic input lead to differences in cognitive development (Bowerman 1981, 137–39; 1989; Gopnik and Choi 1990; Rice 1984).

Other researchers stress the importance of social interaction to the process of language acquisition and category formation (Lakoff 1987, 48–50; Wells 1974). Children interact with caretakers long before they acquire specific linguistic skills. What sort of linguistic skills they acquire, the rate at which such skills are acquired, and to what uses they are put are all influenced by the interactions children have with experienced language users. The cognitivist and social interactionist perspectives are somewhat in the middle of the nature/nurture continuum. Both perspectives acknowledge the significance of the interplay between children and their environment and avoid reducing language acquisition to purely innate ability or to a set of responses to stimuli. The cognitivist perspective emphasizes the importance of the child's internal cognitive structures, while the social interactionist stresses the importance of socialization and education.

Apart from matters of emphasis, most linguists would agree on two broadly stated propositions: first, that language acquisition is an important cognitive skill that develops over time; second, that social interaction plays an extremely important role in shaping many of the characteristics of a developing child's language use. Because I am concerned almost exclusively with the task of learning word meanings, I want to turn now from the general question of language acquisition to the more specific problems of acquiring word meanings and definitions. In so doing, I borrow from both the cognitivist and the social interactionist perspectives.

Language as Abstractive

Regardless of the origins of our linguistic skills, one of the most important functions that language performs is to categorize and, thus, to "make sense" of our experiences. Such a function can be described as the abstractive function of language. Such a function is not unique to language, because our central and peripheral nervous systems must "abstract" specific sensations long before we ever learn a language. As psycholinguist Gunter Senft notes, "Biology has shown that classification abilities are necessary for the survival of every organism. Human beings classify consciously, unconsciously and even subconsciously in all situations" (2000, 11). Because it is literally impossible for humans to process all of the sensory input that offers itself at any given moment, our nervous system reduces that input into manageable bits of sensation. As William James put it, "Out of what is in itself an undistinguishable, swarming *continuum,* devoid of distinction or emphasis, our senses make for us, by attending to this motion and ignoring that, a world full of contrasts, of sharp accents, of abrupt changes, of picturesque light and shade" (1981, 274). Our sense organs are "organs of selection" that respond to certain stimuli but not to others (273). We can see only a certain range of light waves and hear only within a particular set of sound frequencies, for example. Even within the range of possible sensations, at any given point in time only some stimuli are "processed" as sensations through the nervous systems. To avoid what is commonly called sensory overload, our nervous system acts as a sort of filter that attends to some stimuli (such as the markings on this page or a sudden pain) and, in effect, ignores the rest. As James put it: "We actually *ignore* most of the things before us" (1981, 273).

Communication scholar Richard B. Gregg points out that the neurophysiological process of abstracting specific sensations from a rich environment of potential stimuli involves categorizing: "It is important to recognize that the patterned activation of sensory neuronal systems is an act of classification. That is, the information in the external environment which is attended to by the human nervous system is 'noticed' in light of certain characteristics that the neuronal structure groups together, establishing relationships among segments of information. . . . Because the patterned firing occurs in response to orders from motor neurons in the brain, an act of abstraction always precedes an act of specification" (Gregg 1984, 30–31). Abstracting sensation from stimuli is a habitual process that typically does not require conscious reflection. We do not think about it; we just do it. But what is it that our brains and sense organs "do"? Much remains unknown about how the human brain processes sensations, and it would take us far afield from the topic of definition to explore what is known. For present purposes, the most important theory is that our sensory-perceptual activity *forms* experiences through a process of abstraction and categorization: "The grouping of discriminably different stimuli into categories on the basis of shared features is an adaptive way of dealing with what would otherwise by an overwhelming array of unique experiences" (Bowerman 1976, 105–6; see also Mervis and Pani 1980, 496–97). Our nervous system "manages" all of the manifold possible sensations and cognitions that one could have into specific experiences identifiable as "seeing a circle," "hearing a noise," "going for a walk," or "reading a book" or describable in answer to questions such as "What has your experience over the past five minutes been like?" From these examples, it should be clear that an experience can be simple or rather complex. Furthermore, because I have represented the previous examples linguistically, it bears emphasizing that it is possible to have experiences that one cannot find adequate words to describe. Spatial and sensorimotor knowledge, for example, is described as "resistant to verbal expression" (Rice 1984, 145). In any event, by "experience" I refer to the constellation of sensations and cognitions that a person *produces* in any given segment of time. I stress the word "produces" because sensations and cognitions must be created by the nervous system. Precisely what the "link" is between "external" stimuli and "internal" sensations, I set aside. The point emphasized here is that human experience is *formed* experience, organized through a continual process of abstraction and categorization (Gregg 1984, 25–51).

Key to the practice of classification is the ability to identify certain sensations as "the same" and others as "different." James describes our perceptual experience as a constant flux: what makes that flux manageable is our ability to segment or compartmentalize specific sensations into categories (1981, 442). Psychologists Carolyn B. Mervis and Eleanor Rosch stipulate that "a category exists whenever two or more distinguishable objects or events are treated equivalently" (1981, 89). Through classification, "the whole rich world of infinite variability shrinks to manipulable size" (Tyler 1969, 7). Philosopher Willard V. O. Quine suggests that we think of physical objects as "postulated entities" that "round out and simplify our account of the flux of experience" (1980, 18). After all, as James argues, no two sensations are exactly the same, since at the very least their location in time and space distinguishes them as "different" sensations. What is the same are the categories that such objects, qualities, relations *count as:* "We hear the same *note* over and over again; we see the same *quality* of green, or smell the same objective perfume, or experience the same *species* of pain" (1981, 225).

James's examples point out that not all of our categories are linguistic. As important as language is, language is not the only way we "think" (for a discussion of the research, see Bowerman 1981, 133–37). At a remarkably early age, infants are able to distinguish the facial expression of "happy" from "surprise" (Caron, Caron, and Myers 1982), a specific female face from female faces in general (Cohen and Strauss 1979), and male from female faces (Fagan 1976) and to discriminate among colors (Bornstein, Kessen, and Weiskopf 1976). Regardless of the question of origins (where such skills "come from"), there is no reason to doubt that preverbal children acquire a set of categories to which, at a later age, they learn to attach specific words: "food," "no," "mama," and so on. One might object that, prior to language acquisition, such categories are largely instinctual and hence do not really "deserve" the label of thought. But if by "thought" we intend to refer to mental operations that allow individuals to have influence over their environment, then the instinct/thought binary is a difference without a distinction: "The power to think things, qualities, relations, or whatever other elements there may be, isolated and abstracted from the total experience in which they appear, is the most indisputable function of our thought" (James 1981, 447). For this reason, many psychologists would insist that "most if not all of our thought" involves categories (Lakoff 1987, xvii).

A study by two linguists documents that nine-month-old infants are able to form a prelinguistic category of "bird" after being shown a series of prototypical exemplars (Roberts and Horowitz 1986). The researchers monitored the infants' eye movements, and by measuring the duration of sustained gazes by which the infants became "habituated" to visual images (familiar images are gazed at for shorter lengths of time than novel ones), they found that infants initially shown good examples of "typical" birds (robin, sparrow, blue jay) demonstrated evidence of later recognizing parakeets and cranes as part of the "same" (familiar) category, while those initially shown bad examples (atypical birds, such as an ostrich or chicken) did not form a functional category and did not recognize parakeets and cranes as the "same." Regardless of whether one is inclined to call such processes evidence of thought, it is clear that preverbal children can and do develop nonlinguistic categories (see also Clark 1977).

Thus, language is one way, though not the only way, that we categorize sensed stimuli into concepts and ideas. The English word "abstract" is derived from the Latin *abstractus*—"drawn off from" or "drawn away" (cf. Burke 1984b, 104). Just as our nervous system draws from available stimuli to form specific sensations, one of the abstractive functions language performs is to manage or make sense of our experience by selectively focusing attention. When we use language to describe an experience to ourselves or to others, the experience is not duplicated. By this I mean no more than to point out that a verbal description of a roller coaster ride is not the same as experiencing the ride. No matter how vivid the description, it must focus on one aspect of the experience at a time (the rushing air on one's skin, the sensation of falling, or the sounds). Through a series of descriptions that selectively focuses on different aspects of the experience, a listener or reader may be able to put together the account in such a way as to understand better what the original experience was like. The process will be long and laborious, however, for human languages cannot recreate the multidimensionality (what all our senses process at once) of experience in anything remotely like the speed at which the nervous system works: "For all the complexity and richness of language, experience is immeasurably more complex, and richer in information [stimuli]" (Barnes 1982, 28).

Of course, complex experiences can be summarized by simple phrases. I could spend years trying to describe in minute detail all the aspects of my experience of the past hour, but if asked, I am more likely to say simply that "I have been working on a book." Similarly, of all the things that you are doing now (breathing, sitting or standing, aging, learning, and so on), the simplest way to make sense of your experience would be to say, "I am reading." Such accounts, however, are not particularly revealing. At best, they identify a broad category with which the listener/reader is familiar, and depending on the circumstances under which such an account was offered, a broad category may be sufficient. The point is that when any particular experience is described, some aspects of that experience are selected or "drawn from" to the neglect of others. Such a process of abstraction is not faulty or malevolent; rather, it is vital to the ordering and comprehension of reality. Philosopher Calvin O. Schrag contends that "selection is not in itself a mark of distortion or falsification. Selection is simply an implication of the finitude of human knowledge" (1980, 65).

I turn now to the more pragmatic (and difficult) question of how we create linguistic categories. Some of our earliest linguistic acts involve pointing and gesturing to objects and learning what objects are called. Long before we learn more formal means of defining words, we acquire ostensive definitions, such as when an adult points to an object and says to a child "apple." Initially, it would be more accurate to say only that a child is learning the name of specific items or events, but from the very earliest stages of learning a language, naming facilitates categorizing, and it has been argued that "the abstraction of categories cannot be separated, in practical terms, from the problem of language acquisition" (Smith 1988, 37; see also Bowerman 1976, Rice 1984).

When a child learns to identify a specific class of objects such as the category of "apples," that child learns a set of *similarity/difference relationships* (SDRs). That is, the child learns to identify a set of respects in which apples are similar to one another and different from non-apples. Two important examples of SDRs that children use to form categories are *perceptual* and *functional* (Bowerman 1976, 123–27; Smith 1988, 30). An example of a perceptual SDR is when children identify apples based on visual sensations (red, round, and so on). Objects also are given a common label when they are functionally similar—that is, capable of acting or being acted upon in similar fashion—such as when children call anything they think they can eat "food" and all liquids "drink."

One of the basic premises guiding this book is the belief that SDRs are learned. There is a body of research that indicates that there are some categories that can be found in virtually all cultures and may be rooted in a common human neurophysiology (Allan 1977; Clark 1977; Rosch 1973, 1974, 1975). Nevertheless, there remains a potentially infinite number of ways language can categorize stimuli. Although not all vocabularies are equally valuable (Mervis and Rosch 1981), there is, nonetheless, an enormous degree of freedom in the way words can be used to classify. One way to appreciate that freedom is to learn a foreign language. Very early on, one learns that not all of the categories reflected in the English language are duplicated in other languages. Indeed, one of the most interesting aspects of learning a foreign language is to learn those words that cannot be rendered into English without losing the SDRs entailed by those words (see, e.g., Bowerman 1981, 139; Kuhn 1983, 679–81).

Sorting Things Out: Classification and Its Consequences (1999), by communication scholars Geoffrey C. Bowker and Susan Leigh Star, is a fascinating study of the social uses of categories and classification. Their examples are categories used typically in public policy and professional settings, but much of what they have to say applies to ordinary language acquisition. For example, they note that learning "the ropes and rules of practice in any given community" entails learning its categories. Just as children are taught to accept as "natural" the categories of ordinary language, socialization into a particular community or institution involves the "naturalization" of its categories: "The more at home you are in a community of practice, the more you forget the strange and contingent nature of its categories as seen from the outside" (1999, 294–95). The same can be said about the classifications and categories of ordinary language.

Another way to recognize the range of possible schemes of classification is to note the sorts of "mistakes" children make when learning a vocabulary. "Underextension" is when a child fails to apply a term to what adults agree is an appropriate referent. For example, if a child learns that apples are red, round, and of a particular size, that child might hesitate to call a green or yellow apple by that name. "Overextension" is when a child uses a term too broadly, according to adult standards, such as when a tomato is called an apple because it is red, round, and of the appropriate size. In both of these examples, it is easy to identify the source of the error and to correct it. The SDRs used by the child to distinguish apples from non-apples require further elaboration in order to match the use of such terms by adults (Miller and Gildea 1987). Nevertheless, there was nothing patently wrong with the process these "mistaken" children went through (Kamhi 1982). To say that their system of classification must be altered to bring it into conformity with adult classifications does not deny that, had the English language evolved differently, their "childish" classification system might have turned out to be right (cf. Lakoff 1987, 48–50).

An oft-cited example of a "mistaken" categorization by a child is reported by Melissa Bowerman (1976, 119–20). Bowerman's daughter Eva first used the word "kick" at about eighteen months "in connection with herself kicking a stationary object." She used the term "then while looking at a picture of a cat with a ball near its paw, for a fluttering moth, for cartoon turtles on TV kicking their legs up, as she threw an object, as she bumped a ball with her trike wheel, making it roll, as she pushed her chest up against a sink, and so on" (119). Bowerman believes that the use of "kick" by Eva was based on one of three different perceived similarities with the original utterance of "kick": "a waving limb," "sudden sharp contact," or "an object propelled." By adult standards, Eva's use of "kick" is a clear case of overextension, but it would be misleading to say that Eva had no idea of what she was saying. She had a working category of "kick" informed by a set of SDRs that she found useful to make sense of her experiences. The cognitive processes involved with the learning and use of such a category is functionally no different than that for the "right" words used by adults (Smith 1988, 29–34).

The previous example underscores that language users must learn to categorize in similar ways; that is, they must "abstract" aspects of a set of stimuli in a manner similar to other language users if their vocabulary is to be shared. How does this happen? Again, this is a matter over which there is considerable difference of opinion. A purely behaviorist theory would suggest that children must learn when to use or not to use a term through a series of positive and negative reinforcements. Such a theory gives little credit to "the young child's constructive abilities and potential to make sense out of sound and referent objects" (Smith 1988, 28–29). A more promising explanation of how children learn the denotative meaning of words (what the word "points out" or refers to) focuses on the cognitive role of *exemplars*. From a linguistic perspective, an exemplar is a prototypical denotation that demonstrates a category to a language user.

What Bowerman calls the "original or *prototypical* 'kick' situation" initially taught Eva the category of "kick" (1976, 120). Her later denotative use of the term was based on what she saw as similar situations based on an identifiable set of SDRs. Such denotations are performed by analogy; that is, later instances of "kick" were based on what Eva thought kicks were *like*. As Eva's case demonstrates, it typically takes repeated uses of a term to learn the "licensed" SDRs such that the term is used "correctly." According to the best-example theory of categorization, persons exposed to good exemplars learn a new category more quickly and accurately than those exposed to bad exemplars. Thus, a child is more likely to learn how to refer correctly to "birds" after being shown robins and sparrows rather than penguins and ostriches (Roberts and Horowitz 1986). There is support for the best-example theory in research conducted both with adults (Rosch 1973) and children (Mervis and Pani 1980; cf. Merriman, Schuster, and Hager 1991).

Learning to use words to refer correctly, therefore, involves learning the SDRs that are commonly recognized within a given language community. Definitions, especially those found in dictionaries, are efforts to describe the category of experiences to which words refer; thus, they are linguistic guides to the SDRs that individual words entail. In the next section, the relationships among definitions, exemplars, and SDRs are discussed at greater length.

Before turning to an examination of the processes involved in learning the specific skill of defining words, I should point out that the previous discussion has been about words used to denote or "refer." Not all words fall into this category (Alston 1964, 14–16), including expressive words and phrases such as "Oh!" or "Hello"; conjunctions such as "and," "if," or "but"; modal terms such as "would," "could," or "might"; and such prepositions as "at" or "with." Although these and other categories of words play important syntactical and communicative roles, by themselves they do not refer to objects or actions to which one could point. The primary focus of this book is on how people define words used to denote classes and individual instances of things (such as "art," "phlogiston," or "mass"), events (such as "death" or "war"), qualities (such as "obscene"), and actions (such as "rape" or "sexual harassment"). Such words are not all that make up a language, but they are central to what can be called "the politics of meaning."

Defining Is a Learned Ability

Paradoxical as it may seem, I want to begin this section by pointing out just how unnecessary formal definitions are. Formally defining words is a specialized linguistic practice that is by no means ubiquitous among language users. The practice of definition flourishes primarily (if not exclusively) in literate cultures in which language is materialized and becomes a more accessible object of analysis (Havelock 1963). Whether literate people have radically different cognitive skills than nonliterate people is a hotly contested issue that need not be resolved here (see Finnegan 1988; Scinto 1986; Street 1984). My point is that defining words is a specialized task that one must learn to perform. Facilitated by the technology of writing, definitions "fix" or "freeze" language in order to function as a sort of road map demarcating what words mean. These road maps depict the definer's reality; they function as claims about the way language and the world are. Absent such written road maps, other means of negotiating shared meaning must be substituted. Just as one often can arrive at familiar destinations without a road map, so too language communities can master a lexicon without formal definitions. The contingent status of formal definitions in five different contexts of language use can illustrate the point: fifth-century BCE ancient Greece, children's language use, nonliterate adults' language use, color terms, and scientific settings.

In ancient Greece, for example, it was not until the late fifth century BCE that anyone attempted to produce anything quite like a formal definition. Most of the so-called Greek enlightenment took place at a time in which definition was unknown. The historical narratives of Herodotus, the philosophical texts and fragments of the pre-Socratic philosophers, the plays of Aeschylus and Sophocles, all were composed at a time when formal definitions of words were unheard of. Almost all important communication transactions were conducted orally (Thomas 1989), a medium that encourages face-to-face confirmation and clarification of intention. In fact, only a small percentage of the Greek population was literate (Harris 1989), and books were exceedingly rare (Turner 1977).

One reason the practice of defining words developed slowly is that Greek grammar, prior to Plato, did not encourage propositions of the form "X is Y" (Havelock 1963, 1978). A key component in the syntactical construction of definitions is the word "is" (Sera, Reittinger, and Pintado 1991, 137–40). The Greek verb for "to be," *einai,* was used as a copula to connect subject and predicate, but prior to Parmenides one does not find what can now be called a philosophical use of "to be" as the subject of a sentence or as a bare predicate (Kahn 1973). The latter use facilitates asking questions of the form *ti esti* or "What is X?" that are tantamount to asking for a real definition: statements that identify what X necessarily *is.* Prior to Plato, it has been argued that the more common uses of *einai* were to indicate such qualities as presence, location, or status, or for acoustical value in the composition of rhymes (Havelock 1978, 233–48). It is not that proper Greek excluded locutions like "Achilles is running," but locutions like "Plato runs," without a copula, are more common in pre-Platonic Greek usage.

The earliest efforts to distinguish the specific meanings of words are credited to Prodicus of Ceos, with whom Socrates is reported to have studied. Prodicus is reputed to have distinguished between words we now consider synonyms or near synonyms, although there was no term for "synonym" at the time. For example, Plato portrays him in one dialogue as saying to Socrates and Protagoras, "I myself think it right that you agree with each other to *debate* but not to *dispute.* For friends debate with friends in a spirit of goodwill, but enemies and rivals dispute with one another." Later he distinguishes between "satisfaction" and "pleasure": "For satisfaction attends the learning experience when we are exercising our understanding and our reason, while pleasure accompanies eating or some other enjoyable accommodation of the wants of the body" (*Protagoras* 337a in Sprague 1972, 76). As these examples illustrate, one can distinguish between word meanings without formally defining them or using the verb "is." Similarly, we find no trace of "is" in one of earliest statements that could be categorized as a stipulative definition: Gorgias of Leontini, a contemporary of Prodicus, declared, "All poetry I regard and name as speech having meter" (*Encomium of Helen* §9 in Kennedy 1991, 286).

It is Socrates who apparently took the next step to ask questions such as "What *is* pleasure?" and "What *is* satisfaction?" The descriptions of Socrates by Plato and Xenophon are quite different, but both make it clear that Socrates wanted to understand what such "things" as Courage, the Beautiful, Wisdom, and the Good are. During Socrates' lifetime, there was no Greek word for "definition." Socrates probably used the word "hypothesis" in a sense that is consistent with its current use to describe claims about the way "things" really are (Guthrie 1971, 113n). Plato and Aristotle, of course, had a profound effect on subsequent philosophical thought about definitions and describing "the nature of things." An important part of their contribution was wrestling with, and changing, the dominant syntactical practices in order to express new forms of philosophical analysis—definition being the relevant example. There were other philosophers who were interested in definition, such as Antisthenes, but it is Plato and Aristotle to whom we are most directly indebted for our current attitudes toward, and practices of, defining.

Aristotle's writings about definition are many and diverse; it is somewhat misleading to refer to a single "Aristotelian" theory of definition (Le Blond 1979). Nevertheless, Aristotle is credited for the standard definitional form involving genus and difference: An X is (a kind of) *class name* that has such-and-such *attributes*. This procedure is not solely Aristotle's invention—"[I]t is close to Socratic definition and to the Platonic method of division" (Le Blond 1979, 67)—but Aristotle elaborates different processes of definition; thus, it is to him that the formula is usually attributed. It is worth noting that none of the Greek thinkers mentioned was interested in what would later be called "definition" purely for the sake of communicating more clearly. Even Prodicus— whose contributions are often downplayed on the mistaken assumption that he was motivated solely by the desire to use language persuasively— approached problems of language and meaning to understand "reality" better, that is, to produce what later would be called real definitions (Bett 1989, 154–61). More often than not, the fruits of his labor, like those of Socrates, produced results considerably at odds with the contemporary usage (Kerferd 1954, 253–54).

Just as ancient Greece reached its cultural zenith without definitions, so children can use language with great success without the assistance of a dictionary. Noting that defining is a "literate metalinguistic task," psychologist Marilyn A. Nippold points out that the ability to produce "correct" definitions should not be equated with verbal knowledge: "Youngsters often know more about words than they can actually explain" (1988, 43; see also McGhee-Bidlack 1991, 417). On the basis of her research involving young children's responses to requests for definitions, Bonnie Litowitz suggests that children's efforts to define words can be divided into five categories or "levels" (1977). The first is "nonverbal statement or a verbal statement which is semantically empty," such as pure gesturing or pointing (294). Her example is a child defining the word "snap" by ostension by saying "like *this*" and snapping his fingers. Engaging in a sort of "ritualized dialogue" with a teacher or primary caregiver who produces many such statements as, "X," "It's an X," "That's an X," "Look at the X," is the way most children learn to label (Ninio and Bruner 1978). That they would use similar behaviors to provide a requested definition, therefore, is no surprise.

The second level of definitional activity children learn is to associate specific words with the word being defined. Litowitz notes that these responses, "while verbal and not semantically empty, lack an ordered form" (1977, 294). So a child might supply the single word "sock" to define "shoe," or "head" to define "hat." There is a potential connection between the "definition" and the word defined, but the child has not yet learned the appropriate form to express that connection. The third level includes a "concrete example of actual experience" associated with the word being defined (295). At this point, children have learned to identify specific attributes with the word-thing being defined, but they are fairly idiosyncratic by adult standards. A child might define "knife" as "sharp," "bicycle" as "you ride on and you fall off," or "nuisance" as "when people are bad" (295). These children have linked the word to a finite category of experience, but they have not yet learned to identify verbally what an adult would call a specific class or an "essential" attribute.

Litowitz describes the fourth level as indicating "some awareness of a definitional form (a set predicate) and a beginning abstraction from the individual experience towards general social information" (1977, 296). Litowitz suggests that this level is characterized by a child's recognition of the *social* function of defining, which is identifiable by the use of more hypothetical and, hence, more generalizable descriptions: "A knife is when you cut with it," for example (296). At this level, children's definitions may give a somewhat clearer idea of the ways they have learned to categorize sensations; object-categories that are formed by functional similarity, for example, are likely to produce functional definitions of the form "An X is for Y-ing" or "An X is to Y with" (297).

The fifth level is identified by Litowitz as producing "pure" Aristotelian definition (1977, 297–98). In her study of children between four and a half and seven and a half years of age, none was able to produce level-five definitions. As children grow and develop cognitively and linguistically, their definitional skills improve to reflect "an advanced conception of a word's socially shared meaning" (Nippold 1988, 44). Research by Betty McGhee-Bidlack suggests that children learn to define concrete nouns by class and attribute "from age 10 to 18," yet it is "not until participants are 18 years old that they begin to define abstract nouns as they define concrete nouns" (1991, 425).

Clearly, then, people learn to be effective language users long before they learn to define many words "correctly," that is, as they are defined in dictionaries. Children must learn to define words according to the conventional Aristotelian form of "An X is (a kind of) *class name* that has such-and-such *attributes*"; for example, "A bed is a piece of furniture used for sleeping" (Nippold 1988, 40; Litowitz 1977, 297). In other words, the cognitive skill involved in learning word meaning—exposure to good exemplars and learning to refer to similar stimuli correctly (by adult standards)—is related but not identical to the linguistic skill of producing definitions in the correct propositional form (Ninio and Bruner 1978, 15). Children can acquire a powerful lexicon without recourse to dictionaries.

Dictionary definitions not only are unnecessary for acquiring a lexicon but also, it has been argued, might interfere with young children's efforts to learn new words because using a dictionary requires considerable sophistication. "Interrupting your reading to find an unfamiliar word in an alphabetical list, all the while keeping the original context in mind so that you can compare it with the alternative senses given in the dictionary, then selecting the sense that is most appropriate in the original context—that is a high-level cognitive task. It should not be surprising that children are not good at it" (Miller and Gildea 1987, 97). When fifth and sixth graders were given new words along with dictionary definitions and asked to use the words in a sentence, they produced sentences such as "[She] *stimulated* the soup" and "Our family *erodes* a lot" (Miller and Gildea 1987, 97–98). Although these children have learned that dictionaries can provide synonyms, they do not yet have the requisite experience using the terms to understand *which* synonym may be appropriate in a given context. So, when one child found "stir up" as a definition of "stimulate" and another found "eat out" and "eat away" for "erode," it is not surprising that they "mapped" the new word into sentences that made sense to them in light of the definitional categories that were most familiar. Children typically learn how to denote by using words to refer to things, actions, or events with which they have direct experience. In the process of acquiring a larger lexicon, they learn about language and the world simultaneously. That is why prototypical exemplars are so useful for children to learn new words, while traditional dictionary definitions are largely superfluous.

Today, as in ancient Greece, nonliterate people virtually never produce formal definitions. Not unlike children in the early literate stages,
nonliterate adults with otherwise fully functional communicative abilities generally do not learn how to define words formally. Rather than
identifying classes or categories of objects and specifying required attributes, nonliterate people typically describe the referent as they experience it. Aleksandr Luria's study of nonliterate Russian peasants elic-
ited responses not unlike American and British schoolchildren's responses
to requests for definitions. For example, when asked "What is a car?,"
Luria's subjects answered as follows (1976):

> "When it screeches, goes screaming down the road, moves this
> way and that, and has fire burning inside it." (87)

> "It uses fire for its power and a person drives it. If it has no oil
> and no one to drive it, it won't move." (87)

> "A car? It's called a car, and a kukushka [dinkey] is a kukushka."
> (88)

> "If someone asks me I'd say it makes work easier. If you don't
> have any flour or firewood, a car can get them to you very
> quickly." (89)

Two subjects with a rudimentary education produced the following:

> "A car is a thing that moves fast, uses electricity, water, and air.
> It covers great distances so it makes difficult work easier." (88)

> "It's made in a factory. In one trip it can cover the distance it
> would take a horse ten to make—it moves that fast. It uses fire
> and steam. . . ." (90)

Although the last two answers come closer to what would be considered the correct form of a definition (class, attributes), none of the responses is likely to be confused with a dictionary account. Even more
interesting were the responses that resisted definition altogether. One
villager, asked to explain what a tree is, answered, "Why should I? Everyone knows what a tree is, they don't need me telling them" (Luria
1976, 86). When asked, "What is the sun?," several subjects responded
that it would be impossible to answer the question for anyone who had
not seen it (87–90).

The point of these examples is that defining words is not a universal linguistic practice, unlike labeling and categorizing. Whole societies have developed and flourished without the aid of definition, and children acquire an impressive level of communicative competence without necessarily learning how to put together a "correct" definition. Although our ability to communicate *does* require an ability to recognize sets of SDRs that other people recognize and link to a specific lexicon, it does not necessarily require a common ability to articulate those SDRs into a specific propositional form.

As a final example of "ordinary" language use, consider how virtually all people learn to use color words. As children, we learn what is "red" or "blue" initially through a series of prototypical denotations. If asked to define a color, most of us would revert to what Litowitz described as a level-one definition: pure ostension. Ludwig Wittgenstein often used color words to illustrate how learning about "language" and "the world" is often inseparable: "How do I recognize that this is red?— 'I see that it is *this;* and then I know that that is what this is called.' This?—What?! What kind of answer to this question makes sense? . . . How do I know that this colour is red?—It would be an answer to say: 'I have learnt English'" (1958b, 117; cf. 1958a, 130–41). One can, of course, describe "red" metaphorically or locate it in the specialized vocabulary of light-waves, but such definitions are unlikely to help a nonnative speaker learn how to use the word. Either the word "red" must be mapped onto a preexisting category (in French, for example, *rouge*), or one would learn it through ostension. Different languages categorize colors differently, and even within a given culture and language some people may have a far more sophisticated color vocabulary than others. In any case, it is hard to imagine anyone learning how to use primary color words by referring to a standard dictionary definition. Like so many words, words for colors have to be learned through repeated exposure to appropriate stimuli, guided by prototypical exemplars and coaching by more experienced language users.

So far, I have argued that there are various contexts of ordinary language use in which definition plays a negligible role. What about a specialized context of language use, in particular, the so-called hard sciences? In part because physical science is so often seen as the paradigm of sound knowledge, it comes as a surprise to many to hear that language learners in the physical sciences do not rely on definitions. In the process of acquiring new terms in science, Thomas S. Kuhn, noted historian and philosopher of science, contends that "definition plays a negligible role.

Rather than being defined, these terms are introduced by exposure to examples of their use, examples provided by someone who already belongs to the speech community in which they are current" (1989, 15; see also 1977, 178). Such exposure may be to exemplary situations in the laboratory, or via "a description conducted primarily in terms drawn from the antecedently available vocabulary," or both (Kuhn 1989, 15–16). Just as all language users do, scientists must learn to recognize categories based on SDRs acquired through repetition. Language acquisition in science is no different in kind from language acquisition outside of science (Kuhn 2000, 246–48). Repeated exposure to terms is necessary for novice scientists just as it is for children learning their native language, because "a single exemplary situation seldom or never supplies enough information to permit the student to use a new term" (Kuhn 1989, 16). One learns about language and the world at the same time in science and elsewhere through a combination of category formation and linguistic "mapping."

Definitions are not as important as the ability to use the term appropriately (cf. Vervenne and De Waele 1985). As Quine argues, "Language is socially inculcated and controlled; the inculcation and control turn strictly on the keying of sentences to shared stimulation" (1969, 81). In the hard sciences, such socialization is often aided by instrumentation. "Mass" to a physicist is not an abstract concept but what one measures with certain instruments (Kuhn 1977, xviii–xix). If a physicist "ever discovers the meaning of terms like 'force,' 'mass,' 'space,' and 'time'," claims Kuhn, he or she does so less from "definitions in his [or her] texts than by observing and participating in the application of these concepts to problem-solution" (1970, 47). Similarly, once a construct is fully operationalized in the social sciences, definitions are either unimportant because the measuring instrument replaces their function, or they become tautologies (such as economists' definition of "demand").

My argument has been that learning to define words is not the same as learning how to use words successfully; the skills may be related, but they are clearly distinguishable in theory and in practice. Furthermore, producing definitions in the conventional Aristotelian form is an acquired ability that typically follows well after a range of other communicative competencies is developed. Defining is, therefore, a specialized linguistic skill, the practice of which varies considerably from context to context, culture to culture. None of this should be interpreted as implying that definitions are unimportant or unnecessary. Indeed, definition is an indispensable tool of social coordination in technologically advanced mass societies. As a socially variable practice, defining warrants investigation, evaluation, and improvement.

Definitions as Persuasive

At the outset of this book, definitions were described as "rhetorically induced" to call attention to the persuasive processes on which definitions rely. Persuasion is involved both when definitions are "mundane" and when they are "novel." A definition is mundane when it is used unproblematically by a particular discourse community. Thus, the vast majority of standard dictionary definitions are mundane. The persuasion involved with a mundane definition directly parallels the persuasion involved in teaching a child the "correct" meaning of a word. Consider a child who is learning to use the word "dog." As Bowerman points out, prototypical denotations are polysemic; that is, they are open to various interpretations: "Even in the relatively straightforward case of ostensive definition, when, for example, an object is shown to the child and he is told 'dog' or 'that is a dog,' much is left unexplained. What features are the critical ones that determine what new objects could or couldn't be called 'dog'? The fur? The presence of four legs? The color? The size? The bark? People's reaction to it?" (1976, 114). If the child forms a category of "dog" based on the "wrong" set of features, according to adult standards, then that child must be persuaded to alter his or her category of "dog." Correct references to dogs will be reinforced; incorrect uses will be ignored or discouraged. The intended result is to bring that child's behavior into line with adults' usage of the word "dog." Although such a process of persuasion may not actually involve turning to a dictionary definition (though, in theory, it *could*), the objectives are the same. The child has been taught to understand what a dog really is when the child uses the word "dog" as adults do. When a language user acquires an understanding of what a dog *is* that is shared by other members of the discourse community, that language user has added to his or her stock of social knowledge. Linguistically, the child has been taught to bring his or her verbal behavior into agreement with adult language use. Such intersubjective agreement can be described as *denotative conformity.*

Referring to the process of teaching children how to use a word as "persuasion" may seem unusual, but anyone who has struggled to convince a child that "a wolf is not a dog," "a lion is a kind of cat," or "that is not a toy!" realizes that not all such efforts at persuasion are successful. That such persuasion is usually successful with children does not alter the fact that children are being induced to change their verbal behavior. All else being equal, it would be foolish of children not to believe adults whom they trust when they are told that one animal is a dog and another is not. Children gain a shared understanding of the world around them as well as social acceptance by accepting adults' persuasive efforts to bring their behavior into denotative conformity (Quine 1969, 81). These gains are powerful persuaders, to be sure.

Just as children normally take for granted the "givenness" of word meanings that come from more experienced language users, so adults typically reflect a natural attitude toward definitions (described in chapter 1). That is, unless provided with a motive to do otherwise, the standard reaction to a mundane definition is acquiescence. Confronted with unfamiliar words, we are inclined to accept a standard dictionary definition as reliable social knowledge and bring our understanding and linguistic behavior into line accordingly. Dictionary definitions thereby persuade us to see and talk about the world in certain ways and not in others. The rhetorical interaction is analogous to the persuasion involved in choosing to accept the "teaching" of someone we regard as more knowledgeable in a particular context. Thus, if a doctor dubs a certain pain one feels the result of a "myocardial infarction" or a mechanic points to an object and calls it a "solenoid," someone unfamiliar with such words is unlikely to argue. The more knowledgeable language user—in these contexts, a doctor and a mechanic—normally persuades us as easily as an adult persuades a child to call a particular animal a "dog." Of course, one can imagine a patient disagreeing with a doctor or a customer reluctant to take at face value every utterance of a mechanic. We must be persuaded to agree; such persuasion may be simple and direct or complicated and time-consuming.

Two somewhat different definitional interactions are described in the previous paragraph. The first situation involves learning the meaning of a word "in general" as it is recounted in a dictionary. Such formal definitions have an almost unique credibility in highly literate cultures that make common dictionaries extremely potent persuaders. The second situation involves learning how to use a word apart from a dictionary based on exposure to a prototypical denotation. Such informal (typically ostensive) definitions rely on a very different set of factors to be persuasive, such as the relative age and experience of the people involved, the confidence expressed by the more experienced language user, the various social and personal implications associated with accepting his or her use as valid, and so forth. Nevertheless, the motivations involved in both types of interaction are very similar: one accepts a particular pattern of usage to understand some part of the world better and to coordinate one's linguistic behavior with other people. Formal and informal definition thus can be understood as persuasion aimed at shared understanding and denotative conformity.

The persuasive processes involved with "novel" definitions are somewhat different, although the end result is the same. Novel definitions are introduced when a person feels that the dominant mundane definition (formal or informal) is wrong or unhelpful. Thus, someone introducing a novel definition wants to change other people's understanding and linguistic behavior away from the conventional patterns and toward new behaviors and understanding. Definitions are dominant (for example, canonized in a dictionary) only as long as most people continue to adhere to them. Thus, dominant definitions are conventional and remain "factual" only "so long as they remain unchallenged" (Perelman and Olbrechts-Tyteca 1969, 211).

Novel definitions are not part of the ongoing effort of language "purists" to encourage the "proper" use of English. To the contrary, novel definitions are introduced when someone feels that the "proper" meaning of the word is no longer correct. When the first philosophers of language in ancient Greece taught how to form a "correct account" of things (orthos logos), their primary concern was to improve students' understanding of the world as that understanding was expressed in language (Kerferd 1981, 68–77). Similarly, Socrates' and Plato's efforts to define important concepts were motivated by a belief that most people do not really understand many important parts of their world. Some of Plato's dialogues end in a failure to define a concept, while others explicitly defend a new definition of highly valued terms such as "justice" and "the good" (in Republic and Philebus, respectively). Charles L. Stevenson describes Plato's arguments as persuasive definitions: "The purport of the definition is to alter the descriptive meaning of the term, usually by giving it greater precision within the boundaries of its customary vagueness; but the definition does not make any substantial change in the term's emotive meaning" (1944, 210). Accordingly, one of the argumentative objectives of the dialogues was to critique the conventional usages of certain terms and—at least in some dialogues—to offer an alternative conceptualization based on Plato's understanding of the world (225).

Plato's dialogues often portray the way the world is through the vehicle of arguments about definition. These definitions (or anti-definitions, in some cases) constitute claims that, if accepted, result in altered understanding and behavior. If "sophists" are paid hunters after young men, then they are people to be avoided. If "rhetoric" provides mere opinion and philosophy provides true knowledge, then philosophy is a preferable form of educational training. If we do not really know what "excellence" *(aretê)* is, then we should hesitate before paying someone fees to impart it. In other words, Plato's dialogues are persuasive documents that induce changes in attitudes and behavior by arguing about definitions.

Definitions, then, are persuasive in several respects. Definitions represent claims about how certain portions of the world are. They are conventional and depend on the adherence of language users. Definitions function to induce denotative conformity, which is another way of saying that definitions are introduced or contested when one wants to alter others' linguistic behavior in a particular fashion. A successful new definition changes not only recognizable patterns of linguistic behavior but also our understanding of the world and the attitudes and behaviors we adopt toward various parts of that world. Taken seriously, these persuasive characteristics of definition have important implications for how we should construct and resolve arguments concerned with definitions. It is to those implications that I now turn.

Part Two

What Is X?
Arguments about Definition

Mundane definitions are those conventionally accepted definitions that delineate "the real" for a given discourse community (cf. Rescher 1977). While the natural attitude toward definitions is undisturbed, the congruity between facts of essence (what X really is) and facts of usage (how the word for X is used) is taken for granted. Definitions change, of course, although the types of change vary widely. The meaning of words can change slowly and virtually imperceptibly as a result of localized changes of habit that slowly spread across a broader group of language users, or patterns of usage can change very rapidly. An example of the former is the addition of the word "irritate" for the word "aggravate" in the third edition of the *American Heritage Dictionary*. An example of the latter is when the word "disk" was first used to describe a new piece of computer technology. More often than not, such changes take place informally. No formal arguments take place, nor are any official votes taken over whether to adopt new uses for words—except perhaps in the process of deciding whether to include such new meanings in a particular dictionary. However, there are a good number of occasions—especially in academic, public policy, and legal settings—in which novel definitions are set forth and debated formally and explicitly. If, as I have argued, defining is a specialized and learned ability, then in principle the discursive practices that are involved can be analyzed, assessed, and improved. As Aristotle observes with respect to the *technê* (art or skill) of rhetoric, "It is possible to observe the cause why some succeed by habit and others accidentally" (in Kennedy 1991, 29). Accordingly, the persuasive processes involved in arguments about novel definitions are the focus of this part of the book.

3
Moving Beyond "Real" Definitions: The Case of "Death"

The phrase "real definition" refers to all efforts to define things rather than words, that is, facts of essence rather than facts of usage. When one tries to provide a real definition of "death," for example, one is not reporting how people use the word "death" but is identifying what the defining characteristics of death "really" are. Strictly speaking, dictionary definitions are lexical definitions and not "real definitions," because they merely report how words have been used in the past. According to someone who believes in real definitions, the usage reported in a lexical definition could be in error, since people in the past may not have understood what the thing to which a given word refers "really is." A real definition, therefore, records not how people are using a word, but rather what the defining qualities of the referent "really" and "objectively" are.

Although Plato and especially Aristotle are the philosophers most often associated with the search for real definitions, they were not alone. Benedict Spinoza in the seventeenth century proclaimed that "the true definition of each thing involves nothing and expresses nothing but the nature of the thing defined" (1927, I, prop. 8, n.2; see also Hart 1983, 130–31). In the twentieth century, real definition is the primary activity that Bertrand Russell and G. E. Moore had in mind with their notion of the "correct analysis" of concepts. Moore posited that definitions "describe the real nature of the object or notion denoted by a word" and "do not merely tell us what the word is used to mean" (1903, 7). Russell's and Moore's objective was to enumerate the various empirical constituents of "factual, independently existing" complexes of objects and relations in such a way as to describe "the ultimate constituents" of reality. Accordingly, a "true" or "complete" analysis would yield a real definition that correctly identifies what "time" or "memory" actually are (Weitz 1967, 99–100; see also Russell 1921).

Arguments about real definitions may be viewed as competing answers to questions of the form "What is X?" Our earliest recorded instances of arguments of this sort, as noted earlier, are in Plato's dialogues. Typically, these dialogues begin with someone planning action based on a belief concerning X. So, for example, Euthyphro believes the prosecution of his own father for murder to be pious, although members of his family are calling Euthyphro impious. Because Plato's Socrates believes that one must know what piety really is before one can call a specific action pious or not, he poses the question "What is Piety?" that informs the ensuing discussion.

In the case of Plato, the belief that words are somehow related to essences or Ideal Forms fuels the search for definition; therefore, a real definition of a word is the one that accurately depicts what is "essential" about the word's referent. Although few people still embrace Plato's notion of the Ideal Forms, the search for real definitions continues, and the "language of essentialism" that fills Plato's dialogues still informs many contemporary arguments about definition. The language of essentialism refers to linguistic habits that reflect and depend on metaphysical absolutism: the belief that things have independent, "objective" structures or essences that are knowable "in themselves" (Barnes 1982, 79–83). The most readily identifiable example of such a linguistic habit is described by Belgian philosophers Chaïm Perelman and Lucie Olbrechts-Tyteca as *dissociation:* an arguer's effort to break up a previously unified idea into two concepts, one that will be positively valued by the target audience and one that will be negatively valued (see Perelman and Olbrechts-Tyteca 1969, 411–59). Arguers enact dissociation through the use of "philosophical pairs," one of which is usually considered metaphysically, epistemologically, or ethically superior to the other. The prototypical philosophical pair is appearance/reality. An arguer uses this pair by claiming that one definition is the real or true instance of X, whereas competing definitions point to an illusory appearance. In definitional disputes, closely related pairs include essential/accidental and necessary/contingent.

Whenever a novel definition is offered and defended as a real definition, some sort of dissociation is unavoidable. When a novel real definition is put forth, we immediately have competing claims about what some part of the world "really is": the claim made by the current mundane definition and the claim made by the new definition. There are now two competing claims about what is the "essence" or "real nature" of X. The worldviews that defend the notion of real definition maintain that both claims cannot be true. If the essence of X is Y, it cannot be anything else (X is not-Y). To claim that X is Y and also that X is not-Y violates a fundamental premise of traditional ontology, the principle of noncontradiction: "It is a property of being itself that no being can both have and not have a given characteristic at one and the same time" (MacIntyre 1967, 542). An advocate of a novel real definition must resolve the contradiction, and this is usually done through dissociation. An act of dissociation breaks X into two referents: X is really Y; it only appears to be not-Y. Only through such a dissociative act can the advocate of a novel real definition defend the claim "X is Y" as "real" while explaining away counterdefinitions, including the claim made by the dominant, mundane definition.

The definition of human death constitutes a useful and typical case study of the use of dissociation in an argument about definitions. For many centuries, death was indicated "by a physician feeling the pulse and putting a mirror under the patient's mouth. If there were no signs of life—no pulse, no breath—death was certified" (Humphrey and Wickett 1986, 277). Technological advances in the late twentieth century, most notably organ transplants and life-support machinery, have made traditional medical definitions problematic. New technology created a definitional rupture by calling into question the belief that someone without a pulse is "really" dead, because life-support machinery can restore and maintain a person's heart and lung functions for many years. Are patients who have massive irreversible trauma to the brain and who are unable to keep their own organs functioning "dead" or "alive"? Doctors were no longer as sure as they had been previously, and doctors are the class of people in our society authorized to pronounce someone legally dead. Denotative conformity in such matters could no longer be taken for granted; thus, an extremely important bit of social knowledge—the difference between life and death—was thrown into doubt. Beginning in the 1960s, a number of philosophers, attorneys, and physicians turned their attention to the problem of redefining death. The primary clash is whether or not new conceptions of "brain death" ought to supersede the traditional definition of death as the cessation of cardiorespiratory functions (Bernat 1999).

Many of the arguments proffered so far in the debate by philosophers, physicians, and law professors have been in behalf of what the authors posit as real definitions. That is, they are efforts to define what death really is. David Lamb defends the concept of brain death in part because the *"essence"* of being human, having a personality, is "in the head" (throughout this analysis, the emphasis added is my own). Furthermore, using the analogy of a decapitated individual, Lamb suggests that "the *essential* characteristics of life reside in the brain" (1985, 39). Without the "neurological integration" that the human brain provides, Lamb claims, the continued machine-assisted functioning of a patient "only *mimics* integrated life" (37). In opposition to brain death, M. B. Green and D. Wikler claim that the brain is just one of many organs that "could conceivably be replaced by an artificial aid." Thus, even irreversible cessation of brain activities is a "non-essential" characteristic of death (1982, 57).

Although he acknowledges the difficulties in defining death, philosopher Douglas Walton characterizes the question in Platonic terms: "What is death?" (1980, 53, 64). Agreeing with the notion that "the *essence* of the animal's personality is in the head," Walton wishes to distinguish between cases in which "it is clear" that the patient is alive and those where there is only a "semblance" of life: "It may be a *semblance* that has a powerful *emotional* force to a loved one of the deceased, but, *intellectually,* perhaps it is a force that should be resisted" (62). Note here that Walton's argument is doubly strategic—he combines a metaphysical pair (semblance/reality) with an epistemological pair (emotional/intellectual).

Some attempts to define death shift the focus to the true nature of human *life*. Robert M. Veatch offers the following as his "formal definition" of death: "a complete change in the status of a living entity characterized by the irreversible loss of those characteristics that are *essentially* significant to it" (1989, 17). Frank J. Veith et al. argue that the "nature" of being human is such that when the brain is dead, the capacities to think, perceive, and regulate bodily functions cease, which are "*essential* to human nature" (1977, 1653).

Perelman and Olbrechts-Tyteca observe that a dissociative definition is at work when a characteristic becomes the criterion for the correct use of the concept. An example is Lamb's claim that "*essential* to any *valid* concept of death is the prediction of irreversibility" (1985, 13). In other words, a requirement of any valid definition of death is that it preclude the dead person from coming back to life, which is another way of saying the person must be "really" dead. A number of authors distinguish between the "ambiguous," "vague," "ill-defined," "indeterminate," "philosophical" *concepts* of death and the authors' own "practical," "scientific," "technical" *criteria* for diagnosing whether a patient is dead (Gervais 1986; Walton 1980). The dissociations at work here function strategically to dismiss rival definitions and encourage their audiences to act favorably toward their proposals. These proposals usually are legislative definitions of death, a fact that suggests that the only practical difference between a "concept" and a "criterion" in this instance is that one is backed by the power of law.

Dissociation can be used to suggest that a new definition is not a threatening break from tradition; thus, it is a particularly powerful tool to use to maintain a given lexicon while changing its referents. The revised meaning of a concept is the "true" or "essential" definition, while opponents' (including past users') counterdefinitions are explained away as imperfect realizations of the real definition. For instance, Lamb claims that brain death is not "an alternative form of death" but rather what death has been all along: "The traditional cardio-respiratory concept never provided adequate criteria for death . . . irreversible cardio-respiratory arrest was *merely an indication* that brain death was imminent" (1985, 19). Similarly, Culver and Gert suggest that "permanent loss of whole brain functioning *has always been* the underlying criterion of death" (1982, 187).

The preceding survey of some of the arguments about defining death has shown that competing real definitions depend on dissociation and the language of essentialism and are informed implicitly by a theory of metaphysical absolutism. I now want to argue that there are serious problems with such an approach to definition. One problem is philosophical: dissociations that use certain metaphysical pairs are based on an untenable theory of language and meaning. The other problem is pragmatic: the language of essentialism obfuscates important social needs involved with defining.

To reiterate, metaphysical absolutism is the belief that the world consists of independent, objective "real" objects or essences that can be known directly as they "really are." For Plato, philosophy in general and dialectic in particular are the only ways to a correct understanding of reality, that is, the Ideal Forms. Aristotle rejected Plato's theory of Forms but maintained the belief that philosophy and what we would now call science provide direct access to the true nature of things. For over two thousand years, most (though not all) Western philosophers maintained a belief in some sort of metaphysical absolutism or "direct" realism. Such absolutism may be applied to transcendent universals (as with Plato), the real essence of things (as with Aristotle), or the nature of concrete particulars (as with William of Ockham). In any event, the proper "objects" of philosophical investigation are "things-as-they-really-are," or "things-in-themselves" and not things as we merely think they may be.

Metaphysical absolutism should be rejected for two related reasons. The first objection is that the idea of grasping the "essence" of things or understanding "things-in-themselves" is unintelligible. In his *Critique of Pure Reason,* Immanuel Kant called "things-in-themselves" *(Dinge an sich)* noumena and argued that they are unknowable in principle; all we can know are phenomena—things as we perceive and experience them (1965). We literally cannot speak of things of which we have no experience or sensation. As philosopher John W. Yolton notes: "To say objects in themselves are unknown simply means . . . that to think of an object without thinking of it, to perceive it (or know it) without perceiving it is of course impossible, even a manifest contradiction" (2000, 140). Thus, noumena are even less intelligible than the proverbial tree that falls in the forest with no one there to hear the hypothesized noise. Noumena are more like a hypothetical alien: a being you have never met, will never meet, and of which you can have no knowledge.

What about phenomena? Might *they* have definable "essences"? William James's critique of essentialism is particularly relevant here. He argues that our assertions of "essence" are guided by human purposes that change over time, and "there is no property *absolutely* essential to any one thing"; rather, "the same property which figures as the essence of a thing on one occasion becomes a very inessential feature on another" (1981, 959). Our inability over the centuries to agree on definitions that identify the essence or nature of a phenomenon is less a failure to follow some correct methodology than a reflection of our variable needs and interests. If our linguistic categories are formed according to specific salient attributes (functional or perceptual, for example), then James's point that which attribute is deemed "essential" is a matter of relative, not absolute, choice has considerable force. For example: "A substance like oil has as many different essences as it has uses to different individuals. One man conceives it as a combustible, another as a lubricator, another as a food; the chemist thinks of it as a hydro-carbon; the furniture-maker as a darkener of wood; the speculator as a commodity whose market price today is this and tomorrow that. The soap-boiler, the physicist, the clothes-scourer severally ascribe to it other essences in relation to their needs" (962n). Furthermore, James is unwilling to accept the notion that a scientific description of a phenomenon somehow is closer to its true nature: "Readers brought up on *Popular Science* may think that the molecular structure of things is their real essence in an absolute sense, and that water is H-O-H [H_2O] more deeply and truly than it is a solvent of sugar or a slaker of thirst. Not a whit! It is *all* of these things with equal reality, and the only reason why *for the chemist* it is H-O-H primarily, and only secondarily the other things, is that *for his purpose of deduction and compendious definition* the H-O-H aspect of it is the more useful one to bear in mind" (961n). In other words, a thing-as-experienced may have as many essences as we have interests: "The essence of a thing is that one of its properties which is so *important for my interests* that in comparison with it I may neglect the rest" (961).

The second objection to metaphysical absolutism is that "knowledge" is limited to what we can say about reality (cf. Rorty 1979; Lakoff 1987). What we know must be put into language or some sort of symbol system if it is to be shared with others. To make this claim does not deny the importance of nonlinguistic ways of knowing or the personal and "tacit" components of human understanding (Polanyi 1958). But definitions are linguistic expressions, and most of the time when we speak of knowledge, we refer to propositional statements, which are also linguistic. Because real objects are nonlinguistic, we are doubly removed from any sort of unmediated or direct access to reality. Or, to return to the terminology presented earlier, our shared accounts of experience are twice removed from some hypothetical "pure" reality: first, our sensations are abstracted from available stimuli; second, our linguistic utterances can only re-present a portion of our sensations. As Senft notes, *first* the nervous system and brain must selectively process available stimuli, *then* "if we want to communicate about this perceived, classified and filtered input, we have to classify once more: we have to transform this input into classes and categories" that constitute our language (2000, 11).

Just as metaphysical absolutism fails to account for the variability of human experience, linguistic absolutism fails to account for partiality of language. George D. Romanos describes linguistic absolutism as positing that "although there may be no way in which the world *really is,* there is still a way (or ways) that we *really say* it is, or *conceive* it to be" (1983, 32). Philosopher Hilary Putnam has critiqued what he calls the quest for "a God's Eye point of view" of reality. The ideas that "the world consists of some fixed totality of mind-independent objects" and that there "is exactly one true and complete description of 'the way the world is'" lead to the search for a God's Eye point of view (1981, 49). As Putnam points out, however, no such perspective is possible because we are limited to our experiences and our different ways of representing those experiences given historically situated beliefs and vocabularies: "There is no God's Eye point of view that we can know or usefully imagine; there are only various points of view of actual persons reflecting various interests and purposes that their descriptions and theories subserve" (50).

In the next chapter, I discuss efforts to preserve a version of linguistic absolutism via empirical methods, but for now it is sufficient to note that almost all philosophers of language now consider definitions strictly "lexical" (reports about how words are being used) rather than "real" in the sense advocated by metaphysical absolutism. The sort of essentialism found in Plato's works mostly has been abandoned as a guide to definitions, and both Anglo-American and continental philosophers now reject the sort of "direct" or "naïve realism" that informs the notion of real definitions and "correct analysis" (Weitz 1967).

A more thorough summary of contemporary critiques of metaphysical absolutism is unnecessary, at least for the moment. Few philosophers calling themselves "realists" even discuss the concept of real definitions anymore, let alone defend them, even though one could argue that any deeply held philosophy of realism *ought* to lead to a theory of real definitions (Lakoff 1987, 173). Many contemporary "metaphysical realists" still defend the idea that reality consists of independent, objective "real" objects that can be known, but they have abandoned an absolutist or "direct" realism for approaches that acknowledge that our accounts of the world are mediated by historically situated languages and technologies. Rom Harré, for example, defends metaphysical realism but not direct or absolutist realism: "Close examination has shown that the descriptive vocabulary of a scientific community is controlled by a shifting, historically contingent network of contexts, conceptual clusters, material practices, and social influences" (1986, 106). William P. Alston (1996), Michael Devitt (1996), Helen E. Longino (1990), Joseph Margolis (1986), Christopher Norris (1997), Hilary Putnam (1990), Nicholas Rescher (1987), Sean Sayers (1985), and Roger Trigg (1980) are other philosophers who defend various forms of non-absolutist metaphysical realism while abandoning essentialism and the notion that language provides direct access to reality. None of their works (at least those cited here) explicitly address or defend the status of real definitions. Jerry A.

Fodor declared recently that there is now "something like a consensus" that "the notion of a definition has no very significant role to play in theories of meaning" (1998, 44). Real definitions, which arguably at one point in Western history were the *point* of philosophical analysis, have been set aside by most professional philosophers.[1]

Even if real definitions have lost favor with philosophers, the examples provided here suggest that the language of essentialism and metaphysical realism persists in the social arenas outside of the confines of professional philosophy. My position is that proponents of new definitions can produce better arguments if they recognize that definitions do not and cannot describe things-in-themselves but report or advocate functional relationships between words and people. In other words, along with Richard Robinson I advocate abandoning real definitions and turning toward a self-conscious, lexical approach to defining.

Attempts to define what things "really are," as Robinson notes, are fueled by the intuitive reasonableness of questions of the form "What is X?" (1950, 190). The reasonableness of such questions results from the degree to which our language is still permeated by Platonic/Aristotelian terminology and assumptions. An implicit metaphysical absolutism in our ways of speaking reinforces the natural attitude toward definition. Breaking from real definitions, therefore, must be part of a departure from metaphysical absolutism.

I turn now from the more purely philosophical objections to real definitions toward more pragmatic concerns. The first objection is that real definitions unnecessarily narrow one's argumentative focus. As I argue at some length in the next chapter, conflicting definitions in general are perspective or theory bound. That is, the truth or appropriateness of a particular definition is dependent upon the truth or appropriateness of interrelated beliefs, values, and concepts. In most situations, one cannot deny the truth or appropriateness of a rival definition without presuming the truth or appropriateness of one's own. When an arguer uses dissociation to contrast one definition with an inferior one, there is an important sense in which the defense of the "realness" of one's definition is circular. If an arguer has, to his or her satisfaction, arrived at an understanding of what X actually is, then of course rival definitions merely represent what X merely appears to be. The upshot is that there is no theory- or perspective-independent means of arbitrating between conflicting real definitions.

Two examples can illustrate the circularity of dissociative strategies in defense of a real definition. In the wake of growing support for rede-

fining death as "brain death," Bethia S. Currie argued that the "redefinition of death as 'irreversible coma' is dangerous and should be opposed" (1978, 196). The basis of her argument was a series of examples
of patients who would have been declared dead by new proposed guidelines but who recovered from their comas. These are cases in which "the
prediction of outcome of coma may *seem* clear," but the *"facts"* are that
the patients lived (196). Walton, a defender of redefining death by brain
activity, responded in three ways. He argued that the *"actual"* documen-
tation of these cases "is questionable"; Currie's expert testimony was
from Soviet scientists "whose findings have apparently been challenged
by neurologists from other countries"; and her examples did not meet
his "criteria" for death because they fell under specified "exceptions"
(1980, 26–27). Walton was confident that these patients were not "really" dead according to his definition. He dismissed Currie's evidence
as only apparent (not "actual"), as coming from questionable (pseudo-)
scientists, and as representing exceptions (not the rule). Through these
dissociations, Walton was able to keep his definition and its justification intact. If any of these patients had been "really" dead—that is, dead
according to Walton's definition—they would have stayed dead.

Veatch begins the defense of his definition of death, quoted above,
by noting the apparent fuzziness of the word in common usage in a series of stories about a sports figure involved in a serious automobile
accident: "*The Washington Post* ran a story the next day with the head-
line 'Flyers Goalie Lindbergh is Declared Brain Dead.' . . . The coverage of the story for the next two days continued to refer to him as 'brain
dead,' yet spoke of him as 'being kept alive on life-support systems,' as
'hovering near death,' and as having 'no chance to survive.' One account reported that he was declared 'clinically dead' on Monday. . . .
The *Times* reported on Wednesday that he 'died yesterday afternoon at
the conclusion of a five-hour operation to remove his organs for trans-
plant'" (1989, 15).

Veatch relates the anecdote to pose the question: "What can it mean
to say that a person is declared 'brain dead' on Sunday morning, 'clinically dead' on Monday, and 'dead' on Tuesday afternoon?" (1989, 15).
The inference is that if people use the word "death" in such an inconsistent manner, they must not understand what death itself "really" is.
Although one could argue that each of the claims concerning the patient's
death is correct according to the particular perspective being used, advocates for new definitions contend that only one of the usages is correct—the one that corresponds to their perspective and definition.

Alternatively, an advocate can take on the burden of satisfying *all* competing perspectives. Lamb suggests that "the only wholly satisfying concept of death is that which trumps other concepts of death in so far as it yields a diagnosis of death which is *beyond dispute*. It follows that any criterion which, when fulfilled, leaves it possible for someone to *say* that the patient is still alive, is unsatisfactory" (1985, 13). Although Lamb's standard is rather open-minded, its execution is not as flexible. He later attacks a rival's attempt to define death as a "process" rather than as an "event" on the basis that his opponent's concepts are "flawed" and have "never found acceptance in any medical community" (77). Apparently, it is not enough for someone to be able to say that a patient is still alive; it is not someone's ability to dispute a case but the profession of medicine that must precisely define the "moment of death" (82).

Needless to say, a good deal of argument and evidence has been left out of my reading of the authors' arguments defining "death" discussed so far. They are not as unreasonable as my analysis might imply; however, it is the point of contact between competing arguers' positions that is of interest here. When rival definitional perspectives conflict, arguers must make explicit or implicit comparisons. In so doing, circular defenses may be inevitable.

The second pragmatic objection to real definitions is that they are dysfunctional to the extent that they direct attention to "is" claims and away from "ought" claims. The proponent of a novel definition is proposing a new way of using a particular word. The proponent seeks to change our linguistic behavior and thereby alter patterns of denotative conformity. Accordingly, the question arguers should be asking is not "What is X?" but rather "How *ought* we use the word X?" or "What should be described by the word X?" Normative questions of this sort cannot be answered acontextually; they virtually compel interlocutors to address the pragmatic needs of a given community of language users located in a particular historical moment. Viewed rhetorically, proponents of new definitions seek to alter the behavior of a specific audience. Perelman and Olbrechts-Tyteca declare that "it is in terms of an audience that an argumentation develops" (1969, 5); definitional argumentation is no exception. An arguer defending a definition is just as culpable for the pragmatic and ethical results of his or her arguments as is any other advocate seeking to move an audience to action.

The debate over defining death would not have occurred had medical technology not advanced to the point that old linguistic practices became problematic. Current life-support technology can maintain the cardiorespiratory functions of a person even when all brain activities have ceased. Is such a person "alive" or "dead"? If the person is alive, then the removal of organs, such as the heart, would "kill" him or her, and the surgeon could be criminally charged with murder or sued in civil court for wrongful death. Such a case took place in Virginia in 1972. In *Tucker v. Lower,* the judge initially instructed the jury using the traditional cardiorespiratory definition of death found in *Black's Law Dictionary.* Before sending the jury to their deliberations, however, the judge's new instructions allowed them to consider brain damage as a possible cause of death in the case (Converse 1975). By the traditional definition, the doctor clearly "killed" the patient; however, the jury opted for the brain death definition and cleared the doctor. Interestingly enough, although "brain death" is now the commonly accepted legal definition of death, a definitional debate continues over precisely what constitutes brain death (Youngner, Arnold, and Schapiro 1999).

The case of *Tucker v. Lower* is not unique (Humphrey and Wickett 1986, 283–85). In fact, "as a matter of social, historical and cultural practice and as a matter of law, a variety of social and legal consequences are linked with an individual's death" (Brock 1999, 295). It is clear in the literature examined for this study that the desire to "harvest" donor organs without suffering legal penalty is one of the motivations for defining death as the cessation of brain activity. Additionally, the ability to maintain cardiorespiratory functions following the cessation of brain activity raises concerns about the removal of remaining medical treatments, the time for mourning, the transfer of property to the deceased's inheritors, and marital status (Brock 1999; Charo 1999). Yet the discussion of practical issues is often treated as secondary. That does not mean that the arguers feel that the practical motivations are unimportant, but it may mean that such motivations are driven underground and are not discussed in a full and open manner. The thrust of my argument is that circular arguments about the "essential" or "true" nature of life and death should be set aside in order to focus more clearly on the social and ethical implications of defining death one way (brain death) as opposed to another (cardiorespiratory failure). The choice of definition is what will guide a physician's practical decision to pronounce a patient dead. After all, a central goal of defining is denotative conformity: we want to be in a position in which *all* doctors would make a similar diagnosis of life or death and in which one is not motivated to make a "premature" pronouncement owing to pressures for organ donorship, for example.

The sort of pragmatic orientation advocated here[2] is evident in an argument offered by Alexander Morgan Capron and Leon R. Kass on behalf of a specific statutory definition for determining human death (1972). Capron and Kass note that terms such as "defining death" and "definition of death" are problematic, and they carefully distinguish between different uses to which theory- or perspective-bound definitions could be put. They offer their own "definition" as a proposal for action; specifically, as a means of stipulating when it is appropriate for physicians to pronounce a patient dead. Their defense includes such practical matters as public acceptance, protection of patient rights, and concern for doctor liability. At the same time, the authors point out that certain practical considerations ought *not* be covered by a law that is designed to define death. Admitting that the need for organ donors is a source of pressure for changing current definitions of death, they suggest that "[if] more organs are needed for transplantation than can be legally obtained, the question whether the benefits conferred by transplantation justify the risks associated with a broader 'definition' of death should be addressed directly rather than by attempting to subsume it under the question 'what is death?' Such a direct confrontation with the issue could lead to a discussion about the standards and procedures under which organs might be taken" (1972, 107–8). Capron and Kass demonstrate that it is possible to address a question involving denotative conformity without using dissociation strategies or defending a real definition. Their definition is consistent with the apparent intent of those defining death as an irreversible cessation of brain functions, yet the wording of their proposal, "A person will be considered dead if . . . ," suggests that their focus is on influencing linguistic behavior more than determining what death itself "really" is.

According to Stevenson, persuasive definitions seek to alter the "descriptive" meaning of a word while retaining its emotive meaning. Perelman and Olbrechts-Tyteca modify Stevenson's position because they believe the descriptive and emotive meanings of a term are inseparable (1969, 447). Stevenson's position can be reformulated as suggesting that advocates of a new definition of X seek to alter *which* "things" (or "set-of-sensations") we denote as X while preserving past patterns of action or behavior taken *toward* the "things" (or "set-of-sensations") called X. In this sense, virtually all proposed novel real definitions are persuasive definitions, because "all those who argue in favor of some definition want it . . . to influence the use which would have been made of the concept had they not intervened" (Perelman and Olbrechts-Tyteca 1969, 213).

Robinson's critique of persuasive definitions neatly parallels the point made here about real definitions substituting pseudo-*is* claims for normative considerations. Robinson suggests that arguments proposing new and nonconventional definitions should be seen as stipulative rather than as "real" (1950, 59–92). It is simply more intellectually honest, according to Robinson's analysis, to stipulate a new definition for a word and defend its practical utility than it is to argue in behalf of a "real" definition. A persuasive definition is "at best a mistake and at worst a lie, because it consists in getting someone to alter his valuations under the false impression that he is not altering his valuations but correcting his knowledge of the facts" (1950, 170).

In the case of the word "death," how the word is defined has obvious and profound implications. In other definitional disputes, the stakes may seem smaller, but they are still significant. Definitions identify the scope of our daily endeavors, and it is not an exaggeration to say that they often demarcate our available "reality." Calls to adopt new definitions are calls to change our attitudes and behavior. For these reasons, arguments about definitions should be conducted in as ethical and productive a manner as possible. The first step toward improving our argumentative practices concerning definitions is to acknowledge their unavoidably persuasive and argumentative features. The second is to eschew "real" definitions as ethically suspect and philosophically problematic.

4
Definitions as Prescriptive and Theory Bound: The Case of "Rape"

A definition is always a matter of choice. (Perelman and Olbrechts-Tyteca 1969, 448)

The purpose of this chapter is to illustrate some of the ways in which definitions are prescriptive and normative. In the process, a second theme concerning the way in which definitions depend on larger clusters of beliefs, or theories, is developed.

As noted earlier, mundane definitions found in dictionaries report facts of usage, how words have been used in the past. Dictionaries are repositories of previous usage that are treated by most language users as factually correct. Many people assume that matters involving "is" and "ought" are so distinct that they require different ways of thinking and arguing about them. Facts involve "is" propositions (X is Y), and because facts are "objective," they must be verified through appropriate empirical methods. Values involve "ought" propositions, and because values are "subjective," they can only be accepted or rejected, but not empirically proven. Facts are descriptive; values are prescriptive and normative.

As simple as the previous distinction may sound, the is/ought dichotomy is highly problematic. There have been many critiques of the is/ought dichotomy, but at the moment only one needs discussion. Mundane definitions, understood as facts of usage, can be described as "institutional facts." Philosopher John R. Searle describes institutional facts as those dependent on the existence of certain human institutions (1969, 50–53). He writes that it is only "given the institution of marriage that certain forms of behavior constitute" one person marrying another, and it is "only given the institution of money that I now have a five dollar bill in my hand. Take away the institution and all I have is a piece of paper with various gray and green markings" (51). Searle claims that "every institutional fact is underlain by a (system of) rule(s) of the form 'X counts as Y in context C'" (51–52). Explicit and implicit rules are both descriptive and prescriptive. The laws governing the institution of marriage both delineate what marriage "is" and what one must do to marry; those laws therefore both describe and prescribe what "counts" as "getting married." Similarly, by learning about the U.S. institution of money, one learns when to say that a particular piece of paper is a five-dollar bill.

Dictionary definitions can be understood as prescriptive guides to what counts as correct usage. By describing the dominant uses of a word in the past, dictionaries prescribe how the term ought to be used now. Part of learning any given language is learning what counts as what—when one ought to call a certain animal a "dog" or a "cat," for example. Although initially we learn what to call an X or Y informally, dictionaries represent a sort of formal rule book of the "institution" of a particular language. Definitions guide the choice of "*what* we should say *when*" and thus offer prescriptive answers to questions of the form "What is X?" (Cavell 1969, 20).

The prescriptive character of mundane definitions is fairly straight-forward. Just as adults informally correct children's overextension or underextension of a word to teach them how they ought to use a word, dictionaries are the more formal source language users typically consult to verify the correct ways to use a word. Dictionary definitions report institutional facts of usage with which we ought to comply if we are to use words correctly. If one does not agree to participate in a particular language institution by choosing to adopt nonstandard usage such as regional dialects, speaking a language other than English, or simply renouncing dictionaries as obsolete, then the normative force of an English dictionary is rendered ineffective. One is not obliged to follow the rules of an institution from which one has walked away (Searle 1969, 184–86).

The prescriptive character of novel definitions is even more obvious. New definitions are "proposals for future usage" (Robinson 1950,

10). When an advocate wants others to adopt a new definition, that person must persuade people that they ought to alter their future linguistic behavior. As noted in the previous chapter, Capron and Kass (1972) offer their definition of death as a proposal for action, specifically as a means of stipulating when it is appropriate for physicians to pronounce a patient dead. "Real" definitions are criticized on the basis that the persuasive appeals on which they are typically defended are pragmatically and philosophically problematic. Lexical definitions are not without problems as well, but I argue in the pages that follow that lexical definitions are superior to real definitions, in part because novel lexical definitions are defended in a more explicitly prescriptive and normative manner. I support these claims through the example of changing definitions of "rape."

Changing Definitions of "Rape"

Rape has been described as a nationwide epidemic. Noting that "violence against women should be treated as a significant social problem," the National Institute of Justice Centers for Disease Control and Prevention reports that one in six women in the U.S.—more than 300,000 per year—has experienced an attempted or completed rape (Tjaden and Thoennes 1998, 11). Reported rapes "more than doubled from the early '70s—at nearly twice the rate of all other violent crimes and four times the overall crime rate" (Faludi 1991, xvii). The rapid increase is not a result of an increase in the percentage of rapes reported; studies have not shown any increase in women's rate of reporting rape, which still hovers around only 10 percent of all cases (Faludi 1991, 465). Nearly nine out of ten women in a 1989 poll considered rape the "most important issue for women today" (Faludi 1991, 321–22).

How is "rape" defined? Here it is appropriate to pause long enough to note the differences between legal and ordinary dictionary definitions. The latter are supposed to report facts of usage—how a given word has been used by a general population. A legal definition is typically more precise and has no necessary connection with how a word is used by a general population. Legal dictionaries, such as *Black's Law Dictionary,* also are supposed to report facts of usage, but for a very specific population of language users, namely legal institutions. Legal definitions generally are derived from one of two sources. Legislative definitions are stipulative definitions as to what particular words mean within the context of a given law. Judicial definitions are stipulative pronouncements

of how specific courts have chosen to define particular words. Both
become prescriptive guides within legal institutions about the ways legal terms are to be used and enforced.

Legal definitions generally are self-consciously lexical and prescriptive. That is, when a legal definition of X is set forth, there is no pre-
tense that this is what X really is (a fact of essence) or even much concern about the ways that the term X has been used previously (a fact of
usage). Previous usage is obviously a factor, but not a determining one,
in decisions about how to define a term for the purposes of a law or court
case. Many statutes include a section labeled "definitions," which state
that "for the purposes of this law, X means so-and-so"; otherwise, the
law is usually written in a form similar to "X counts as Y in context C."
For example, in 1988 the Indiana state law against rape read, in its en-
tirety, as follows:

Indiana Code 35-42-4-1 Rape

Sec. 1. (a) A person who knowingly or intentionally has sexual
intercourse with a member of the opposite sex when:
   (1) the other person is compelled by force or imminent
       threat of force;
   (2) the other person is unaware that the sexual intercourse is
       occurring; or
   (3) the other person is so mentally disabled or deficient that
       consent to sexual intercourse cannot be given;
commits rape, a Class B felony. However, the offense is a Class
A felony if it is committed by using or threatening the use of
deadly force, if it is committed while armed with a deadly
weapon, or if it results in serious bodily injury to any person
other than a defendant.   ·
 (b) This section does not apply to sexual intercourse between
spouses, unless a petition for:
   (1) dissolution of their marriage;
   (2) a petition for their legal separation; or
   (3) a protective order under IC 34-4-5.1;
is pending and the spouses are living apart.

It is an institutional fact, then, that certain forms of sexual intercourse
count as rape in the state of Indiana (X counts as Y in context C). Trans-
forming the law into an abbreviated Aristotelian definition is a simple
matter: rape is heterosexual intercourse (class name) that is nonconsen-

sual (attribute). A more elaborate Aristotelian definition would include the specific constituents of "nonconsensual" sexual intercourse: coercion, marital status, and lack of ability to grant consent.

Three aspects of the Indiana law are noteworthy. First, only heterosexual intercourse is included. Homosexual activities are governed by other laws; by definition, rape is impossible between two people of the same sex. Second, the sex of the rapist is not specified. Until recently, almost all state laws concerning rape defined it explicitly as a crime that men commit against women. In the 1999 edition of *Black's Law Dictionary*, for example, the first definition for rape is "unlawful sexual intercourse committed by a man with a woman not his wife through force and against her will" (Black 1999, 1267). Third, the law specifically excludes sexual intercourse between people married to each other prior to certain legal proceedings, including filing for separation or divorce. "Spousal rape" is an oxymoron, according to such a definition. Put yet another way, the word "rape" simply has no referent within the context of a marital relationship in areas governed by such a law.

Although there have been many changes in state rape laws over the past several decades, the one of primary interest here is the definitional change to include coerced sexual intercourse within a marital relationship. Whereas twenty-five years ago, no man could be charged with raping his wife, today it is some form of crime in all fifty states for a husband to rape his wife (Connerton 1997). Typically, the change is effected by omitting those portions of the law that define rape as "committed by a man with a woman not his wife." For example, in 1989 the state of Indiana changed the rape law quoted above simply by omitting the entire (b) section. However, not all states have implemented such a comprehensive change in definition (Russell 1982, 375–81); while seventeen states have completely abolished the marital rape exemption by deleting words such as "not his wife," "to whom he is married," or "unlawful" from their general rape statutes, the exemption survives in mutated form in the majority of states (Brown 1995, 664–68). Where the marital rape exemption has not been completely eliminated, statutes make spousal rape a lesser crime than nonmarital rape, allowing spouses a shorter time to report a rape than nonspousal victims, or require the victim to prove bodily injury or threat of bodily injury without a similar requirement when the accused is not the spouse of the victim (Brown 1995). The difference is a classic case of competing definitions: certain behaviors between married people in some states count as rape, while in other states the same behavior is not rape.

The rationale for defining rape as involving an act committed by a man "with a woman not his wife" is "as ancient as the original definition of criminal rape, which was synonymous with that quaint phrase of Biblical origin, 'unlawful carnal knowledge.' To our Biblical forefathers, any carnal knowledge outside the marriage contract was 'unlawful.' And any carnal knowledge within the marriage contract was, by definition, 'lawful'" (Brownmiller 1975, 380). The modern legal definition has been inherited directly from English common law. Lord Matthew Hale declared in the late 1600s that "the husband cannot be guilty of a rape committed by himself upon his lawful wife, for by their mutual matrimonial consent and contract the wife hath given up herself in this kind unto her husband, which she cannot retract" (1778, 629). Throughout most of the history of U.S. jurisprudence, Hale has "stood as the accepted authority" on coerced sex within a marriage ("To Have" 1986, 1256; see also Augustine 1991, 560–62). His explanation has been described as the "implied" or "irrevocable consent" theory and is still influential two centuries later: "A husband cannot be guilty of an actual rape, or of an assault with intent to rape his wife even if he has, or attempts to have, sexual intercourse with her forcibly and against her will. The reason for this, it has been said, is that when the woman assumes the marriage relation she gives her consent to marital relations which the law will not permit her to retract in order to charge her husband with the offense" (Silberstang 1972, 775). Sir William Blackstone's influential *Commentaries,* originally published in 1765, provide a somewhat different justification for not counting coerced marital sexual intercourse as rape. Known initially as the "unities" theory and later, more critically, as the "woman-as-property" theory, Blackstone's argument is that "by marriage, the husband and wife are one person in law: that is, the very being or legal existence of the woman is suspended during the marriage, or at least is incorporated and consolidated into that of the husband" (1859, 442). As a result, a husband cannot grant "any thing to his wife . . . for the grant would be to suppose her separate existence" (442). In matters that treat the husband and wife as separate, she is "inferior to him, and acting by his compulsion" (444). Because marriage put a woman "under the protection and influence of her husband, her *baron,* or lord . . . her condition during her marriage is called her *coverture*" (442). The very "body of the wife was, at least historically, the property of the husband in Anglo-Saxon law" (Bessmer 1984, 84). The husband "may enforce sexual connection" because, by marriage, "she has given her body to her husband" ("Rape" 1918, 1175). Rape thus understood is a type of property crime of man against man, since "the law protected a father's interest in his daughter's virginity and a husband's interest in his wife's fidelity. Rape of an unmarried woman rendered her unmarriageable because her value to future husbands was destroyed, while rape of a married woman brought disgrace upon her husband and family" ("To Have" 1986, 1256–57). Despite changes in the nineteenth century that radically challenged the legal standing of "unities" or "coverture" theory, its spirit lived on. An anonymous author argued in 1954 that "historically," rape "has had great importance in destroying the acceptability of an unmarried girl as a bride" and suggested the continued exclusion of coerced marital sexual intercourse from the legal definition of rape ("Rape and Battery" 1954, 724).

Explicitly and implicitly, the "irrevocable consent" and "women-as-property" theories have formed the basis for the laws and court decisions excluding coerced sex within a marriage from the legal definition of rape (Augustine 1991). The two theories are closely related and can be usefully treated as two aspects of the "male sexual prerogative" theory of marital sex. Such a combined rationale can be detected in an 1888 ruling by Justice Pollock in *Regina v. Clarence:* "The husband's connection with his wife is not only lawful, but it is in accordance with the ordinary condition of married life. It is done in pursuance of the marital contract and of the status which was created by marriage, and the wife as to the connection itself is in a different position from any other woman, for *she has no right or power to refuse her consent*" (cited in "Rape and Battery" 1954, 723n, emphasis added).

The beliefs that inform the male sexual prerogative theory have not gone unchallenged. Advocates of women's rights have successfully overturned many aspects of coverture laws, especially in the area of women's property and contract rights ("To Have" 1986, 1257–58). Prior to 1977, there is no record of any serious legal challenge to Lord Hale's assertions regarding irrevocable consent. In the wake of reforms of other aspects of rape laws, courts in New Jersey in 1978 harshly criticized Hale's notion of irrevocable consent as "tantamount to 'bondage of a wife' . . . [that] was 'fatally anachronistic' given the changes in the status of women since the seventeenth century" (Augustine 1991, 564–65). The objection to the male sexual prerogative theory is simple: the theory is sexist and its application in law discriminates unfairly against married women. As Susan Brownmiller notes in her classic *Against Our Will:* "[C]ompulsory sexual intercourse is not a husband's right in marriage, for such a 'right' gives the lie to any concept of equality and human dignity. Consent is better arrived at by husband and wife afresh each time, for if women are to be what we believe we are—equal partners—then intercourse must be construed as an act of mutual desire and not as a wifely 'duty,' enforced by the permissible threat of bodily harm or of economic sanctions. . . . A sexual assault is an invasion of bodily integrity and a violation of freedom and self-determination wherever it happens to take place, in or out of the marriage bed" (1975, 381).

As beliefs about married women's rights have changed, contradictions have become evident in the justice system's language use. In the 1977 case of *State of New Mexico v. Bell,* for example, the court held that the husband was "legally incapable of raping his wife" because the "wife is irrebutably presumed to consent to sexual relations with her husband even if forcible and without consent" ("Rape" 1992, 97). In short, the woman in this case was held to have both *consented* and *not-consented!* Such linguistic anomalies signal a definitional rupture; in this case, two conflicting notions of "consent" are at work and, by implication, two conflicting definitions of rape.

Consent is granted through the agreement to marry, according to the male sexual prerogative theory; thus, "marital rape" is definitionally impossible. Viewed as an institutional fact, rape is no more possible within a marriage than kicking a field goal is possible in a baseball game. According to such a theory, the idea expressed in the phrase quoted previously—"even if forcible and without consent"—simply does not make sense. That the utterance can and does make sense points to a rival theory and definition of rape, one that stipulates that rape is intercourse (class name) that is nonconsensual, that is, involves coercion or lack of ability to grant consent (attributes). For simplicity's sake, such an approach will be called the "consent" theory or definition of rape.

Although legal definitions bring into focus the conceptual differences between the male sexual prerogative and consent theories of rape, the conflict between the two can be understood in part by noting how people initially learn to use the word "rape." As demonstrated earlier, most words are not acquired by reference to a dictionary but rather by reference to a prototypical exemplar. We learn to use words in later contexts based on the perceived similarities and differences to earlier uses (SDRs). Most people learn to use the word "rape" by reference to the "classical" rape situation: "the ambush of a lone woman by one or more strangers in a deserted place at night" ("Rape and Battery" 1954, 723–24). Just as different children may pay attention to certain characteristics of a dog the first time they see one and later "wrongly" apply it to a cat or wolf, so can people develop their respective category of rape based on different aspects of the most common exemplar. For example, an opponent of the consent definition notes that married couples are not strangers and probably have been intimate on prior occasions, thus "in the ordinary marriage relationship the classical form of forcible rape is not probable" ("Rape and Battery" 1954, 724).

On the other hand, advocates of the consent definition argue that the more important characteristic to note is lack of consent. Once lack of consent has been stipulated as the most valuable defining attribute of rape, the appropriateness of the "classical form of forcible rape" is called into question. Using consent as the guide to classifying specific acts, a far wider variety of behaviors has been categorized as rape. Such labels as "date rape," "acquaintance rape," and "marital rape" typically are not intended to designate separate categories of rape. Indeed, most advocates of a consent definition of rape espouse slogans such as "Rape is rape," and "If she says 'no,' it's rape." Rather, labels such as "marital rape" are valuable as additional exemplars to teach language users what to designate as rape. By juxtaposing a prototypical notion of "date" to the classical notion of rape, we are encouraged to think of rape in a different way. Adding terms such as "date," "acquaintance," and "marital" to "rape" act like linguistic crowbars to expand the range of situations in which the behavior "rape" can be denoted. Once our conceptual category has been reshaped so that consent is the definitive attribute, the "crowbars" are no longer necessary, and we can see that "rape is rape," regardless of social context or previous relationship status. How we understand the conceptual category of rape has changed.

Using a fairly straightforward definition of rape (sexual intercourse obtained by the threat or use of force, or that occurs when the victim is incapable of granting consent), Diana E. H. Russell's study suggests that at least 14 percent of women, or one in seven, who are or have been married have been raped or sexually assaulted by their spouses (1982, 57–60). Of the victims interviewed by Russell, 85 percent were subjected to "completed penile-vaginal rape by their husbands or ex-husbands," an act that would clearly violate even the most conservative state law governing rape were the perpetrator not the woman's husband (57). Once the effort was made to listen to victims of marital rape, their accounts revealed that such attacks involved "brutality and terror and violence and humiliation to rival the most graphic stranger rape"

(Finkelhor in "To Have" 1986, 1261). Rape by someone supposedly in a loving and caring relationship can be especially devastating. Contrary to the belief that rape victims who know their attackers do not suffer the same sort of ill effects as victims of "stranger rape," research demonstrates that the short- and long-term traumatic effects are typically worse for victims of marital rape (Russell 1982, 190–205; Augustine 1991, 571–72; "To Have" 1986, 1261–62).

Given that the male sexual prerogative theory leads to such contradictions as claiming that women have both consented and not-consented, and given that victims of nonconsensual marital sexual intercourse suffer as much or worse as victims of nonmarital rape, the consent definition makes sense as a prescriptive and normative guide to the use of the word "rape." The widespread use in ordinary discourse as well as in academic and legal publications of "marital rape" clearly signals the need to address an important definitional rupture. Nonetheless, there has been a great deal of resistance to eliminating the so-called marital rape exemption. In fact, at one point about one-quarter of the states have moved in the opposite direction by expanding the exemption to cover unmarried cohabiters and even "voluntary social companions" (Russell 1982, 21–22). Such expansions indicate that the male sexual prerogative theory is still very much alive and well: "[T]he expansion of the exemption beyond the marital relationship reflects the deeply discriminatory vision of women inherent in the theories used to justify the exemption; in particular, the expansion reflects a modern version of Hale's theory that women who enter into relationships with men give an implied consent to sexual intercourse or that those who consent to intercourse once are forever bound" ("To Have" 1986, 1260).

Defenders of the marital rape exemption offer arguments that can be grouped into two categories: definitional arguments and arguments "from consequence." The latter type of argument includes the following (see Sallmann 1980, 79–80; Marsh, Geist, and Caplan 1982, 15, 92):

1. Prosecuting husbands for raping their wives will destroy marital harmony and impede reconciliation efforts.
2. Marital rape is less harmful than other rapes.
3. Alternative legal remedies are available for victims of marital rape, including assault charges, an order of protection, separation, or divorce.
4. Prosecutions of marital rape face difficult problems of proof.

5. Vindictive wives may fabricate rape charges when no rape has occurred.
6. The court system could become overloaded with charges of spousal rape.
7. Rape laws violate the privacy of marital relations.

These arguments all concede that coerced sexual intercourse within a marriage is appropriately labeled rape. There is no definitional gap or rupture; there is simply a disagreement about what ought to be the legal approach to the category of marital rape. Such arguments concede the consent definition of rape and argue, in effect, that husbands ought to be able to get away with rape because of problematic consequences of criminalizing marital rape. Not surprisingly, this line of argument has been sharply criticized:

> Item 1 is absurd, since it is not the prosecution of rape but the act of rape itself that is far more devastating to a marriage.
>
> Item 2 has been empirically disproved.
>
> Item 3 fails to provide women the right to legal redress for the specific crime committed, the alternatives fail to provide an adequate legal deterrent to marital rape, and such options are simply not a viable option for many women.
>
> Item 4 is a red herring in the sense that there are many crimes (including "stranger rape") that are difficult to prove; furthermore, there have been enough successful prosecutions in states that have changed their laws to disprove the point.
>
> Item 5 is highly unlikely given the traumatic experiences associated with rape trials for the accuser and the low rate of success in prosecution of rape.
>
> Item 6 has been empirically disproved in states in which the laws have been changed.
>
> Item 7 confuses marital sex with marital rape; privacy rights do not shield violators of criminal laws.[1]

I also note that items 1, 2, 4, and 7 were rejected as a defense of the marital rape exemption by the Court of Appeals of New York in *People v. Liberta* (474 N.E. 2d 567), the oft-cited case that declared that state's spousal exemption unconstitutional.

In contrast to arguments from consequence, definitional arguments against the elimination of the marital rape exemption do not concede the consent definition of rape; that is, they deny the utility of the idea of marital rape. In the 1954 British case of *Regina v. Miller,* a woman brought rape and assault charges against her husband ("Rape and Battery" 1954). At the time of the attack, she had been separated from her husband for a year and had initiated divorce proceedings. The charge of rape was thrown out based on the common law theory of implied consent, although the wife had long since left her husband. In defense of the ruling, one commentator suggested that forcible sexual intercourse can be a form of marital passion: "Forcible rape between unmarried persons is the culmination of a desire whose very inception is disapproved; between married persons it is a loss of control over an explosive but encouraged situation" ("Rape and Battery" 1954, 725). Such patently sexist thinking replicates the rationale of a 1905 case that also exonerated the husband's behavior based on the implied consent theory. In *Frazier v. State of Texas,* the court described a husband's coercive efforts toward sexual intercourse with his estranged wife as "a rather vigorous" insistence "upon what he believed to be his rights as a husband" (quoted in Augustine 1991, 564). The 1954 commentator quoted previously also notes that resistance may not accurately reflect the true wishes of the woman, "since a seeming lack of consent may be simply a manifestation of the fact that resistance during preliminary love-making greatly increases the sexual pleasure of some women" ("Rape and Battery" 1954, 728). Throughout the comments, the author clearly makes the prescriptive argument that the legal definition of rape ought not include coerced marital intercourse: "[R]ape is a category ill-suited to marriage" (725).

Even in jurisdictions in which the consent definition of rape has been adopted, there has been resistance by some to treating all nonconsensual sexual intercourse as rape. Putting new laws on the books does not ensure that all individuals responsible for enforcing those laws will immediately assimilate the new definitions and categories. Language users must *learn* to restructure their categories and may resist efforts to alter or replace old exemplars. After the rape laws were reformed significantly in Michigan in 1974, many criminal justice officials continued to distinguish between "real rape," committed by sexual psychopaths preying on strangers, and other sex crimes considered less serious (Marsh, Geist, and Caplan 1982, 107). It may be concluded that coerced marital sexual intercourse is not rape because "in the minds" of those who firmly believe in the male sexual prerogative theory, "nothing wrong has happened" (Bessmer 1984, 308).

The temptation to dismiss out of hand such sexist attitudes is great, particularly when the language use of advocates of the marital rape exemption is contradictory regarding the issue of consent. To the advocates of the consent definition, coerced marital sex is so obviously rape that opponents' definitional squabbles may appear to be "mere semantics," or worse, a cynical twisting of the truth. If marital rape really is rape, then opponents to reform are either out of touch with reality or lying, or both. As the previous sentence suggests, however, such declarations resurrect the metaphysical absolutism discussed and criticized in the previous chapter. The point of definitions, especially those adopted for use in legal contexts, is to designate what counts as rape for purposes that are both shared and practical. Lexical definitions remind us that the relevant question is not "What *is* rape?" but "What shall we call 'rape'?" The answer to the latter question requires us to articulate and defend competing definitions with prescriptive and normative arguments. If we find ourselves persuaded that the consent theory is preferable because it does not unfairly discriminate against married women, then it is easy to "see" that coerced marital sex *is* rape. It is no longer merely a "theory" that at least 14 percent of married women are raped, but an empirical observation.

The Theory/Observation Distinction: From Metaphysics to Social Agreement

The preceding discussion illustrates that the choice to label or define certain behaviors as rape depends on a larger set of beliefs, or theory, about human interaction in general and rape in particular. What I am describing as the theory-dependency of definitions is extremely important and can be best understood through an account of the rise and fall of the notion of "observation statements" in science.

The philosophers of the so-called Vienna Circle of the 1920s and 1930s gave rise to a philosophical approach known as logical positivism. These philosophers, including Moritz Schlick, Rudolf Carnap, and Otto Neurath, were profoundly influenced by what later came to be called the "picture theory" of meaning presented in Ludwig Wittgenstein's 1921 book, *Tractatus Logico-Philosophicus* (1974). The "early" Wittgenstein of the *Tractatus* believed that the world possesses a fixed and knowable structure. The world is represented to us by language that, for Wittgenstein, is a picture of reality. Because language pictures reality, there must be a similarity between "that which pictures and that which pictured" (Phillips 1977, 21). In other words, language must accurately correspond to the structure of reality. There are several important corollaries to Wittgenstein's picture theory of language. To begin with, the theory clarifies the basis for a referential theory of meaning. Language has meaning because it refers to objects or "states of affairs" in the world. Names are representatives or "simple signs" of objects (Wittgenstein 1974, §3.144–3.221). "Propositions" are pictures-in-language of that in the world to which they refer:

> A proposition is a picture of reality.
> A proposition is a model of reality as we imagine it. (1974, §4.01)

Wittgenstein also provided a language-based rationale for what is commonly referred to as the correspondence theory of truth. The theory posits that truth consists of some form of correspondence or agreement between belief and fact, between a person's subjective opinion of what-is and what objectively "really is." The correspondence theory combines epistemological and metaphysical considerations: The True is The Real. According to Wittgenstein:

> Reality is compared with propositions.
> A proposition can be true or false only in virtue of being a picture of reality. (1974, §4.05–4.06)
> If an elementary proposition is true, the state of affairs exists: if an elementary proposition is false, the state of affairs does not exist. (§4.25)

If we think about the way we learn language as children, we can understand why Wittgenstein's picture theory of meaning was so influential. Except for blind children, most learning by ostension is visual. We initially learn words by literally matching visual sensations (pictures) with certain sounds (words). Many studies have documented that adults talk to children quite differently than adults talk to each other. Many of the differences are aimed at avoiding ambiguity and teaching words that have the most referential utility: "cat" as opposed to "mammal," for example. Learning simple names of particular objects is the first step, followed by learning names of classes of objects. At least while we are children, the idea that particular objects can be grouped into multiple categories—even apparently conflicting categories—could be very dysfunctional and hence is avoided. Most people become socialized into an implicit picture theory of language that they never find necessary to challenge or modify; a fixed world, as pictured and "given" through language, is taken for granted. Early language education and socialization avoids the idea that our understanding of the world is relative and contingent; rather, "diversity and uncertainty are perceived as extensive but only temporary conditions" (Heffernan 1975, 496; cf. Perry 1970).

Whatever the reason for Wittgenstein's persuasiveness, by the 1930s philosophers such as Carnap (1936, 1937) and A. J. Ayer (1936) suggested that scientists describe phenomena using language that would not logically depend on any particular theory (see also Reichenbach 1953). Such language later would be described as "observation language." The assumption was that what scientists "saw"—sense data—is "concrete" and relatively "fixed and stable" (Barbour 1974, 94; Mulkay 1979, 29–30). Some positivists envisioned two levels of scientific language that differed in kind: "an unproblematic lower level of unchanging, objective data, describable in a pure observation language on which all observers can agree; and a separate upper level of theoretical constructs, acknowledged as products of [hu]man's creative imagination" (Barbour 1974, 94). What came to be called the "verifiability theory of meaning" is described by Quine as the "dogma" of reductionism, which is "the belief that each meaningful statement is equivalent to some logical construct upon terms which refer to immediate experience" (1980, 20).[2]

The distinction between observation and theory language came to be rejected by most philosophers. One of the most famous critiques of this distinction can be found in Quine's 1951 essay, "Two Dogmas of Empiricism" (1980, 20–46). Quine noted that philosophers had, by now, focused attention on the verification of observation sentences or statements because "it was in practice extremely difficult to distinguish observational terms, whose meanings were 'derived from experience,' from speculative theoretical terms" (Mulkay 1979, 32). Accordingly, the "statement," rather than individual words, came to be "recognized as the unit accountable to an empiricist critique" (Quine 1980, 42). Quine argues that individual observations are not meaningful in isolation but depend on prior conventions of linguistic behavior and a host of beliefs about the world that are related to the individual statement. Thus, Quine and others suggest that the world is made meaningful to us holistically rather than in the sort of atomistic way the reductionism of the verification theory of meaning posits. The "empirical content" that informs the statements of science is shared in "clusters" and "cannot for the most part be sorted out" among individual statements (1980, viii). Citing Pierre Duhem's influential work (1954), Quine contends that "our statements about the external world face the tribunal of sense experience not individually but only as a corporate body" (1980, 41). Our beliefs about the existence of physical objects and events are "cultural posits" that make sense as part of a larger "conceptual scheme" that is adjusted, over time, to meet our pragmatic needs (44). Put simply, the meaning of an observation statement depends on a larger, historically situated set of beliefs, or theory.

Philosopher Norwood Russell Hanson argues that even though the same visual stimuli or "sense data" may impinge on two scientists' retinas, they may not "see" the same thing. A "retinal reaction is only a physical state—a photochemical excitation," Hanson notes (1958, 6). Seeing is an "experience" that is influenced by the observer's past experiences, training, and beliefs; "there is a sense, then, in which seeing is a 'theory-laden' undertaking" (19). Similarly, Kuhn points out that a vast amount of "neural processing" takes place between the receipt of a stimulus and the awareness of a sensation (1970, 192–93; 1977, 308; see also Bronowski 1978, 18–22, 43). Kuhn adds that "very different stimuli can produce the same sensations; that the same stimulus can produce very different sensations; and finally, that the route from stimulus to sensation is in part conditioned by education" (1970, 193).

In light of such critiques, a number of philosophers of science, including Richard Braithwaite (1953, 79–82), Carl Hempel (1965, 112–13), and Mary Hesse (1974, 9–16), agree that the minimum unit of meaning is not the single term or the sentence but rather whole theories. Quine rejects the idea of "absolute meanings" and instead advocates a position he describes as "ontological relativity" (1969). Words have meaning only relative to a certain theory or linguistic framework: "This network of terms and predicates and auxiliary devices is, in relativity jargon, our frame of reference, or coordinate system. Relative to it we can and do talk meaningfully and distinctively" (48–49). According to Quine, this relativity is so strong that it is possible for two rival frameworks or theories to make not only different but also contradictory statements about the world (1960, 73–74). We lack a neutral frame of reference, or impartial observation language, with which to compare the definitions of competing theories. To return to the example of coerced marital sex, it is possible for two observers to describe the same event in a contradictory manner: "It was rape" and "It was not rape." There is no neutral or theory-independent way to decide whether such behavior "really is" rape or not, but such a determination may be readily made once one definition or another is taken as prescriptive.

The meaning of words—whether they appear in legal or ordinary settings—is a relative, not an absolute, matter. What is an "essential" or "accidental" feature of a concept (such as "consent" or "marital status") is the result of one's theoretical, and thus definitional, perspective. Kenneth Burke puts the matter succinctly: "Stimuli do not possess an absolute meaning"; rather, "different frameworks of interpretation will lead to different conclusions as to what reality is" (1984b, 35). Paul Sagal notes that asking "*what is* questions" is tantamount to asking for a "rigorous, consistent, complete theory" that would include "an *implicit definition* of x" (1973, 446–47). Just as in physics where predications about speed and position become possible only relative to a given frame of reference, so our technical concepts become meaningful only relative to a given theory. "Phlogiston" is meaningful and "real" only relative to a particular theory, just as "electrons" are meaningful and "real" only relative to another. As Braithwaite puts it, "[T]o say that theoretical concepts exist is to assert the truth of the theory in which they occur" (1953, 80).

To sum up: A strict theory/observation language distinction has been dropped; instead, most philosophers declare in effect that "all observation is theory bound." Such a declaration is useful as long as we keep in mind that by "theory," all that is meant is an interrelated cluster of beliefs about some aspect of the world. We can have a theory about human interaction just as we can have a theory about quarks or DNA. In any case, the salient point is that what *counts* as an observation statement can be decided only from *within* a particular theory. For example, if one accepts the beliefs that make up the male sexual prerogative theory, then the word "rape" has no objective referent with respect to marital relations; it is a term that can be applied to married people "in theory" only. It is primarily when conflicting theories are juxtaposed that it becomes apparent that an empirical observation according to one theory may become a wrongheaded theoretical speculation from another (Kuhn 1970, 144–59, 198–207).

The significance of the breakdown between observation and theory languages is difficult to overstate. At the very least, the inability to sustain a distinction between terms or sentences that are "observational" or "theoretical" challenges any clearcut metaphysical basis for defending the distinction between words we tend to label concrete or abstract, literal or figurative, objective or subjective, and so on. If a clear distinction between such philosophical pairs as observation/theory, concrete/abstract, literal/figurative, or objective/subjective is not defensible on a metaphysical basis, then the difference is best explained as one of social

practice and group behavior. Based on the prevailing beliefs of a given
social group located in a particular historical context, it may be simple
to say, "That expression is only a metaphor," or, "That description is
rather subjective," but as people and beliefs change, yesterday's metaphor may be literalized tomorrow. Quine suggests that "observation
sentences are the sentences on which all members of [a given language]
community will agree under uniform stimulation" (1969, 87). Similarly,
philosopher of science Helen Longino notes that "what is observational
and what is theoretical *changes* depending on what can be contested or
what can be taken for granted" (1990, 220, emphasis added). Accordingly, I suggest that we think of the difference between observation and
theory language (and closely related concepts) as one of differing levels
of denotative conformity, not one of extrahuman ontological status. The
relationship between the terms employed in these philosophical pairs can
be redescribed as follows:

High(er) Denotative Conformity	*Low(er) Denotative Conformity*
observation statements	theory statements
objective descriptions	subjective descriptions
literal language	figurative language

Within a given shared theory or set of beliefs, such distinctions are typically relatively easy to make, but not across theories, nor when sets of
beliefs conflict. Accordingly, the most useful alternative to metaphysical absolutism strikes me as that of treating such distinctions about kinds
of language use as a matter of social practice, which entails viewing those
distinctions as historically and socially contingent.

Interests Guide Definitions

Novel definitions are defended on the basis of a theory about some aspect of the world. Whether the theories involve "death" or "rape," the
question of which definition to adopt is inseparable from the question
of which theory ought to be believed. Because theories typically involve
a number of interrelated beliefs and attitudes, some definitional disputes
are extremely difficult to resolve. Whole sets of normative and factual
beliefs must be changed before someone may be convinced to accept a
new institutional fact: that X *ought* to be counted as Y in context C.
Whether we are talking about a group of scientists or the citizens of a
community, our beliefs are intertwined with our needs and interests, and
a new theory (whether of quarks or rape) will clash with some needs and

interests and advance others. In almost any arena of human interaction, the prevailing beliefs and interests of those in authority will be defended even to the point of dogmatism (cf. Kuhn 1963).

Political theorist Peter C. Sederberg notes that "definitions of anything must be controlled by the interests of the definer" (1984, 36). "Whose interests are being served?" is always worth asking in definitional disputes. Legal definitions of rape have evolved primarily to serve the interests of men rather than women (Brownmiller 1975; Estrich 1986). "One must explain the shape of [rape] laws made by these people in terms of their motives, drives, intentions, and attitudes" (Bessmer 1984, 352). William Blackstone defended the unequal treatment of women under British law as for women's own good: "[E]ven the disabilities which the wife lies under are for the most part intended for her protection and benefit: so great a favourite is the female sex of the laws of England" (1859, 444). Today it is argued that the marital rape exemption "ruthlessly reinforces woman's subordinate position in marriage" (Coonan 1980, 43). The controversy over redefining rape, over counting marital rape *as* rape, continues because the marital rape exemption enforces the male sexual prerogative theory. Men who believe that they are entitled to sexual access to their wives or live-in lovers regardless of women's wishes and men who fear the consequences of empowering women with access to the legal system benefit from continuing the marital rape exemption. The most stubborn resistance to redefining rape in consent terms comes from those individuals, men and women, who embrace the political theory or worldview that informs patriarchy, a belief system in which men are seen as superior to women and thus should "naturally" have power over them. Breaking from such sexist attitudes is difficult, in part, because patriarchy has privileged and thus benefited men. That some states have adopted the consent definition suggests that at least some sexist attitudes can be overcome when they result in contradictions such as "a wife can consent and not consent."

The consent definition may not have a significant effect on the rate of marital rape in the short run (Sallmann 1980, 82). Reconstructing social practices and attitudes is a slow process but one that the law and legal definitions undeniably can affect positively (Ryan 1995). Public debates over how rape ought to be defined legally raise consciousness. Definitional ruptures have the potential to bring attention to the attitudes and beliefs that inform specific proposals for definitions. By encouraging "an intense and exhaustive examination of the nature and scope of what is meant by 'rape'" (Sallmann 1980, 83), proposals for redefining rape not only may result in empowering married women but also can call attention to the ways in which the legal system affects the sexes unequally. Regarding the efforts in Australia to remove the marital rape exemption, one advocate noted: "We knew that much of the social value of the rape-in-marriage reform lay in the debates, arguments and discussions that follow up public debate—in pubs, in front of television, in buses, in the corner deli, between husbands and wives, between wives and wives, in discussions between men in the workplace, between women in the workplace. I now believe that this process has had some lasting effect" (Treloar 1980, 193).

Once metaphysical and linguistic absolutism are set aside, definitions can be appreciated as part of our creative and ever-changing efforts to make sense of the world. Once in place, definitions become "institutional facts" that guide our understanding of the world. Members of the legal profession "see the world in terms of categories which have meaning within their culture" (Bessmer 1984, 357). To the extent that definitions of rape encourage denotative conformity, they encourage a common understanding of what rape *is* and what ought to be done in response. Thus, even if attitudes cannot be eliminated overnight, changes in legal definitions are important because they "act to socialize" members of the legal profession; they also "act to enforce conformity in those who disagree with the assumptions and values which lie behind the rules" (Bessmer 1984, 354). Because definitions affirm or deny specific interests and encourage particular linguistic and nonlinguistic behaviors, the choice of definitions is always normative and prescriptive. Put another way, the choice of definitions is always political: "Definitions are tools, not truths, their value determined in use, not in terms of their approximation of some transcendent ideal. This pragmatic view of definition highlights its essentially political function: successful definition shapes mutual response and thereby helps to establish and maintain communities of shared meaning. Disputes over appropriate definitions are thus political conflicts" (Sederberg 1984, 94). For lexical definitions no less than real definitions, we can agree with Stevenson's point that "to choose a definition is to plead a cause" (1944, 210) and Chesebro's proposition that "definitions are a form of advocacy" (1985, 14).

5
When Are Definitions Political?
Always: The Case of "Wetlands"

This chapter extends the thesis that disputes over definitions are political conflicts by examining a controversy over the appropriate definition of "wetlands." My argument is that all definitions are political, specifically in two respects: first, definitions always serve particular interests; second, the only definitions of consequence are those that have been empowered through persuasion or coercion. The latter point does not say that "Might makes meaning" but rather that for a particular definition to be shared, people must be moved to adapt their linguistic and nonlinguistic responses according to the understanding instantiated in the definition (Sederberg 1984, 56). Such responses "may be shaped through the application of various forms of power from logical or moral suasion, through bribery, to coercion" (7).

A sweeping generalization that all definitions are political should be qualified if it is not to be dismissed out of hand. Obviously, not all definitions are equally important. Some definitions involve life and death decisions, others are trivial, and most fall someplace in between. Usually, picking up a dictionary to look up a definition is not seen as equivalent to political activism, but it would be a mistake to think that inaction or trivial actions that leave the status quo unchallenged are politically irrelevant. If we look hard enough, all definitions serve some sort of interests, even if those interests are as simple as coordinating our linguistic behavior so we know how and when to use a word in a socially acceptable manner. Defining what is or is not part of our shared reality is a profoundly political act (Frye 1983). The establishment of authoritative definitions by law or custom requires a political *process* involving persuasion or force that generates political *results* by advancing some views and interests and not others.

Definitions devised by scientists usually are not thought of as "political." Scientific definitions usually are described as more "objective" (that is, more real) than nonscientific definitions and as informed by "rational" and "neutral" criteria rather than by value-laden political factors. I believe that such distinctions are misleading and unproductive. Just as what is "really" rape differs from one theory of human interaction to another, what is considered "objectively real" varies from one scientific theory to the next. A growing number of philosophers, sociologists, and rhetorical theorists agree that there is no compelling theoretical or practical reason to treat definitions by scientists as more "objective" or "real" forms of knowledge than definitions by nonscientists (see, for example, Barnes 1982; Gilbert and Mulkay 1984; Gross 1996; Latour and Woolgar 1979; Rorty 1991, 21–62.). Accordingly, I avoid using the usual rubric "scientific definitions" and instead refer to definitions "by scientists" to emphasize that social practice, not metaphysics, distinguishes definitions offered by one group or another.

The belief that scientific definitions are different from and more stable than nonscientific definitions often is based on the idea that the *referents* of scientific analysis are objective and, thus, can be classified into "natural" kinds. As Jerry Fodor describes this belief, "Science discovers essences, and doing science thereby links us to natural kinds *as such*" (1998, 158). The natural sciences in particular are assumed to be relatively immune to the problems of category change and redefinition: "Their truths (and falsities) are thought to transcend the ravages of temporal, cultural, and linguistic change" (Kuhn 1989, 23). Accordingly, if scientists have done their job correctly, scientific terms are "rigid designators" that necessarily correspond to natural kinds. To borrow an example from philosopher Saul A. Kripke, "[P]resent scientific theory is such that it is part of the nature of gold as we have it to be an element with atomic number 79" (1980, 125). In light of such scientific knowledge, gold "is a rigid designator, whose reference is fixed by its 'definition'" (136; cf. Norris 1997, 156). Such an account of scientific language has been challenged directly by Kuhn. Although he agrees with Kripke that "gold" is "among the closest approximations we have to an item in neutral, mind-independent observation vocabulary," he insists that all so-called rigid designators are vulnerable to revision because the theoretical beliefs that make such terms meaningful may change (1990, 309). He notes that the concept of an atomic number is a term from the lexicon of atomic-molecular theory, and only while such a "system endures do the names it categorizes designate rigidly" (315). Kuhn's position is that, viewed historically, the referents of linguistic categories change in science just as they do elsewhere: "'Planet' and 'star' now categorize the world of celestial objects differently from the way they did before Copernicus, and the differences are not well-described by phrases like 'marginal adjustment' or 'zeroing in.' Similar transitions have characterized the historical development of virtually all referring terms of the sciences, including the most elementary: 'force,' 'species,' 'heat,' 'element,' 'temperature,' and so on" (313). Precisely because our categories are always open to revision, philosopher Nelson Goodman has suggested that we think of language as sorting the world, not into "natural," but into "relevant" kinds (1978). That is, we sort out the world not from a God's eye point of view but in order to meet various relevant human needs and interests.

Indeed, even *within* science the world may be classified and understood in different ways to meet the relevant needs of particular groups. Kuhn provides an anecdote that illustrates this point. Two scientists were asked whether a single atom of helium is or is not a molecule: "Both answered without hesitation, but their answers were not the same. For the chemist the atom of helium was a molecule because it behaved like one with respect to the kinetic theory of gases. For the physicist, on the other hand, the helium atom was not a molecule because it displayed no molecular spectrum" (1970, 50). These were two different theory-driven answers to the question "What is a molecule?" What counts as a molecule differs according to the current needs and interests of chemistry and physics. It is pointless to ask which answer is "really" correct because the implicit definitions involved are theory dependent, and, of equal importance, what may be the most appropriate conceptualization for one group of specialists may not be for another. The question of what ought to count as X for a particular language community is a normative and prescriptive question; what we consider X "really" to be is the result of our answer, not its cause.

In a similar line of thought, linguistics theorist George Lakoff notes that a chair "can be viewed *correctly* in many ways. From the molecular point of view, it is an enormous collection of molecules and not a single undifferentiated bounded entity. From the point of view of wave equations in physics, there is no chair, but only wave forms. From a human point of view, it is a single object" (1987, 262). Of course, all three points of view are "human" in the sense that molecular theory and wave theory are human creations, but the point Lakoff is making is that there is no reason to treat a "scientific" point of view as any more "real" or "correct" than the nonscientific description.

Definitions proffered by scientists may serve different interests than those put forth by nonscientists, but they serve interests nonetheless. Typically, "scientific" interests can be described as those "internal" to the language community to which a scientist belongs. How well a definition serves the shared purposes of the community might be discussed in terms of coherence with other concepts, clarity, amenability to quantification, or other predictive and explanatory interests. Intentionally or otherwise, "external" interests also are served by scientific definitions, from deciding what is death to determining who is male or female to delineating what should be called rape. Both internal and external interests are involved in the dispute over the authorized definition of wetland.[1]

Although words such as "bog," "marsh," and "swamp" have been in use for centuries, the collective term "wetland" "came into broad usage only during the late 1960s and early 1970s" (Golet 1991, 635). Generally speaking, the term denotes areas "sufficiently saturated by water that only specially adapted plants can grow there. Saturation with water prevents oxygen from working its way into the soil and therefore creates conditions of no oxygen" (Tripp 1991, 203). Only hydrophytes, vegetation that has adapted to such anaerobic conditions, can survive in wetlands. Furthermore, because the soil in such areas is periodically or permanently saturated with water, it has higher than average moisture content and is classified as hydric soil. The degree or type of water saturation of an area is known as its hydrology. These three factors— hydrology, hydric soil, and hydrophytes—are the traditional defining characteristics of wetlands.

Wetlands are "open systems." That is, wetlands interact with other ecological systems, such as groundwater tables and rivers, in a way that enhances the overall environment and, in particular, water quality. When water flows in and out of the wetland area, "sediments and other pollutants tend to remain, and the nutrients are converted into plants" (Tripp 1991, 195). Wetlands produce vegetation that photosynthesize at much higher rates than nonwetlands, which creates material vital to the aquatic food chain. A wide variety of plant and animal life flourishes in wetlands. U.S. Representative Robert Davis summarizes the value of wetlands as follows:

> Long perceived as wastelands with few redeeming characteristics, wetlands today are being recognized as valuable natural resources. They provide habitat for a wide variety of plants and animals, probably the most commonly recognized value of wetlands. But they have been shown to provide many other valuable functions such as the maintenance of water quality. They can retain, at least temporarily, nutrients that would otherwise reach streams, rivers, or lakes and contribute to increased growth of algae. Sediments that are suspended in running water can also be removed by wetlands. Wetlands interconnected with the groundwater table can recharge groundwater while in other areas discharge groundwater. Wetlands also provide a valuable function by reducing the severity of floods. They are effective as a storage basin during times of heavy rainfall and ease in the flooding of rivers. Finally, wetlands provide a multitude of uses for recreational activities; hunting, fishing, and a number of nonconsumptive uses of wetlands are enjoyed by many Americans. (in U.S. Congress 1992, 2)

So-called drier wetlands are areas that are saturated for relatively short periods of time but still perform some of the important ecological functions of wetlands. Ironically, drier wetlands are among the most valuable of wetland areas from an environmental perspective: "Many have a powerful intuition that the wetter the wetland the more valuable it is. This intuition is false" (Tripp 1991, 201). Among the valuable functions of drier wetlands are the following: (1) They are particularly effective natural flood controls: "Their relative dryness gives them greater capacity to absorb floodwater. Their strong vegetation slows down floodwaters and limits their destructive force" (201). (2) They are especially useful filtration systems because they "trap and absorb pollutants before runoff can mix with deeper waters. Scientific studies have confirmed that many drier wetlands provide the most effective treatment of water quality" (201). (3) Certain animals can live in shallow wetland areas when the "wetter" wetlands become too deep: "Loss of these areas leaves these animals nowhere to go in periods of high water" (201). (4) During dry periods, a good deal of plant and tree growth occurs. Then, during seasonal or temporary periods of saturation and flooding, certain plant material is carried into deeper waters where it becomes an important food supply for various fish species. In sum, certain wetlands appear to be "dry" much of the time. Nonetheless, the saturation they receive is sufficient to facilitate valuable ecological functions that distinguish them from nonwetlands.

Specific definitions of wetlands differed somewhat from state to state when the term first became popularized in the late 1960s. It was not until the mid-1970s that efforts were made to produce a standardized definition that could be used nationwide (Golet 1991, 635). Virtually from the beginning, those most interested in defining wetlands were interested in identifying and preserving their ecological functions. In strictly academic settings, conflicting definitions can coexist without serious problem, for example, in rival textbooks. It is assumed that there is sufficient overlap in the competing definitions that no harm results from a lack of strict uniformity. Besides, normally no one in academic settings has the authority to declare one specific definition to be the one that everyone in a given discipline must follow. Public laws, on the other hand, are aimed at precisely this sort of denotative conformity. Section 404(f) of the 1977 Clean Water Act was designed to halt widespread wetland destruction. The subsequent definitions put into service by the relevant federal agencies at that time were backed by the power of federal law. In 1979, a standard ecological definition was published by the U.S. Fish and Wildlife Service: "[W]etlands are lands where saturation with water is the dominant factor determining the nature of soil development and the types of plant and animal communities living in the soil and on its surface. The single feature that most wetlands share is soil or substrate that is at least periodically saturated with or covered by water. The water creates severe physiological problems for all plants and animals except those that are adapted for life in water or in saturated soil" (Cowardin et al. 1979, 3). Such a definition includes all three factors mentioned previously: hydrology (wetness), hydric soil, and hydrophytes. Although the temporary or permanent presence of water is what makes a given area a wetland ecology, the total amount of water *on* and *in* the soil varies tremendously over the seasons and is difficult to document directly. Accordingly, the 1979 definition, like most of those that have followed, defines wetlands as areas that have any *one* of three features— wetland vegetation, soil, or hydrology: "For the purposes of this classification, wetlands must have one or more of the following three attributes: (1) at least periodically, the land supports predominantly hydrophytes, (2) the substrate is predominantly undrained hydric soil, and (3) the substrate is nonsoil and is saturated with water or covered by shallow water at some time during the growing season of each year"

(Cowardin et al. 1979, 3). Because the amount of water necessary to produce wetlands is highly variable and difficult to measure, most efforts to define wetlands throughout the 1980s focused on hydric soil and hydrophytes. Hydric soils have been defined as those that receive sufficient saturation to produce anaerobic conditions—conditions that sharply limit the types of vegetation and animal life that can live in or on the soil. Hydrophytes are those plants that have adapted to such anaerobic conditions. A specific list of hydrophytes was drafted by the U.S. Fish and Wildlife Service in 1977 and has been reviewed and updated many times since (Golet 1991, 637).

Based on these early ecological definitions, it has been estimated that wetlands in the contiguous states are being destroyed by natural and human causes at a rate of nearly 300,000 acres annually. An additional 4,250,000 acres of wetlands were predicted to be at risk between 1990 and 2000 (U.S. Department of the Interior 1990, 13), although national data for that time period still are not available. Given that approximately 56 percent of wetlands has already been lost over the past two centuries (Dahl 1990), the cumulative losses are enormous: "Society pays for the loss of wetlands in very direct ways. Wetland losses increases the need for water treatment facilities and multi-billion dollar flood control projects. Wetland losses also represent the loss of habitats of animals and plants of aesthetic, commercial, recreational, and medicinal value. Society pays for the loss of wetlands that had helped replenish and cleanse bays, estuaries, and rivers that contribute significantly to the spawning and rearing of hundreds of estuarine, anadromous, and oceanic species valued by commercial and recreational fishermen" (U.S. Department of Interior 1990, 15).

During the 1980s, four different federal agencies had jurisdiction relevant to the regulation of wetlands: the U.S. Fish and Wildlife Service (FWS), the Environmental Protection Agency (EPA), the Army Corps of Engineers (CE), and the Agriculture Department's Soil Conservation Service (SCS). All four had the legislative or administrative power to define wetlands according to their respective needs and interests. As noted by Max Peterson of the International Association of Fish and Wildlife Agencies: "At one time Fish and Wildlife Service had a *habitat* classification. Soil Conservation Service had a *soils* classification, and other agencies had a definition based on *water presence*" (U.S. Congress 1992, 43; emphasis added). Each of these regulatory bodies had the statutory or administrative power to designate specific areas as wetlands and to affect people's behavior accordingly. For example, the "Swampbuster" provision of the 1985 Food Security Act required farmers wishing to sell wetland acreage to commercial developers first to obtain a federal permit. If the acreage is classified as wetlands, according to federal definitions, the permit can be denied.

Just how disparate the different federal regulatory agencies' definitions of wetlands were prior to 1989 is a matter of some dispute. Although some contend that the various agencies used "very similar approaches" (Tripp 1991, 199), others complain that the lack of standardized methods "resulted in inconsistent determinations of wetland boundaries" (Environmental Protection Agency [hereafter EPA] et al. 1991, 40449). To ensure a reasonable degree of uniformity, the four responsible federal agencies began a series of meetings beginning in early 1988 to produce a standardized manual for delineating wetlands. In January 1989, the Federal Interagency Committee for Wetland Delineation published the *Federal Manual for Identifying and Delineating Jurisdictional Wetlands* (hereafter *Manual*). According to Francis C. Golet, a professor of natural resources science who has been involved in wetlands research for over twenty years, "[T]he 1989 *Manual* represents the culmination of nearly 17 years of efforts by wetland scientists, soils experts, and land managers from throughout the country. It also represents a consensus of the four leading wetland management/regulatory agencies" (1991, 639).

Like most federal regulations, the 1989 *Manual* received both praise and criticism from those most directly affected. Critics charged that the *Manual* significantly broadened the definition of wetlands such that millions of acres previously *not* considered wetlands would now be so designated (EPA et al. 1991, 40450). Those who defended the *Manual* pointed out that it did not "initiate a significant revision to prior existing standards. Like the other manuals, it most heavily emphasized evidence of soil types and vegetation, and used the limited available evidence of hydrology (of wetness) primarily as a means of verifying the evidence provided by soils and vegetation" (Tripp 1991, 199). Defenders of the *Manual* agreed that there had been problems implementing the relevant federal regulations but argued that the definition of wetlands was consistent with years of experience and needed no revision (Environmental Defense Fund 1992). The implementation of federal regulation concerning wetlands, like all public policy procedures, required an ongoing process of negotiation and mutual adjustment between regulators and those regulated. If not for the campaign rhetoric of George Bush during the 1988 presidential election, hammering out the details concerning the appropriate regulatory definition of wetlands very well might have remained a matter of interest solely to specialists. As a result of campaign promises made in the fall of 1988—promises repeated after Bush took office—how to define wetlands became a controversy attracting nationwide attention and interest.

As part of a bid to be known as "the environmental president," Bush promised in the 1988 presidential election that he would commit his administration to the goal of "no net loss" of wetlands. In October of 1988, as part of a candidate forum in the magazine *Sports Afield,* Bush stated: "My position on wetlands is straightforward: All existing wetlands, no matter how small, should be preserved" (in Paugh 1988, 15). Following his election, in a speech before members of Ducks Unlimited in June of 1989, Bush proclaimed that "any vision of a kinder, gentler America—any nation concerned about its quality of life, now and forever, must be concerned about conservation" (1989, 860). Noting that "our wetlands are being lost at a rate of nearly half a million acres a year," Bush reaffirmed his commitment to "no net loss": "You may remember my pledge, that our national goal would be no net loss of wetlands. And together, we are going to deliver on the promise of renewal, and I plan to keep that pledge. . . . Wherever wetlands must give way to farming or development, they will be replaced or expanded elsewhere. It's time to stand the history of wetlands destruction on its head. From this year forward, anyone who tries to drain the swamp is going to be up to his ears in alligators" (861). Bush described the protection of the environment as "a moral issue. For it is wrong to pass on to future generations a world tainted by present thoughtlessness" (862). Encouraging his audience to judge their actions in light of the verdict of future generations, Bush asked those present to imagine what might be said in forty years: "It could be they'll report the loss of many million acres more, the extinction of species, the disappearance of wilderness and wildlife. Or they could report something else. They could report that sometime around 1989 things began to change and that we began to hold on to our parks and refuges and that we protected our species and that in that year the seeds of a new policy about our valuable wetlands were sown, a policy summed up in three simple words: 'No net loss.' And I prefer the second vision of America's environmental future" (862).

The efforts to codify the different federal definitions of wetlands began in early 1988, well before Bush was elected president. Nevertheless, by making "no net loss" a centerpiece of his administration's environmental policy, Bush energized governmental efforts to protect wetlands. As Congressperson Gerry E. Studds noted, "[T]his is the first instance I know of where campaign rhetoric rises to the level of statutory law. No loss of wetlands originated in a campaign speech; to my knowledge, it is not the law" (U.S. Congress 1992, 31). In his 1990 budget statement, Bush reiterated the goal of no net loss. The U.S. Department of the Interior and the U.S. Fish and Wildlife Service published a "wetlands action plan" in 1990 that was titled *Wetlands: Meeting the President's Challenge;* the publication prominently quoted the above-cited passages from Bush's speech before Ducks Unlimited. Congressional hearings were held in part to explore ways in which to meet the president's goal of no net loss of wetlands (U.S. Congress 1989). The responsible federal agencies already were committed to enforcing existing statutory regulations requiring the protection of the nation's wetlands; their efforts to produce a unified manual for delineating wetlands were part of that ongoing effort. Bush's policy of no net loss created heightened awareness of such federal efforts so that when wetland protection came into conflict with other policy objectives, public controversy was virtually inevitable.

The goal of no net loss probably was deemed a politically viable promise because it sounds flexible and absolutist at the same time, thereby placating environmentalists who demand commitment and pro-growth developers who want flexibility. Thus, environmentalists tended to emphasize the "no loss" part of the promise, while developers emphasized "no *net* loss." In practice, however, the effort to placate both constituencies proved impossible. Congressional hearings held in 1989, 1990, and 1991 document that pressure was mounting from both directions. On one hand, Bush's call for no net loss generated considerable enthusiasm for protecting wetlands. Almost all policy makers endorsed the goal; the only question was how to implement it. When is it appropriate, for example, to drain a valuable wetland in one location with the expectation that another wetland will be created elsewhere? Pressure mounted on the different regulatory agencies to articulate clearly how they would meet the president's challenge for no net loss. On the other hand, the coincidental pledge for no net loss and the publication of the official *Manual* to delineate wetlands galvanized opponents of federal environmental regulation. Opposition to the protection of wetlands comes most often from farmers wanting to sell their land and from developers wishing to buy, drain, and develop wetlands. They argued that the regulatory agencies had run amok, applying the label "wetlands" much too broadly, and that regulators were not adequately taking local economic needs into consideration.

The Bush administration found itself in a dilemma: Either Bush could modify his commitment to no net loss, thereby breaking a highly visible and useful campaign promise, or he could stand by the promise and risk alienating pro-business, pro-development constituents. Bush's "solution" was simple and, had it worked, politically ingenious. In January of 1990, White House press secretary Marlin Fitzwater announced that "[a]t the President's direction, the Domestic Policy Council, which has created a task force on wetlands, is in the process of examining how best to implement the President's goal of no net loss" (Bush 1990b, 73). "How best to implement the President's goal of no net loss" turned out to be a proposed redefinition of wetlands. By sharply narrowing the scope of the regulatory agencies' definition of wetlands, Bush would be able to claim that he kept his promise of no net loss of wetlands while allowing the development of areas previously designated as wetlands.

In August of 1991, the four agencies charged with protecting wetlands published in the *Federal Register* a document entitled "'Federal Manual for Identifying and Delineating Jurisdictional Wetlands'; Proposed Revisions" (EPA et al. 1991). Although bearing the name of the relevant regulatory agencies, the document was produced under the direction of the vice president's task force on wetlands and was intended to be codified as a Presidential Executive Order with the force of law. The "Proposed Revisions" were presented and explained as a clarification and refinement of the 1989 *Manual,* but in effect the revisions represented a major departure from the *Manual*'s procedures for delineating wetlands. The practical result of the proposed redefinition, if implemented, would have been to decrease dramatically the amount of acreage that could be designated as protected wetlands. The most modest estimate was that "as much as a third of the 38.4 million hectares (95 million acres) of wetlands in the lower 48 states will be considered wetlands no more and thus will be vulnerable to development" (Lemonick 1991, 53). The Environmental Defense Fund's extensive study of the effects of the proposed changes to the *Manual* suggested that an even larger percentage—50 percent or roughly 50 million acres of land previously designated wetlands—would be excluded by the proposed redefinition (1992, x). That estimate corresponds to that by the National Wetlands Technical Council, a group of "independent wetlands scientists" (U.S. Congress 1992, 661–63).

There are two primary differences between the 1989 *Manual* (which represents the traditional practices of delineating wetlands) and the Bush administration's proposed redefinition. First, whereas the 1989 *Manual* allowed an area to be designated a wetland if any one of several criteria were met clearly, the 1991 redefinition required that all three criteria (hydrology, hydric soil, hydrophytic vegetation) be met and proved independently. Second, the specific standards by which each criterion was judged were made more stringent. For example, the 1989 *Manual* required seven consecutive days of inundation or saturation "at or near the surface," while the 1991 redefinition more than doubled the length of time necessary (fifteen to twenty-one days) and specified water *at the surface,* not just near it.

The codification of definitions of wetlands in the 1989 *Manual* was implemented by the relevant federal agencies without additional authorization by the White House or Congress and without inviting public comment. The *Manual* was considered a "technical guidance document which is not required by law to go through Administrative Procedure Act rulemaking procedures" (EPA et al. 1991, 40446). In other words, the relevant federal agencies were empowered to enforce the *Manual*'s definition of wetlands without additional authority, because the power to regulate wetlands was given already under current federal law. Opponents of wetland regulation responded in two ways. First, a rider was successfully attached to the Energy and Water Development and Appropriations Act of 1992 that cut off funding for further delineation of wetlands using the 1989 *Manual*. The action temporarily disempowered the federal agencies from requiring conformity to the *Manual*'s definition. Second, opponents criticized the agencies for creating and enforcing the "new" definition without inviting public comment. The Bush administration could have enforced the proposed 1991 redefinition by Executive Order or through the same input-free process by which the 1989 *Manual* was adopted. However, having criticized the federal agencies for having acted without inviting public comment, the administration felt compelled to extend such an invitation regarding the proposed redefinition (EPA et al. 1991, 40446; see also Hilts 1991, A10). The response was overwhelming. Over ten thousand documents were sent to the EPA, requiring the agency to hire an outside consulting firm to collate the input provided.

Although not without supporters, the proposed redefinition was met mostly with intense opposition and condemnation. *Sierra* magazine claimed that the administration's "evisceration of existing wetlands policies demonstrates—more conclusively than any previous actions in this arena—the abandonment" of the no net loss pledge (Pope 1991, 22). The Bush administration's proposed redefinition "broke his most specific campaign pledge" (23). The redefinition was seen as a cynical ploy: "A teensy redefinition of what constitutes a wetland, and presto—the administration jeopardizes 30 million acres of them, an area about the size of New York state" (Dworetzky 1992, 9). The Associated Press reported that "[g]overnment wetlands experts have concluded that the Bush administration's proposed redefinition of the term is unworkable, unscientific and would leave 'many obvious wetlands' unprotected" ("Papers" 1991, 7). By late November of 1991, criticism from inside and outside the administration had grown so intense that a spokesperson for the president's Competitiveness Council admitted that the proposed redefinition would have to be revised "to honor President Bush's 1988 campaign pledge" (Hilts 1991, A1).

Before discussing the specific arguments lodged against the administration, I want to draw attention to a rhetorical strategy that emerged in the criticisms that is particularly relevant. The proposed redefinition was branded "political" and contrasted to the current "scientific" definition. Representative Lindsay Thomas complained that policy makers had no business defining wetlands: "The problem is not how to define wetlands. That is a science" (U.S. Congress 1992, 24). Similarly, scientist Francis C. Golet suggested that "the definition of wetland is wholly a scientific issue." Although political input is unavoidable, "in matters of science, such as the definition of wetland, scientific arguments must prevail" (U.S. Congress 1992, 640, 654). The image of an objective, bias-free science was invoked frequently to help justify continuing the 1989 *Manual*'s definition as opposed to the administration's proposed redefinition. James T. B. Tripp, general counsel to the Environmental Defense Fund, ended his testimony to Congress as follows:

> The attack on wetlands programs has proceeded from a number of factual misconceptions. The proposed revisions to the manual represent this callous approach to science taken to an extreme— as nonscientists believed they could draw up a manual that would be usable and would accurately cross off some unarticulated category of wetlands that did not perform important functions. The need for more dispassionate, unbiased science has rarely been greater on any environmental issue. I urge this Committee to make an important priority the assurance that accurate science guide public policy on this issue. (U.S. Congress 1992, 208)

Because few, if any, scientists engaged in environmental studies were willing to support the administration's proposed redefinition, it is tempting to interpret the dispute in the simple terms of politics (subjective and biased) versus science (objective and unbiased). As an editorial in the *New York Times* put it: "Mr. Bush's scientists have one definition of what a wetland is, his political advisers another" ("Back in the Bog" 1991, A20). Consistent with contemporary philosophical pragmatism, however, I believe that we are better off without such a dichotomy. The dispute over defining wetlands can be understood as a matter of *competing interests*. When science and politics are treated as wholly distinct, the tendency is to slip into the rhetoric of "real definitions." "A wetland is a wetland is wetland," as one environmentalist put it (Seligmann 1991, 49). Real definitions, for those who believe in them, ought to be provided by those who are most expert with respect to the slice of reality being defined. Reality is to be defined by the experts—By Those Who Know, just as Plato would have suggested. "The natural sciences, given the frequent presence of a scholarly consensus on the means and ends of inquiry, often approximate the rational ideal of definition," notes Peter Sederberg (1984, 94). If we accept this cliché, then it is an easy step to granting definitional hegemony to a technocratic elite. One witness to a congressional hearing on wetland protection claimed that "the 1991 revisions represent a knee jerk reaction to political pressure rather than reason" (U.S. Congress 1992, 244). Another witness suggested that the definition of wetlands "probably needs to be turned over to the National Academy of Science because an independent objective standard needs to be used" (62–63). The problem with such a solution is that it turns "experts" into a technocratic ruling elite. "These technocrats," Sederberg observes, "would be the functional equivalent of the philosopher kings" (1984, 57). Rather than relegating the task of defining reality to philosopher kings, it is more productive and ethical to see definitional disputes as a matter of competing interests, while insisting that some interests are better than others. Accordingly, the questions to ask are "Whose interests are being served by a particular definition?" and "Do we want to identify with those interests?"

In the case of wetlands, the competing interests are fairly easy to identify and to contrast. In the simplest of terms, the 1989 *Manual*'s definitions represent the interests of ecologists; in contrast, critics argue that the proposed redefinition of wetlands is "devised by developers, timber companies, and highway departments" (Pope 1991, 23). Just how fair and accurate such a simple contrast may or may not be is illustrated by looking at the specific interests identified in arguments for and against the proposed redefinition. The most thorough critique was provided by the Environmental Defense Fund (hereafter EDF). Together with the World Wildlife Fund, the EDF published *How Wet Is a Wetland?: The Impacts of the Proposed Revisions to the Federal Wetlands Delineation Manual* in January of 1992. According to the EDF, forty scientists and specialists were involved in preparing the 175-page report. The EDF claims that "an estimated 50 percent of America's remaining wetlands" would be excluded by the proposed redefinition (1992, x). The long-term result would be "severe environmental and economic impacts." The report identifies five specific areas of harm: flooding, water quality, biological diversity, waterfowl, and fisheries. In each area, the EDF directly challenges the administration's belief that only "wet" wetlands deserve protection. As noted earlier, "drier" wetlands sometimes protect the most important ecological interests. The EDF notes that the proposed redefinition's criteria for determining hydrology have "virtually no relevance to flood control." In fact, "compared to the more permanently flooded wetlands, the wetlands excluded by the proposed manual actually have greater capacity to detain floodwaters because they are less likely to be filled with water before the flood event" (x). A specific example demonstrates the costs of the new definition: "In the eastern portion of DuPage County, Illinois, the loss of wetlands has led to frequent severe flooding that caused $120 million in damages in 1987 and will cost up to $50,000 per damaged residence to remedy. The proposed manual would exclude 86 percent of the similar kinds of wetlands in the western portion of the county—an area that today retains many wetlands and suffers from little flooding" (x–xi). The report proceeds to document similar harms to water quality, biological diversity, waterfowl, and fisheries. In each area of harm, the report specifies the sort of damage that would occur if the new definition were utilized. The problems described are precisely those identified in documents such as the Department of the Interior's *Wetlands: Meeting the President's Challenge* and discussed by Bush himself in addresses such as the one given to Ducks Unlimited in 1989. The difference is that the EDF documents in detail how much of the damage from loss of wetlands comes from the loss of so-called drier wetlands that the proposed redefinition was designed to exclude.

The arguments set forth by the EDF are openly pragmatic. There is little or no effort to invoke the sort of circular rhetoric typically associated with "real definitions." Although chapter 1 is titled "What Are Wetlands?," the answer is pragmatic and functional. The EDF notes that "because wetlands are diverse, few generalizations about them are always true" (1992, 2). Instead of looking for unchanging qualities or an essential nature of wetlands, the EDF identifies the valuable ecological functions that various sorts of wetlands serve. The current definition, fueled from the beginning by ecological interests, ought to be preserved because the consequences of the proposed redefinition are undesirable. The EDF rejects what they call "the misconception that only areas that are wet at the surface for extended periods are 'real' or 'valuable' wetlands" (xiii). In the process of defending the claim that "wetter wetlands are not better wetlands," the EDF does not adopt the position that there are real versus apparent wetlands but instead focuses on the many valuable functions such lands perform and notes that surface hydrology—the primary defining characteristic of the proposed revisions—has little to do with such functions.

Interestingly enough, both sides in the wetlands definition controversy were interested in producing a definition that would delineate wetlands accurately, consistently, and predictably. Both sides wanted, in other words, *denotative conformity* with respect to the word "wetlands" in order to enforce current statutes. Accuracy, consistency, and predictability are often considered "scientific" values (Kuhn 1977, 320–39). Indeed, in the proposed redefinition, the Environmental Protection Agency claims that "[o]f paramount importance to us . . . is to maintain and improve the scientific validity of our delineation methods" (1991, 40446). In a general sense, then, both sides were interested in their definition being considered "scientific." When critics of the proposed redefinition called it "unscientific," as they often did, to what were they referring? The scientists who charged the administration with being "unscientific" were not *merely* interested in accuracy, consistency, and predictability. They *also* wanted to continue to study and protect wetlands for their ecological significance. Being "unscientific" in this context translates as "abandoning what scientists have been doing with respect to wetlands." Accordingly, when a scientist such as Francis Golet charges that the redefinition "disregards more than 15 years of scientific research" (U.S. Congress 1992, 639), I believe his criticism is best understood as a complaint that the redefinition breaks faith with those responsible for many years for our understanding of the ecological importance of wetlands and abandons the values and interests that current statutes were drafted to protect. The EDF's studies concerning the amount of loss of wetlands protection suggest that the EDF, in fact, is able to utilize the new definition to delineate wetlands accurately, consistently, and predictably. The problem with the new definition is not so much that it is "unscientific" but rather that it abandons the values and interests of scientists traditionally associated with the study of wetlands. If this constitutes a flaw, it is a social one, not a metaphysical one.

The interests pursued by those in favor of the proposed redefinition were fairly straightforward. Organizations such as the Tidewater Builders Association, the Forest Farmers Association, the National Association of Homebuilders, Weyerhaeuser Company, Associated Builders and Contractors, and the National Association of Realtors testified before Congress in favor of the administration's proposed redefinition. The National Association of Realtors noted that they had advocated in early 1989 the policy "that *all three parameters* (which include hydrophytic vegetation, hydric soils and hydrology) be utilized in delineation of a wetland"—precisely the policy proposed by the Bush administration (U.S. Congress 1992, 368; emphasis in original). The arguments offered by such organizations boil down to one basic complaint: the 1989 *Manual* prevents people from developing land in the manner of their choosing. As a result, the right to use one's property profitably is obstructed by federal regulations that these developers feel "go too far." A representative of the Tidewater Builders Association complained that real estate "estimated at $50 billion" potentially met the *Manual*'s criteria for wetlands and thus could not be developed (U.S. Congress 1992, 60). A county commissioner from Georgia claimed that "economic growth has been drastically curtailed" by the 1989 *Manual:* "Engineers, architects, home builders, developers, contractors and their employees were impacted" (U.S. Congress 1992, 226).[2]

A related and persistent justification for the proposed redefinition was that the 1989 *Manual* drastically expanded the amount of land regulated as wetlands. The argument is controversial; as noted earlier, environmentalists as well as government officials claimed that such accusations were ungrounded and were the result of misunderstandings that subsequently had been clarified (EDF 1992, 13–18). Nonetheless, advocates of the proposed redefinition consistently argued that the 1989 *Manual* expanded protection to far too many areas that are not "true" wetlands. Robert W. Slocum of the North Carolina Forestry Association argued that "identifying dry land that has no resemblance to *true* wetland ecosystems as 'wetlands' only confuses the public and the landowners and hinders protection of *true* wetlands" (U.S. Congress 1992, 109; emphasis added). Slocum praised the administration's proposal as offering "a more *realistic* definition" that protects "*true* wetland ecosystems" (113). Similarly, the National Association of Realtors stated that they were "pleased with the consensus definition of protected wetlands reached by the Bush administration, which more accurately and clearly defines a *true* wetland" (366). More often than not, advocates of the proposed redefinition expressed their belief that "true" or "real" wetlands still would be protected (see, e.g., U.S. Congress 1992, 336, 367, 386). Explicitly or implicitly, the 1989 *Manual* was condemned for protecting lands that are not "really" and "truly" wetlands.

I have argued previously that such dissociative claims in defense of a definition are circular and unhelpful. To claim that one definition is superior to another because it captures what is "really and truly" a wetland simply avoids the pragmatic question of what ought to count as a wetland for the purposes of federal regulation. Typically, advocates of the proposed redefinition relied on a "wetter is better" logic. The Delaware Council of Farm Organizations, for example, argued that "farmers are not, in general, opposed to protecting wetlands; that is, land that is *truly wet*" (U.S. Congress 1992, 409). The problem with such arguments is that they fail to clash with the case offered by ecologists concerning the value of so-called drier wetlands. Rather than invoking the dichotomies of "true" versus "false" wetlands, or "scientific" versus "political" definitions, a more productive discussion would focus on the relative costs and benefits of protecting the lands included by the 1989 *Manual* and excluded by the proposed redefinition. Such a discussion is precisely what the EDF offers in *How Wet Is a Wetland?* The pragmatic question, therefore, is whether the benefits of protecting the disputed lands are considered more important or valuable than maintaining the property rights of those who own and wish to profit by developing them. So far, the values and interests expressed and implied by existing legislation would warrant the conclusion that the answer be "yes."

Even setting aside the question of which interests are more important to protect, the Bush administration's attempt at redefinition was logically inconsistent as well as ethically suspect. Bush's early declarations about wetlands, in his role as "the environmental president," depended on traditional definitions of wetlands. For example, in his statements about the quantity of wetlands being lost each year, he relies on statistics that utilize a definition of wetlands codified in the 1989 *Manual*. Yet his later statements clearly retreated from those definitions. While insisting that "I am committed to no net loss of wetlands," Bush also said, "I am not committed to decisions that take productive land out of production." He complained that "you've got zealots in various levels of the bureaucracy" that require control "from the top on down" (1990a, 632). Bush effectively abandoned his identification with the agencies charged with protecting wetlands who had been working toward a consistent definition of wetlands for over a dozen years. In so doing, he rejected his previous alignment with the interests those agencies represent. Not surprisingly, Bush relied on the rhetoric of real definition to defend the revised policy. When speaking to an agricultural organization with pro-development sentiments, Bush made his interests clear: "My direction to Vice President Quayle's Council on Competitiveness was to protect environmentally sensitive wetlands and protect the property rights of landowners. I've asked the board [of the Farm Bureau Federation] to send in specific recommendations during this hearing period. Our new guidelines will distinguish between *genuine* wetlands which deserve to be protected and *other* kinds of land, *including your farmlands*" (1992c, 83; emphasis added). Noting that "the extreme environmentalists are not happy" with his new wetlands policy, Bush claimed that the answer is "to try to balance all of these interests" (1992b, 1177). Yet by dramatically narrowing the standard definition of wetlands, Bush clearly tipped the balance away from environmental interests. Complaining again that "we were too far over between the Corps [of Engineers] and EPA on the regulatory side," Bush warned that we must "be wary of the extremes" (1177). His own definition was simple and direct: "I've got a radical view of wetlands. I think wetlands ought to be wet" (1177). By identifying himself with the "wetter is better" criterion espoused in the proposed redefinition, Bush explicitly distanced himself from the environmental interests reflected in the traditional definition upon which his pro-environmental statements depended. It is ironic but fitting that Ducks Unlimited—the organization before which Bush gave his most important and influential wetlands address—came to oppose the proposed redefinition (U.S. Congress 1992, 88–90, 311–27). That Bush's attempts to balance interests were unpersuasive is suggested by a steady decline in approval ratings of his handling of environmental issues (although it is impossible to know how much of this had to do directly with wetlands policy). In March of 1991, at the peak of his popularity as president, Bush had a 52 percent approval rate for his handling of environmental issues. By June of 1992, that rate had fallen to 29 percent with 58 percent of those polled expressing disapproval (Saad 1992, 1).

I conclude with two comments about the wetlands controversy. First, the dispute is a useful case study because it throws into relief that definitions are interest-driven and saturated with questions of power and persuasion. What makes wetlands unusual is the amount of media coverage the controversy received, but the fact that definitions *matter*—that

there are pragmatic and political results of our choices of definitions—
is not unusual at all. Power to define is power to influence behavior. All
proposed definitions are devised for specific purposes that can be evaluated according to the interests that they advance. The success of any
definition depends on how effectively its advocates persuade (or coerce)
members of a given community to conform and use the term "properly."
In the case of wetlands, the Bush administration was unable to persuade
enough regulators and citizens to support the proposed redefinition and
was unwilling to coerce them to do so. Such disputes over the scope of
government regulation highlight the political dimension of defining that
is, I believe, ubiquitous.

Second, note that none of the interests identified so far need be classified as exclusively "scientific" or exclusively "political." Scientists constitute a specific social group that is identifiable, in part, by their common
interests and values (Longino 1990). Accordingly, it sheds little light to
describe such interests and values as "nonpolitical." As noted in the cases
of defining death and rape, a variety of social interests are advanced by
achieving a level of denotative conformity with certain words. Thus,
politicians and scientists share the goal of denotative conformity with
respect to wetlands. The dream of escaping politics altogether and let-
ting experts define tough concepts for us is a powerful one, but the dream
potentially ends in a technocratic nightmare. If one considers the outcome of this particular wetlands controversy a happy ending, it is because one identifies with the interests of the winner. The results could
have been otherwise; politics is responsible for what we now call wetlands and for what we will treat as wetlands forty years hence. Interests
always are served by definitions; the only question is *whose* interests.
Prudence requires that, as a society, we learn to tell the difference between
the definitional disputes that are exclusively "scientific," in the sense that
the outcome only affects the community of scientists, and those disputes
that involve us all—scientists included. Both sorts of conflicts are political; recognizing them as such may prompt us to take greater responsibility for defining the reality we impose on ourselves and others.

6

Reformulating the "What Is X?" Question: The Case of "Person" vis-à-vis the Abortion Debate

In this chapter, I review some of the arguments made in earlier chapters and point to some specific ways that definitional questions can be productively reformulated. In particular, I suggest that when we hear questions of the form "What is X?" that we distinguish between "gap" and "rupture" situations, and that ruptures be addressed in part by re-asking such questions as "How should we use the word X?" As noted earlier, definitional gaps can be filled by referring to current beliefs about X. So, if we hear an unfamiliar word or are faced with an unfamiliar stimuli (say an odd noise), a question such as "What is that?" can be answered without the need to revise our current beliefs. If I have never heard the word "ephod" before, I can learn something about it by looking it up in a dictionary, where I would find that it is a kind of Hebrew priestly vestment. Unless I had previous beliefs about Hebrew vestments, it is unlikely that learning about ephods will change any current beliefs; I only add a little about ephods to the total sum of my knowledge. Similarly, if I had never seen a particular species of bird—say, a puffin—my first reaction upon seeing one might be to ask, "What is that?" Learning that it is a puffin is unlikely to require me to change many of my current beliefs but takes what is common knowledge for others and adds that to my understanding of the world. Such additions normally do not disrupt our "natural attitude" toward the world—the belief that the objects of our world (including language) are simply "there" and can be taken for granted. Accordingly, a variety of questions of the form "What is X?" can be considered mundane simply because they merely ask that X be located, or in some instances translated, into a relevant language game.

A definitional rupture, by contrast, calls the natural attitude into question. A fact of essence (what X is) or a fact of usage (how word X is used) may be challenged such that only through revising certain beliefs can the difference be resolved. The rhetoric of real definitions (facts of essence) is unproductive, so we turn to issues of usage; yet in doing so, we should treat such issues as value-laden (ought) policy propositions rather than as fact (is) propositions. As a practical matter, such a normative approach requires us to turn questions of the form "What is X?" into "How should we use the word X?" and, similarly, turn efforts to formulate definitions of "facts of essence" of the form "X is Y" into a request for *proposed institutional norms:* When should X count as Y in context C? In this shift of emphasis, practical questions come to the fore: What are our shared purposes in defining X? What interests and values are advanced by competing definitions? Who should have the power to define or decide what counts as what? How much coercion— if any—is acceptable to further the end of denotative conformity? A pragmatic approach to definition encourages these sorts of questions, which are the questions I want to pursue through a reading of selected arguments over the definition of "person" and "human life" in constitutional disputes over abortion.

The Debate over Personhood in *Roe v. Wade*

Although controversies concerning abortion have a long and complicated history, I want to focus initially on how the questions of "What is a person?" and "What is a human life?" have been addressed in recent constitutional arguments. Because abortion opponents believe that abortions kill unborn babies, an important part of their case against establishing constitutional protection for abortion rights in the famous *Roe v. Wade* case (hereafter *Roe*) was that the fetus should be recognized as a person under the Constitution. The Fourteenth Amendment to the United States Constitution says that states shall not "deprive any person of life, liberty, or property, without due process of law; nor deny to any person within its jurisdiction the equal protection of the laws." If the Supreme Court recognized a fetus as a person, according to anti-abortion advocates, then abortion must be prohibited because it deprives persons of their life without due process and denies them equal protection (against murder) under the law. Accordingly, many of the briefs filed with the Court in *Roe* provided extended arguments to support the belief that a fetus is a live human being that is a person within the meaning of the law.

The importance of the question of whether a fetus is a person is clear in the transcripts of the oral arguments conducted before the Court in 1971 and 1972. Justice Byron White asked Sarah R. Weddington, the attorney arguing in favor of abortion rights, whether it was "critical to your case that the fetus not be a person under the due process clause." Weddington answered that "it is critical, first, that we prove this is a fundamental interest on behalf of the woman . . ." White pressed, "Well, yes. But about the fetus?" Weddington again tried to refocus the question on the issue of whether there is a "compelling State interest" in regulating abortion. White persisted:

> *The Court:* Yes. But I'm just asking you, under the Federal Constitution, is the fetus a person, for the protection of due process?
> *Mrs. Weddington:* All of the cases—the prior history of this statute—the common law history would indicate that it is not. The State has shown no—
> *The Court:* Well, what about—*would you lose your case if the fetus was a person?* . . . [I]f it were established that an unborn fetus is a person, with the protection of the Fourteenth Amendment, you would have almost an impossible case here, would you not?
> *Mrs. Weddington:* I would have a very difficult case. (Kurland and Casper 1975, 813–17, emphasis added)

The same sort of exchange took place repeatedly between Justice White and Robert C. Flowers, the attorney arguing on behalf of Texas's right to outlaw abortions:

> *The Court:* Well, if you're correct that the fetus is a person, then I don't suppose you'd have—the State would have great trouble permitting an abortion, would it?
> *Mr. Flowers:* Yes, sir. (Kurland and Casper 1975, 820)

The Court: The basic constitutional question, initially, is whether or not an unborn fetus is a person, isn't it?
Mr. Flowers: Yes, sir, and entitled to the constitutional protection. (Kurland and Casper 1975, 827)

The Court: Do you think the case is over for you? *You've lost your case, then, if the fetus or the embryo is not a person?* Is that it?
Mr. Flowers: Yes, sir, I would say so. (Kurland and Casper 1975, 822, emphasis added)

These and other exchanges in the oral argument before the Court underscore that for certain members of the Court, the decisive issue in *Roe* was the definitional question of whether a fetus is a person. Indeed, in the Court's decision, Justice Harry Blackmun wrote, "If this suggestion of personhood is established, the appellant's case, of course, collapses, for the fetus' right to life would then be guaranteed specifically by the [Fourteenth] Amendment" (1973, 156–57).

Abortion opponents primarily defended a fact of essence: a fetus really is a person. Regardless of previous legal usage of the term "person," it is a fact that the category "person" includes fetuses because fetuses really are persons. The difficulties with real definitions identified earlier in this book are apparent in the oral argument before the Court; in particular, the theory-dependency of distinctions between what is really X rather than merely apparently X is implicit in the following:

> *Mr. Flowers:* [I]t is the position of the State of Texas that, upon conception, we have a human being; a person, within the concept of the Constitution of the United States, and that of Texas, also.
> *The Court:* Now how should that question be decided? Is it a legal question? A constitutional question? A medical question? A philosophical question? Or, a religious question? Or what is it? (Kurland and Casper 1975, 818)

Implicit in this series of questions is that different perspectives—religious, philosophical, legal, medical, and so on—could yield different answers to the question "What is a person?" Rather than abandoning the effort to provide a real definition of "person," anti-abortion advocates attempted to privilege the medical perspective to make the case that fetuses are persons. Rather than treating different approaches to definition as social practices that serve specific interests of different discourse communities (cf. Olsen 1989), the idea that there are different "perspectives" available toward "personhood" was (and still is) taken quite literally. Medicine, philosophy, and theology, for example, represent different points of view from which to decide what a person is. Because our society generally tends to treat scientists as the most veridical and objective knowledge-producers available, we trust science to see most clearly what the facts about personhood are. Accordingly, the most persuasive avenue available for advocates to pursue was to make the case that the medical perspective supported their claim that fetuses are persons.

Because "person" is not a common medical term, anti-abortion advocates consistently treated certain terms as equivalent: *fetus = live human being = person.* Flowers's statement that, upon conception, "we have a human being; a person" indicates that he considers proof of one to be proof of the other. Similarly, the briefs filed by the State of Texas and by various *amici curiae* (friends of the court) stress such themes as "the human-ness of the fetus," "the unborn offspring of human parents is an autonomous human being," and "the unborn person is also a patient." In these briefs were many photographs of fetuses included to persuade the reader that fetuses, even very early in the gestation period, look like human beings and, thus, should be recognized as persons.

Blackmun's opinion dealt with the question of personhood primarily by defending a fact of usage: previous legal use of the term "person" had not included fetuses:

> The Constitution does not define "person" in so many words. Section 1 of the Fourteenth Amendment contains three references to "person." The first, in defining "citizens," speaks of "persons born or naturalized in the United States." The word also appears both in the Due Process Clause and in the Equal Protection Clause. "Person" is used in other places in the Constitution. . . . But in nearly all these instances, the use of the word is such that it has applicability only postnatally. None indicates, with any assurance, that it has any possible pre-natal application.
>
> All this, together with our observation, *supra,* that throughout the major portion of the 19th century prevailing legal abortion practices were far freer than they are today, persuades us that the word "person," as used in the Fourteenth Amendment, does not include the unborn. (1973, 157–58)

Readers should not assume that anti-abortion advocates only offered arguments in support of facts of essence, because they tried to find legal precedent for fetuses counting as "persons" in previous case law. As one might expect, advocates of abortion rights offered arguments as to why a fetus is not "really" a person. Nonetheless, I think it is a fair generalization to say that the primary thrust of the State of Texas's position with respect to the definitional question of personhood was that fetuses really are persons, while Blackmun responded most directly by reference to established prior usage of the term "person."

Even though Blackmun could make a fairly persuasive argument that previous constitutional discourse did not explicitly count the fetus as a person, he did not avoid arguments about what is "really" a person completely. Because anti-abortion advocates had stressed the linkage *fetus = live human being = person,* the argument could still be made that there is a justification for governments to prohibit abortions to protect the "compelling state interest" in human life. Blackmun shifted away from how the word "person" had been used previously and met the argument directly on its own, "real" terms: "We need not resolve the difficult question of when life begins. When those trained in the respective disciplines of medicine, philosophy, and theology are unable to arrive at any consensus, the judiciary, at this point in man's knowledge, is not in a position to speculate as to the answer" (1973, 159). Blackmun proceeded to survey a range of philosophical, medical, and religious sources "to note briefly the wide divergence of thinking on this most sensitive and difficult question" (159). In other words, because there was no clear consensus among the different perspectives, one could not conclude with confidence exactly when a fetus really becomes a human being and thus a person. The State of Texas merely had adopted "one theory of life," according to Blackmun; it could not claim to know what is really the case (162).

Based on what he perceived to be the scientific consensus, Blackmun articulated the now-famous trimester approach to regulating abortion as a way of guiding states as to when abortions could be regulated or prohibited. "[I]n the light of present medical knowledge," Blackmun argued that the state's "important and legitimate interest in the health of the mother" begins at the end of the first trimester of pregnancy: "This is so because of the now-established fact . . . that until the end of the first trimester mortality in abortion may be less than mortality in normal childbirth" (1973, 163). Having set aside criteria for regulating first-trimester abortions that depend on a specific "theory of life," Blackmun instead depended on the current medical knowledge concerning the relative risks of carrying pregnancy to full term and abortion during the first trimester. Because of the relatively low risks to the woman, prior to the end of the first trimester physician and patient could make a decision regarding abortions free from government interference. During the second trimester, the government could offer only such regulation that furthered the interest of protecting the health of the woman seeking an abortion. Once the fetus becomes "viable," that is, capable of live birth, however, the government could regulate or even prohibit abortions altogether. Instead of defining human life and personhood at conception, as urged by the State of Texas, Blackmun drew the line at that point when a fetus *could be* or actually *is* born: "State regulation protective of fetal life after viability thus has both logical and biological justifications" (163).

As is well known, *Roe* has been praised and criticized endlessly ever since it was announced. The denial of the status of "personhood" to the fetus has been one frequent target of criticism. Objecting to the view that "personhood depends on recognition by the law," John T. Noonan noted the similarity between *Roe* and the infamous *Dred Scott* decision in which the Court found that black slaves were not "persons" under the law (1984, 668). The Court in *Roe,* Noonan complained, "when treating of the unborn, felt free to impose its own notions of reality" (673). Similarly, Guido Calabresi suggested that the Court, "when it said that fetuses are not persons for the purposes of due process, said to a large and politically active group: '*Your* metaphysics are not part of *our* constitution'" (1985, 95).

On the other hand, Erwin Chemerinsky argues that if the Court had held that the fetus is a person, the legal consequences would have been unacceptable. All abortions, even in cases of rape or incest, would have to be prohibited; in fact, "once it is assumed that the fetus is a person, then there is no legal basis for punishing abortion differently than homicide" (1982, 113). Chemerinsky contends that even "birth control methods such as the intrauterine device and the 'morning after pill' would also be homicide since they act after fertilization and thus kill human lives" (114). Furthermore, laws carefully regulating the behavior of pregnant women would be mandatory in order to provide "equal protection" for persons born and unborn (114). Similarly, Laurence H. Tribe suggests that, if the fetus were considered a person, "extraordinary and perhaps unthinkable implications would follow" (1992, 121). In addition to treating all abortions as murder, Tribe argues that (a) birth control measures that do not stop conception but prevent implantation of the fertilized ovum in the wall of the uterus would be prohibited; (b) the use of in vitro fertilization would be prohibited since the "process inevitably results in the accidental but foreseeable destruction of at least

some ova that have been fertilized"; (c) it would be the government's obligation to regulate pregnant women with many less-than-ideal health
conditions (either genetic or environmental), such as by requiring women
to follow stringent state-approved medical practices or even requiring
the transfer of the "fetus-person to a less hazardous womb" (121–25).

The question of whether "person" should be defined in such a way
as to include the fetus would appear to have reached a definitional im-
passe. Anti-abortion advocates insist that the fetus really is a person, yet
such a fact of essence relies on a realist rhetoric that is ultimately circular and self-sealing. Meanwhile, abortion-rights advocates rely on a
wholly different approach to definition. They claim that "person" in
constitutional law has not been used to denote fetuses in the past, nor
should that usage change in the future if we want to avoid undesirable
consequences. Because each position (anti-abortion versus pro-abortion
rights) is defended in part through incompatible approaches to definition (facts of essence versus facts of usage), it is tempting to conclude
that any "appeal to the concept of personhood is entirely unhelpful in
any effort to resolve the fundamentals of the abortion controversy"
(Macklin 1984, 80). Even anti-abortion advocates appear to agree. In
the oral argument of the 1992 abortion case *Planned Parenthood of
Southeastern Pennsylvania v. Robert P. Casey,* Solicitor General Kenneth
W. Starr represented the Bush administration's position favoring the
reversal of *Roe.* When asked, "What is the position of the Department
of Justice on the question whether a fetus is a person within the meaning of the Fourteenth Amendment?," Starr replied simply: "We do not
have a position on that question" (*Official Transcript* 1992, 41–42). The
definition of "person" had evolved from being *the* decisive issue in *Roe*
to "an extraordinarily difficult question which this course need not
address" in *Planned Parenthood* (Starr in *Official Transcript* 1992, 42).

Justice Sandra Day O'Connor's Role
in Redefining the Abortion Debate

I agree with the sentiment that the abortion controversy is not going to
be resolved by the articulation of any particular definition of "person,"
but I believe that the current status of constitutional law regarding abortion provides a useful case study of how a definitional dispute can evolve
over time and how the pragmatics of definition can be confronted directly. Specifically, the opinions of Justice Sandra Day O'Connor, which
have moved from the status of a minority dissent to that of represent-

ing the ruling plurality opinion, can be read as illustrating certain aspects of the pragmatic approach I urge throughout this book. I conclude, however, that the Court has not embraced such an approach fully and, as a result, has allowed coercion where it promised persuasion with respect to exercising the right to define the meaning of the act of abortion.

O'Connor has never commented explicitly on the question of whether the fetus is a person. In fact, no Supreme Court justice, even those opposed to *Roe,* has ever supported the position that fetuses are "constitutional persons" (Tribe 1992, 125; see also Stevens 1992). The Court as a whole apparently has set aside the question of personhood as an unnecessary encumbrance to decisions regarding abortion rights. The primary purpose of the abortion arguments that take place in and before the Supreme Court is to decide what sorts of statutory limits on abortion are constitutional. O'Connor has had many opportunities to disagree with Blackmun's conclusion in *Roe* that "person" in the Fourteenth Amendment does not include a fetus. That she has not implies that she agrees with Blackmun's point or regards the status of "personhood" with respect to the text of the Constitution to be irrelevant. In either case, further defining "person" serves no useful purpose in her decisions and thus is left aside.

At the same time, it is not possible to avoid all questions related to personhood. As noted earlier, anti-abortion advocates often defend the linkage *fetus = live human being = person.* As *Roe* critic John Hart Ely notes, "Dogs are not 'persons in the whole sense' nor have they constitutional rights, but that does not mean the state cannot prohibit killing them" (1973, 926). Even if one severs "person" from the equation, one is left with the notion that a fetus is a live human being; thus, one has to acknowledge that abortions end human lives. We are still left with the definitional question of what counts as a live human being for the purposes of regulating abortion. O'Connor has dealt with this question through what can be described as two "steps" that lead, at least in theory, to an increasingly pragmatic stance.

First, O'Connor appropriated and extended Blackmun's notion of "potential life" from *Roe.* The Court held in *Roe* that the anti-abortion laws of the State of Texas had violated "the Due Process Clause of the Fourteenth Amendment, which protects against state action the right to privacy, including a woman's qualified right to terminate her pregnancy" (Blackmun 1973, 114). Although Blackmun argued that the right to privacy "is broad enough to encompass a woman's decision whether or not to terminate her pregnancy," he declared that it is not an absolute right (153). Where there is a "compelling state interest" to do so, the woman's privacy rights can be tempered. Although unwilling to grant the fetus the constitutional status of personhood under the Fourteenth Amendment, Blackmun repeatedly referred to and affirmed the state's interest in protecting the "potentiality" of human life: "With respect to the State's important and legitimate interest in potential life, the 'compelling' point is at viability. This is so because the fetus then presumably has the capability of meaningful life outside the mother's womb" (163).

O'Connor adopted the notion of "potential life" while effectively repudiating Blackmun's trimester approach to limiting state regulation of abortions. Her critique began in her 1983 dissenting opinion in *Akron v. Akron Center for Reproductive Health* (hereafter *Akron*).[1] The choice of the end of the first trimester as the point at which regulation could be imposed was unworkable, O'Connor suggested, because "of what the Court accepts as technological advancement in the safety of abortion procedure" (1983, 455). However, just as changes in medical knowledge had lengthened the portion of pregnancy during which abortions could be performed safely, thus vitiating the rationale behind the first trimester "stage" of regulation, so too had technology shortened the length of pregnancy necessary for a fetus to become "viable." It was merely a convenient coincidence that medical technology had paralleled the trimesters of pregnancy in 1973. Future changes in medical knowledge, O'Connor declared, meant that the rationale offered by Blackmun could become obsolete: "The *Roe* framework, then, is clearly on a collision course with itself. As the medical risks of various abortion procedures decrease, the point at which the State may regulate for reasons of maternal health is moved further forward to actual childbirth. As medical science becomes better able to provide for the separate existence of the fetus, the point of viability is moved further back toward conception" (458).

O'Connor rejected Blackmun's trimester approach because it is unworkable in practice, not because she opposes the right to an abortion. Following Blackmun, she amended the anti-abortion advocate's equation *fetus = live human being = person* into simply *fetus = potential human life*. Instead of segmenting the government's interest in that potential human life into three stages, O'Connor insists that "[t]he state interest in potential human life is . . . extant throughout pregnancy" (1983, 460). After all, "at any stage in pregnancy, there is the potential for human life. . . . The choice of viability as the point at which the state interest in potential life becomes compelling is no less arbitrary than choosing any point before viability or any point afterward" (461). Since the *Akron* decision, O'Connor has dropped the notion that advances in medical technology could make fetal viability a useless point at which to draw a line for regulation. Subsequent argument to the Court indicated that there is no foreseeable risk that the point of viability is going to move to "within the first twenty weeks of gestation, when ninety-nine percent of the abortions performed in the United States take place" (Olsen 1989, 135). Nonetheless, because a pre-viable fetus could develop into a viable fetus, O'Connor has continued to recognize a government interest in the "potential life" of pre-viable fetuses.

O'Connor's belief that a fetus represents "potential life" throughout pregnancy has meant that she is willing to permit greater state regulation of abortions throughout the entire term of pregnancy than Blackmun, for example, would allow. In a series of abortion cases, she repeatedly has affirmed a woman's constitutional right to an abortion while upholding laws that do not, in her judgment, impose an "undue burden" or "substantial obstacle" to the exercise of that right. One of the most important of these cases is the 1992 case of *Planned Parenthood v. Casey.* In this case, O'Connor takes a second important pragmatic step; namely, she has added to the definitional question the issues of *interests* and *power.*

Many anti-abortion advocates hoped that the Supreme Court would explicitly overrule *Roe* in the *Planned Parenthood* case. O'Connor, writing for a plurality of the Court, held that *Roe*'s basic holding should be reaffirmed. In reexamining that holding, the Court's judgment was informed "by a series of prudential and pragmatic considerations designed to test the consistency of overruling the holding with the ideal of the rule of law, and to gauge the respective costs of reaffirming and overruling a prior case" (1992, 854). In the process of reaffirming abortion rights, the importance of the abortion option to the autonomy and liberty of women is underscored by O'Connor far more explicitly than it had been by Blackmun in *Roe:* "The ability of women to participate equally in the economic and social life of the Nation has been facilitated by their ability to control their reproductive lives" (856). Noting that the Constitution promises "that there is a realm of personal liberty which the government may not enter," O'Connor insists that the Fourteenth Amendment's protection of "liberty" places limits on government's "right to interfere" with basic decisions about "family and parenthood . . . as well as bodily integrity" (847–49).

Having reaffirmed the Court's belief that abortion rights are necessary for women's personal liberty, O'Connor's opinion spends several pages indirectly addressing the definitional issues of "What is human life?" I say "indirectly" because at no point in the opinion is there an explicit statement that affirms or denies a particular definition of "person" or "human life." Instead, the process of definition itself is addressed in a series of passages that directly confronts the impossibility of a theory-neutral, apolitical understanding of what an abortion "means." O'Connor notes that "[m]en and women of good conscience can disagree, and we suppose some always shall disagree, about the profound moral and spiritual implications of terminating a pregnancy, even at its earliest stage. . . . Our obligation is to define the liberty of all, not to mandate our own moral code. The underlying constitutional issue is whether the State can resolve these philosophic questions in such a definitive way that a woman lacks all choice in the matter" (1992, 850). Sometimes, O'Connor notes, when people disagree it is permissible for the government to adopt one position or another, but there are some types of decisions in which to impose one view or another would violate fundamental liberties. As an example, O'Connor refers to two controversial cases in which the Court held that the government could not compel expressions of loyalty to the U.S. flag by requiring the pledge of allegiance or by outlawing all flag burning. In both cases, the flag or its desecration has different meanings to different individuals, and the Court held that in a democracy the government could not, through coercion, impose one particular set of meanings over another. Similarly, O'Connor argued that to impose one particular understanding of human life, personhood, and abortion would deny the fundamental liberties provided by the Constitution: "These matters, involving the most intimate and personal choices a person may make in a lifetime, choices central to personal dignity and autonomy, are central to the liberty protected by the Fourteenth Amendment. At the heart of liberty is *the right to define* one's own concept of existence, of meaning, of the universe, and of the mystery of human life. Beliefs about these matters could not define the attributes of personhood were they formed under compulsion of the State" (1992, 851, emphasis added).

Implicit in O'Connor's opinion is recognition that definitions are "political" in the two respects identified in the previous chapter. First, definitions always serve particular interests, in this case, the state's interests and/or that of the woman. Second, the only definitions of consequence are those that have been empowered through persuasion or coercion. O'Connor neither affirms nor denies the belief that the fetus is a live human being; in fact, she acknowledges the diversity of opinions as to what an abortion *is:* "Abortion is a unique act. It is an act fraught with consequences for others: for the woman who must live with the implications of her decision; for the persons who perform and assist in the procedure; for the spouse, family, and society which must confront the knowledge that these procedures exist, procedures some deem nothing short of an act of violence against innocent human life; and depending on one's beliefs, for the life or potential life that is aborted" (1992, 852).

What O'Connor denies is that the government should have the power to enforce one set of beliefs over others, for the woman "who carries a child to full term is subject to anxieties, to physical constraints, to pain that only she must bear" (1992, 852). Her "suffering is too intimate and personal" for the government to have the right to insist "on its own vision of the woman's role. . . . The destiny of the woman must be shaped to a large extent on her own conception of her spiritual imperatives and her place in society" (852). The "meaning of procreation" is something about which "reasonable people will have differences of opinion" (853). But there is no doubt, O'Connor implies, that "actual" women's liberty would be harmed if the government had the power to impose a particular set of beliefs about abortion.

Part of the process of learning to identify a specific class of objects, as discussed in chapter 2, is learning a set of similarity/difference relationships (SDRs). Because there is a gradual process of growth and change throughout the gestation period, deciding precisely how to categorize the fetus (and its termination in abortion) depends on which SDRs one decides are most important at which stage of pregnancy: "Because the fetus has characteristics both like and unlike those of a human being, the classification of the fetus is a contingent matter"; hence, "we must *choose* how to count the fetus" (Condit 1990, 206–7). Such a choice is difficult, as Ely notes: "Abortion is too much like infanticide on the one hand, and too much like contraception on the other, to leave one comfortable with any answer" (1973, 927). For example, although the early fetus has a "pulse" as a infant does, it is unlike an infant in that the fetus does not have "the four developed major compartments of the human heart or the developed arteries and veins" (Condit 1990, 212). Although anti-abortion advocates point out that an early fetus has measurable "brain waves" and thus is like an infant, abortion rights advocates point out that the measurable electrical impulses are very unlike the brain waves of infants, and that not "until somewhere between the twentieth and fortieth weeks do fetuses even begin to have the kind of brain development that would allow perceptions such as awareness of pain" (Condit 1990, 213). The line of cases from *Roe* to *Planned Parenthood* consistently has held that abortions after viability are too much like infanticide to deny the government the right to ban them. At the same time, because abortions prior to viability are seen by some to be like contraception and are seen by others to be like infanticide, O'Connor's opinion in *Planned Parenthood* denies anyone wholesale definitional hegemony.

Ten years before *Planned Parenthood*, Chemerinsky suggested that one way to "rationalize" the abortion controversy was to focus the debate on "*where* in society the abortion decision should be made" (1982, 163). For Chemerinsky, the question "becomes who should decide whether a fetus is to be regarded as a human person" (163). A decade later, Justice O'Connor's opinion in *Planned Parenthood* comes the closest of any Court decision to addressing the abortion issue in just those terms. O'Connor makes it clear that prior to viability, it is the pregnant woman who must decide, because it is she who bears the responsibility of the decision. In striking down the part of the Pennsylvania law that would have required spousal notification, she notes that "it is an inescapable biological fact that state regulation with respect to the child a woman is carrying will have a far greater impact on the mother's liberty than on the father's" (O'Connor 1992, 896). Only a generation earlier the Court had ruled in *Hoyt v. Florida* that women had "special responsibilities" to home and family that "precluded full and independent legal status under the Constitution" (O'Connor 1992, 897). Thus, for women to have such full and independent legal status, O'Connor argues, they must have the ability to exercise control over their own bodies—control that includes the right to pre-viability abortion.

Although women's liberty is the reason that a total ban on abortion is unconstitutional, that liberty is not "unlimited." In order to delineate that liberty, a line must be drawn between the stage of pregnancy during which the right to an abortion must not face an "undue burden" or "a substantial obstacle" imposed by the state and that stage during which "the right of the woman to terminate the pregnancy can be restricted" (O'Connor 1992, 869, 876–77). In order to give "real substance" to the woman's liberty, some sort of line must be provided: "We conclude the line should be drawn at viability, so that before that time the woman has a right to choose to terminate her pregnancy" (870). Although any act of line-drawing "may seem somewhat arbitrary," drawing a line at viability is the most "workable" option since it is at viability that "there is a realistic possibility of maintaining and nourishing a life outside the womb, so that the independent existence of the second life can in reason and all fairness be the object of state protection that now overrides the rights of the woman" (870). In short, just as *Roe* ruled, it is at the point in the pregnancy where most philosophical, legal, theological, and religious points of view converge to agree that a "potential" life can become an "actual" life that abortion can be prohibited. This line, O'Connor suggests, has "as a practical matter, an element of fairness" to it (870).

In *Planned Parenthood,* O'Connor again criticized Blackmun's trimester approach. She suggested that the trimester framework "misconceives the nature of the pregnant woman's interest; and in practice it undervalues the State's interest in potential life" (1992, 873). That is, because a fetus is "potential life" throughout pregnancy, the government may have a legitimate interest in taking steps that express a preference for childbirth over abortion. Although such steps imply that the government has favored a particular view of pre-viability humanity, they are not unconstitutional steps as long as they do not create an "undue burden" on or "substantial obstacle" to the woman seeking an abortion. To foster and protect "potential life," the government may take steps designed to persuade women to understand the fetus and abortion in certain ways, but the government must stop at the point that it coerces that understanding: It must not impose an "undue burden" or "substantial obstacle" to women seeking an abortion.

Beyond the "What Is X?" Question

I end this chapter by making explicit the connections between the arguments I have advanced about definitional practices and the narrative provided about selected claims advanced in recent abortion cases. It should be obvious that, for the most part, the Supreme Court has addressed the definitional issues involved in abortion in a manner that sidesteps questions of the form "What is X?" At no point has the Court settled the questions "What is a person?" or "What is human life?" Because there are infinite answers to such questions, Richard Robinson describes the "What is X?" question as "the vaguest of all forms of questions except the inarticulate grunt" (1950, 190; cf. 1953, 53–60). The Court has turned the vague question of "What is a person?" into the more productive and answerable question of "What counts as a person with respect to the Constitution?" Robinson commends lexical definition "in which we are explaining the actual way in which some actual word has been used by some actual persons" and urges that we recognize new definitions as stipulative "proposals for future usage" (1950, 10–11, 35). With respect to "person," the Court has been guided by past usage and has shifted attention from "person" to "potential life" for future abortion-related cases. Perhaps because of the sorts of consequences described by Chemerinsky and Tribe, the Court's proposal for "future usage" is that we try not to use "person" as a category relevant to abortion discourse. Furthermore, by emphasizing the notion of the "potential life" of the fetus prior to viability, the Court has managed to avoid stipulating a single answer to the question "What is human life?" while leaving room for citizens and government to offer—through persuasion but not coercion—competing answers as to what should count as a human life for the purposes of our laws.

The Court increasingly has acknowledged that any choice of categorizing the fetus is going to serve particular interests and enact specific inequalities of power. Who decides whether the pre-viable fetus counts as human life for the purposes of our laws? The options are limited: either the pregnant woman is allowed to decide for herself, or others decide for her. In part because women cannot be free without the ability to control their own bodies, and in part because "others" are not wholly in agreement concerning what counts as an actual human life prior to viability, the Court has held that the power to define the meaning of an abortion must reside with the pregnant woman. In so holding, the claim that abortion legislation affects men and women unequally has been conceded. Nonetheless, because not all people are convinced that abortions do *not* terminate human lives, the Court has given the government increased latitude to try to persuade pregnant women how to understand the act of abortion. This should not be construed to say that one could not justify legal abortions even if we were all convinced that "fetuses count as persons" (Tribe 1992, 131), but that is not how the Court has addressed the abortion issue so far.

Despite the generally pragmatic approach of recent Supreme Court decisions, there is still a tendency to paint the debate in "real" definitional terms. Reacting against an article that argued, basically, that the fetus counts as a human life only when those in power value it as such (Olsen 1989, 128), Tribe protested that "the same thing once was said of slaves: the value of black Americans was less than the value of white Americans in the view of people with power" (1992, 119). Such a position is invalid, Tribe insists, because the "members of these other groups, degraded sometimes by the law, simply *are* human beings even though 'people with power' may try to deny it" (120). In this passage, Tribe is trying to distinguish between what Searle calls "institutional" facts and "brute" facts that just are, independent of social agreement. But the belief that black and white Americans are equally valuable is no more theory independent than the anti-abortionist belief that a fetus is a person. Similarly, Celeste Condit's suggestion that "the pro-Life advocates' assertion that the 'fetus is a human being and therefore abortion is murder' is not a 'true' claim but a rhetorical tactic—an effort to establish the claim as a social choice *disguised* as a statement of fact" may be correct, but the same criticism can be made of those who argue the opposite claim (1990, 214). All institutional facts are social choices, because only when a particular claim (X is Y) is accepted or enforced in a particular context (C) is it treated *as* a "fact." Only then can we look back to assert that the claim was true all along, even if folks then did not recognize it as such.

Just because we rejected pro-slavery beliefs and adopted a set of beliefs that sees all races as equal does not make our beliefs "theory free" or literally timeless. Although contrasts such as "simply *are*"/thought-to-be, reality/appearance, essential/accidental, and the like may be used persuasively *intra*theoretically, it is difficult to see how they may be defended *inter*theoretically without engaging in circular arguments. "Concrete" and "factual" data supporting a theory are often defensible only in terms of that theory. The facts that supported the theory of phlogiston, for example, cannot be separated from the theory itself. From the perspective of another theory, those "facts" would not be facts but accidentals, illusions, or faulty appearances. Similarly, whether the fetus counts as a person or actual human life or not depends on a set of beliefs that cannot be scrutinized from an ahistorical, context-free, theory-independent perspective. Just as the Civil War eventually took away slave owners' power to define black Americans as less than fully human, so, too, Supreme Court decisions regarding abortion empower or disempower competing accounts of what counts as human life. When it comes to defining our shared reality, there is simply no escape from questions of power, interests, and historical contingency:

> [S]ociety chooses some period when it decides to attribute human life to its future members. The decision is not arbitrarily made by an individual, but it is socially arrived at through a complex set of negotiations. And whatever is decided comes to seem increasingly "true."

Ultimately, the struggle is not about what status fetal life *does* have but what status it *will* have. Antiabortion laws combine legitimation with force. Antiabortionists present a view of reality—the fetus as person—that they hope will *construct* real-

ity. The same could be said of their opponents. If powerful
people successfully assert that the fetus is not just the same as a
person, this stance too will construct a reality. (Olsen 1989, 131)

For the most part, anti-abortion advocates have relied on the rhetoric
of real definitions rather than on a more pragmatic approach to categorizing the fetus: "Instead of claiming that the fetus should be classified
or treated as a human person, they claim that the fetus IS a human person" (Condit 1990, 210). Accordingly, I would not be surprised if readers
with anti-abortion beliefs are troubled by two concerns: first, that I have
defended a pro-abortion rights position; and second, that I have neglected to emphasize the fetus's interests and lack of power in my discussion. The two concerns should be treated separately. First, I concede
that my own political beliefs incline me to favor the abortion rights
position and that those beliefs have influenced the way I have constructed
the narrative in this chapter. At the same time, I would insist that anyone who writes at length about abortion faces a similar situation. There
simply is no value-neutral vocabulary with which to discuss this or any
other issue. I also believe that public discussion of abortion rights, along
with many other definition-related issues, can be enhanced by a pragmatic turn. As Condit suggests, ultimately our society "may *choose* to
classify the fetus as a human" (213). The process of making that choice
ought to be influenced by such considerations as the consequences of
institutionalizing one understanding of the fetus over others. To date,
anti-abortion advocates strike many as simply repeating circular arguments about what the fetus "really is." I agree with Condit when she
suggests a more productive public debate would focus on "the weigh-
ing process" involved with deciding which similarities and differences
between fetuses and persons are worth backing with legal coercion (213).
Put another way, the public debate would be more fruitful if there was
recognition that definitional categories are human-made, not found;
constructed, not discovered.

The second concern is that the narrative provided here neglects the
interests and lack of power of the fetus. The persuasiveness of such a
charge, of course, depends on the degree to which one believes that the
fetus ought to count as an actual—rather than a potential—human being. The Court has ruled consistently that abortions after the point of
fetal viability can be prohibited. Thus, the government already has the
ability to say that abortions after viability constitute the taking of an
actual human life. Prior to viability, we have a unique category that

counts abortion as something more than mere contraception but something less than infanticide. Few suggest that the government go into the business of encouraging abortions, and the Court has ruled that the government can take various steps to encourage (through persuasion) women to consider alternatives to abortion. If I were convinced that a pre-viable fetus was the same as a fetus after viability, I would see all abortions as killing. I am not convinced that the two ought to be treated as the same, and I am content with the Court's decision to limit the government's actions with respect to the interests in the potential life of a fetus at the level of persuasion. To do more would impose a highly contested definition of human life on pregnant women. To do less would impose a highly contested definition of human life on the potential life of the fetus.

Of course, in the previous paragraph I have said nothing that has not been said in earlier pages. To claim otherwise might lead to the mistaken impression that one can engage the abortion debate from "above"—from a "God's eye view" or the perspective of a disinterested seeker of true essences—and search for the "real truth" about abortion. Once we reject the path of "real" definitions, such perspectives are ruled out. The abortion controversy may be unusually volatile compared to many issues that involve questions of definition. But the intensity of opinions involved helps to throw into sharp relief pragmatic dimensions of definition that I believe are shared in other definitional disputes—not only in legal settings but also in any setting in which new definitions are offered and debated as proposals for future belief and action.

The intensity of opinions should not lead us to conclude, as so many people have, that abortion is an issue "about which people cannot be rational" (Faux 1988, x). The pervasiveness of such of a conclusion is evinced by one Supreme Court justice calling another's opinion "irrational" (Scalia 1989, 536n). In principle, the abortion controversy is no more or less susceptible to "rational discussion" than any other definitional dispute. Good reasons can be adduced for either "side," but that does not make one's choice arbitrary. The debate becomes "irrational" only when we choose to stop listening to others' reasons; that is, when we decide that our opponents' arguments "cannot be taken seriously" (Scalia 1989, 532). We need less hubris of Scalia's sort and more of the humility and sensitivity to the role of persuasion and competing interests of the sort found in portions of O'Connor's opinions (see Courtright 1995; Sullivan and Goldzwig 1995).

Most abortion rights advocates feel that what O'Connor gave to women in her powerfully worded refusal to overrule *Roe* is taken back by an overly expansive view of what constitutes an "undue burden." No one disputes the general definition of an "undue burden" or a "substantial obstacle," but there is disagreement about whether to *apply* such labels to the provisions of the various laws that have been enacted in recent years to discourage abortions. If the Court was willing to empower pregnant women to decide for themselves how much of a burden is "undue," then the promise of allowing women the right to choose would be kept. Because, through a pattern of judicial deference, the Court has largely granted the power to determine what an "undue burden" is to legislatures, the Court has fallen far short of the promise of *Roe* and the pro-woman portions of O'Connor's opinion in *Planned Parenthood*.[2] The important relationship between the establishment of agreed-upon definitions of X and the power to denote specific phenomena *as* X is the focus of the remaining chapters of this book.

Part Three

Naming and Describing
as Entitlements

In the previous chapters, I have described an approach to definitional disputes that emphasizes the normative and pragmatic aspects of deciding how to use socially important words. The focus of the analysis to this point has been a rethinking of how to answer definitional questions of the form "What is X?" When there are competing answers, what follows can be described as an argument *about* a definition. In the following chapters, I discuss arguments *from* and *by* definition, that is, disputes in which a definition of X is generally shared and accepted by interlocutors and the debate turns on whether or not a particular event or phenomenon should or should not be understood as an instance of X.

Rhetorical critic Richard Weaver describes the "argument from definition" as all arguments derived "from the nature of the thing." All such arguments, Weaver suggests, are based on the postulate that "there exist classes which are determinate and therefore predicable. . . . Whatever is a member of the class will accordingly have the class attributes" (1985, 86).[1] The standard Aristotelian form of definition focuses on genus and difference: An X is (a kind of) *class name* that has such-and-such *attributes*. Part of what it means to be "human," for example, is to be a type of being that is mortal. To make the claim that "Socrates is mortal" is to invoke an argument from definition in which "the class of mortal beings is invoked as a predicable" (86). The logic of argument from definition is easily recognizable as the classic form of the syllogism:

> All humans are mortal.
> Socrates is human.
> Therefore, Socrates is mortal.

Or:

> All X are Z.
> Y is an X.
> Therefore, Y is Z.

Arguments about definitions are mostly concerned with the first premise: Asking "What is X?" also amounts to asking "What are the predicable attributes of X?" Once answered, members of the class of objects, actions, or events known as X are generally expected to share those predicable attributes. For example, if we agree to define "rape" as "nonconsensual sex," and it is agreed that in a given instance person A forced person B to have intercourse, then it follows that the given instance is or "counts as" rape. But what happens if we disagree about the middle step in this argument, that is, if we disagree about whether in this particular instance person A forced person B to have intercourse?

In an earlier chapter, I described the "picture theory" of meaning as described in Ludwig Wittgenstein's early work. To those who believe that language pictures reality, there must be a similarity between "that which pictures and that which is pictured" (Phillips 1977, 21). Straightforward "observations" ought to be able to be reported in language that accurately and objectively corresponds to the structure of reality. The description "person A forced person B to have intercourse" is or is not "correct." The picture theory of meaning, it will be recalled, posits that "truth" consists in some form of correspondence between belief and fact: between a person's subjective opinion of what is and what objectively "really is." Accordingly, a description of an event as rape is "objectively" true or false.

Although few philosophers still subscribe to such an account of language, there is something compelling about the idea that language ought to be able to provide an "objective" account of the world that accurately portrays reality. Part of the persuasiveness of such an account of language stems from those instances in which there is a high degree of denotative conformity—where there is virtual unanimity about how a particular phenomenon should be described. But we should not confuse intersubjective agreement—a social phenomenon—with a metaphysical state of affairs. As argued previously, observations are theory bound. If we share a set of beliefs about the United States' monetary system, the odds are good that we will agree on what is a five-dollar bill when we see one. What makes the description "This is a five-dollar bill" function as true is our intersubjective understanding of the institution of U.S. money (Searle 1969). It is our agreement that "entitles" the piece of paper to "be" a five-dollar bill and not the presence of nonhuman metaphysical qualities. Similarly, we must share a number of beliefs about human behavior in order to agree whether, in a given instance, "person A forced person B to have intercourse" and, thus, whether the given instance "counts as" rape. It is not a question of whether a given description is an objective picture of reality but whether a given description receives the intersubjective assent of relevant members of a discourse community. From a pragmatic perspective, what is often called an objective account is one that obtains a high degree of denotative conformity, while a subjective account is one that obtains a low degree of denotative conformity.

When we name or describe a phenomenon, we "entitle" it as some thing, event, action, or whatever. Whether we agree on a description potentially can have enormous consequences. For example, if a jury agrees that person A forced person B to have intercourse and thus decides that the given instance counts as rape, person A is subject to significant penalties under the law. Of course, we do not always agree on how to describe a given phenomenon, and the degree of denotative conformity obtained in various situations can vary widely and change over time. Controversial descriptions, or "disputed entitlements," that argue from or by definition are the focus of the following chapters.

The three chapters in part three describe disputed entitlements at three levels of abstraction. Chapter 7 illustrates the theme that descriptions entitle phenomena in a persuasive manner by examining a dispute over how to identify seven particular objects—in this case, photographs. Are they instances of pornography, or are they entitled to be taken as "art"? Chapter 8 moves up the ladder of abstraction to consider how whole classes of objects and events are named and defined in order to illustrate the theme that naming functions as argument by definition. That is to say, how we name a class of objects can define that class with nontrivial attitudinal and behavioral consequences. In this case, I examine the linguistic practice known as "nukespeak" in order to assess critically some of the ways in which naming persuades. Chapter 9 moves up the ladder of abstraction one more notch to discuss how certain language choices "frame" whole situations. How we define a situation or problem frames, that is, unavoidably limits, our understanding and delineates a limited range of appropriate responses. Based on the view of language advocated throughout this book, it should come as no surprise that I argue that such framing functions persuasively and as a form of social influence. In particular, I look at how the terms "private," "public," and "technical" are used to define distinct "spheres" of human activity.

7
Description as Persuasive Entitlement: The Mapplethorpe "Obscenity" Trial

In this chapter, a case of disputed entitlement that ended up in a court trial before a jury is discussed. In the so-called Mapplethorpe obscenity trial in Cincinnati, Ohio, the question was whether a group of seven photographs should be categorized legally as obscene or not. The case serves as a representative example of disputed entitlement. There was no question in this case about the definition of the key concepts; the legal definition of "obscenity" was not at issue. Rather, the question was how, in this particular case, the phenomena at issue should be described— "obscene" or "art." Prior to, and in the process of, examining this case, I want to develop an argument that all acts of description, naming, or "entitling" are normative and prescriptive and that the notion of a "neutral" or "objective" description of anything is untenable and unhelpful.

Entitling Reality

All language use can be described as persuasive. Just as definitions are persuasive in the sense that they encourage people to use word X in a particular way and understand what X is, so, too, do all descriptions prescribe a view of the way some part of reality is. Nouns and verbs represent categories, and "all category systems are moral and political entities" (Bowker and Star 1999, 324). Sentences are predicative assertions that "have ontological claims" and encourage fellow language users to "see" or understand certain aspects of reality in one way rather than another: "We have no sooner uttered words than we have given impulse to other people to look at the world, or some small part of it, in our way" (Weaver 1970, 224). As explained in chapter 2, efforts to describe are always partial in the sense of being "part" and not the whole and in the sense that any perspective that is selective enacts a sort of bias. As Kenneth Burke puts it, "[T]he mere act of naming an object or situation decrees that it is to be singled out as such-and-such rather than as something-other" (1973, 4). When we label or describe a shared stimuli, we make sense of it by locating it in one shared category to the exclusion of many others (cf. Bowker and Star 1999, 5).

Burke describes the persuasive predicative function of language as a process of "entitlement" (1966, 359–79). He encourages us to think of language use as "the 'entitling' of complex nonverbal situations" (361). There are several ideas at work in Burke's metaphor. Obviously, just as a book's title identifies, denotes, or designates which text is being referred to, so certain words function to identify, denote, or designate "objects" in the world. But it is the selective and abstractive function of titles that Burke wants to emphasize: Just as a title of a novel "sums up the vast complexity of elements that compose the novel, giving it its character, essence, or general drift," so descriptive statements reduce and "abbreviate" in order to make sense of infinitely complex stimuli (361).

The most important aspect of Burke's notion of entitlement is his reversal of the traditional piety that "words are the signs of things" to "things are the signs of words." To "entitle" something—"X"—is not only to give X a title in the simple sense of assigning X a name or label, but it is also to give X a particular status. For example, to describe X as "an object" is to assign X an ontological status somewhat different than labeling X "an event" or "a vague feeling." More specific entitlements provide a more specific status. Calling an object a "dime" is quite different than calling it "a metal object," although both statements could obtain an equally high level of denotative conformity (cf. Brown 1958, 14). Burke points out that we have various categories for words we tend to use to describe different "realms" or orders: words to describe the natural order, the purely verbal order, the sociopolitical order, and the supernatural order (1966, 374). Using words from these different orders entitle reality in different ways that give our experiences different "status" in our belief systems. Attribute a sound to "a ghost" among people who do not believe in ghosts, and they will interpret your statement quite differently than if you were among people who do believe in ghosts. The "status" of "ghosts"—whether they exist and what they are like—can vary among different discourse communities.

Whenever we label a shared stimulus, we make sense of it by locating it in a shared belief system. Without a means to label or name a phenomenon, that phenomenon has no status in our belief system. Although our current beliefs about "gravity" and "carbon" compel us to say that they have existed throughout the history of our planet, we could hold no shared beliefs about gravity or carbon without the linguistic means of identifying or "entitling" them.

The creation of a new word provides a somewhat new way of summing up or entitling a portion of human experience. One rhetorical effect of entitling a new "thing" is that it creates the impression that the thing has been "out there" all along, waiting to be discovered and described. Nouns, in particular, suggest things-that-already-exist: "And that no doubt accounts for the feeling that when one is using nouns, one is manipulating the symbols of a self-subsistent reality" (Weaver 1985, 128). Nouns give one the impression of something stable, even permanent and immutable, or at least beyond the immediate limits of subjectivity (Perelman and Olbrechts-Tyteca 1969, 182, 294).

The idea that language entitles reality also can be described from a psychological perspective. As argued in chapter 2, we know that language affects human perception and cognition. All meaningful human experience is formed experience, organized through a continual process of abstraction, bordering, and categorization. Differences in the way a language encodes a domain of experience influences how individuals conceive reality in that domain. The introduction of a new signifier simultaneously introduces a new signified and thus expands the spectrum of conceptual possibilities for a given linguistic community. Viewing the process in reverse, sans signifier, there is no corresponding signified readily available in the language/belief system. It is precisely this point that Burke is making when he describes nonverbal "things" as "signs" of words. Prior to the coining of a term for a distinct category of phenomena, that phenomena is without form or "meaning." The point here is psycholinguistic, not metaphysical: without the linguistic categories of "art" and "obscenity," for example, the Mapplethorpe controversy would not exist; it would be meaning-less.

The categorizing function of language is a form of persuasion; different terminologies prompt us to perceive the world in different ways (Gregg 1984, 50–51). The position advanced here does not entail the position, usually attributed to Benjamin Lee Whorf, that language pre-determines thought and that meaning is confined to language (1956).[1] Nonetheless, naming has the effect in practice of stabilizing the meaning of that portion of human experience being entitled. Richard Gregg calls this process *linguistic fixing:* "Language helps fix or stabilize tendencies and processes already present in thought and experience" (1984, 87). In fact, empirical evidence supports the relationship between the specificity of a given vocabulary and the degree of analytical sophistication and conceptual retrievability (Brown 1956; Brown and Lenneberg 1954; Rosch 1988; Lakoff 1987, 330–34). A relationship exists between vocabulary and understanding: the more complex the vocabulary or system of entitlements, the more sophisticated the observed learning.[2] Nouns, in particular, "function to introduce and arrange new people or objects in the discourse" (Corrigan 1989, 8).

To summarize the argument so far, naming and describing are acts of entitlement. Through such linguistic practices, we give our experiences meaning and make sense of reality. By entitling a given phenomenon, we locate that phenomenon in a set of beliefs about the world that includes beliefs about existence-status (what things are real or not) and essence-status (what qualities we may reliably predicate about the phenomenon). Because the range of possible entitlements is theoretically infinite, any given act of entitling should be seen as a persuasive act that encourages language users to understand that-which-is-entitled in particular ways rather than others.

The persuasive character of entitlement is particularly clear in the case of the Mapplethorpe obscenity trial. An exhibition titled "Robert Mapplethorpe: The Perfect Moment" opened at Cincinnati's Contemporary Arts Center (CAC) on April 7, 1990. The CAC and its director, Dennis Barrie, were charged by Hamilton County prosecutor Frank H. Prouty Jr. on the exhibit's opening day with pandering obscenity and using minors in pornography. At issue were seven photographs out of 175 in the exhibit. The photographs were of nude subjects, and some depicted sadomasochistic and homoerotic activity. Two of the photographs were of nude or nearly-nude children: one of a nude boy on a chair, another of a toddler with her dress raised and her genitals exposed. The pictures of adult subjects included a photograph of a finger inserted into a man's penis. In another, Mapplethorpe, who had died the previous year of AIDS, had photographed himself with a bullwhip in his rectum; another photograph depicted a man urinating into another man's mouth; and another photograph portrayed a male fist inserted into a rectum. If convicted of the charges, Barrie faced as much as a $2,000 fine and a one-year jail term, while the CAC faced a $10,000 fine. The case was remarkable, in part, because it was the first-ever instance of an art center or museum being charged with obscenity.

The legal definition of obscenity can vary from state to state but can go no further than the definition set forth by the Supreme Court in the 1973 case of *Miller v. California*. The majority opinion of the Court was written by then Chief Justice Warren Burger. He declared: "[W]e now confine the permissible scope of such regulation [of obscene materials] to works which depict or describe sexual conduct. That conduct must be specifically defined by the applicable state law, as written or authoritatively construed. A state offense must also be limited to works which, taken as a whole, appeal to the prurient interest in sex, which portray sexual conduct in a patently offensive way, and which, taken as a whole, do not have serious literary, artistic, political, or scientific value" (1973a, 24). The last sentence quoted here is the most important, as it produces a three-part definition for obscenity that has come to be known as the "Miller test": the work must appeal to prurient interests, depict sexual conduct in a "patently offensive" way, and lack serious value—in this case, as art.

In the Mapplethorpe case, the focal point of the trial was the third part of the Miller test. The key issue was, Were the photographs entitled to be called "art"? If so, then they could not be called obscene under the law. If not, then Barrie and the CAC could be prosecuted and punished. Although, logically speaking, one could imagine the concept of "obscene art," from a legal standpoint "obscenity" and "art" are mutually exclusive categories (Peckham 1969). This opposition is sometimes reflected in popular culture as well, as the cover of the July 2, 1990, *Newsweek* suggests when it posed the question "Art or Obscenity?" about various controversies, including the Mapplethorpe photographs.

The competing sides in the trial attempted to persuade the jury to accept their particular entitlements of the photographs as either art or obscenity. Of course, there is an endless variety of other ways to entitle the objects involved: they could be described by size, shape, color, weight, texture; by emotional response, economic value, political dimensions, religious value; or from any one of a number of other perspectives. To restate Burke's point: "[T]he mere act of naming an object or situation decrees that it is to be singled out as such-and-such rather than as something-other." Thus, to frame the debate as "art" versus "obscenity" is doubly persuasive in that, first, other aspects of the situation are set aside, and then, second, we are encouraged to understand the objects as either art or obscenity, but not both.

What Counts as Art?

Deciding whether a given work is art depends on reaching an agreement about what counts as art. How to define "art" or "work of art" has been a perennial question for philosophers and art critics—so intractable that W. B. Gallie described art as an "essential contested concept" that is impossible to define to everyone's satisfaction (1964, cf. Kekes 1977). Not surprisingly, the theoretical beliefs held by different philosophers in general about language and reality informed their arguments about the problem of defining art. For my purposes, the efforts to define art by philosophers can be described as falling into three categories: essentialist, analytic, and pragmatist.

An essentialist approach is an example of a search for a real definition, fueled by a faith in metaphysical absolutism (critiqued in chapter 3). An essentialist assumes that there is an "essence" or "innate quality" of Art that all particular instances must have in common. Clive Bell, for example, argued that everyone "believes that there is a real distinction between works of art and all other objects" (1914, v). In answer to the question "What is Art?," he declared that "either all works of visual art have some common quality, or when we speak of 'works of art' we gibber" (7). For Bell, that common quality is "Significant Form," and he is identified, historically, as supporting a formalist definition of art. Leo Tolstoy's *What Is Art?* defines art as a specific kind of "infectious" communication of particular emotions (1930, 123). He, along with others such as R. G. Collingwood (1938), is categorized as supporting an emotionalist theory or definition of art. The intuitionist theory claims that it is through art that artists bring intuitive knowledge into aesthetic expression (Croce 1922, 12–21). An organicist definition says that "art is really a class of organic wholes consisting of distinguishable, albeit inseparable, elements in their causally efficacious relations which are presented in some sensuous medium" (Weitz 1956, 29; 1964). These definitions guide their proponents' judgments about what counts as art. Tolstoy contended that ballet, for example, is not art but a "lewd performance" in which "half-naked women make voluptuous movements, twisting themselves into various sensual wreathings" (1930, 179). Royal Cortissoz dismissed the work of Cézanne and bitterly attacked the "Post-Impressionist" paintings of Gauguin, Matisse, and Picasso from an implicit organicist definition he called "common sense" (1913a, 125–38; 1913b), while Clive Bell defended the same paintings as great works of art from a formalist perspective (1914, 215–38).

An "analytic" approach may or may not acknowledge its dependence on metaphysical essentialism but in any case searches for the necessary and sufficient conditions to state that "this is art" (see, e.g., Beardsley 1961). The two most prominent definitions can be characterized as the "functional" and "institutional" theories of art. The most common efforts to define art in terms of the function it performs focus on the aesthetic experience works of art provide (Eldridge 1985; Rowe 1991; Tollhurst 1984). Institutional definitions focus on the recognizable relationships among the artist, a work of art, a public audience, and an institutional "artworld" (Dickie 1974). Both approaches have their critics. What counts as aesthetically pleasing, valuable, or significant is so diverse that such definitions either must remain so abstract as to be useless (Morgan 1961) or else become mired in argument about the aesthetic value of particular works of art. Institutional aspects are declared accidental features of certain works of art that do not identify the necessary or essential requirements of all works of art (Stecker 1986). To the extent that some efforts to articulate a functional or institutional theory of art try to generate definitions that are timeless and eternal, they tend to enact the sort of linguistic absolutism that I argued in chapter 4 fares no better than metaphysical absolutism. Some theorists attempt to provide historical versions of these theories to avoid just such a critique. Noël Carroll (1988) and Jerrold Levinson (1979; 1989) argue that attempts to identify new objects as works of art necessarily involves linking such objects with previously produced artifacts culturally or institutionally acknowledged to be works of art. Robert Stecker suggests that a functional definition of art can be preserved if one admits that aesthetic and other artistic functions change over time (1990). I believe that it is safe to generalize that among those theorists interested in generating definitions of "art," the most productive current approaches focus on artistic functions and institutions from a historical perspective.

A third approach to the issue of defining "art" can be called pragmatist. Such efforts acknowledge that any effort to define art turns out to be a competing theory of art, and that individual observation statements of the type "This is art" or "This is not art" are informed by larger sets of beliefs about—or theories of—art. Some pragmatic theorists maintain that we learn from our definitional efforts about the history and development of art: "Only by taking seriously for a time such slogans

as 'Art is the expression of emotion,' 'Art is significant form,' 'Art is illusion,' 'Art is the decrease in psychical distance without its disappearance,'
'Art is empathy' and other such block-busting blanket definitions, can we
learn anything at all about the kaleidoscopic nature of the most general
of aesthetic concepts, i.e. 'art,' and only by examining the arguments
which are proffered in support of these arrogant, essentialist slogans, can
we learn anything of the quagmires of aesthetics" (Peetz 1987, 143).

Other pragmatists set aside the question "What is art?" altogether
as ill-conceived for many of the reasons that have been described
throughout this book as reasons to reformulate questions of the form
"What is X?" A particularly important influence on these thinkers is the
"later" work of Ludwig Wittgenstein (esp. 1958a, 1958b). Wittgenstein,
as mentioned in chapter 4, abandoned his "picture theory" and argued
that meaning is found in the *use* of terms as parts of "language-games"
and that the use of a word can vary widely according to context and
convention (1958b). Accordingly, pragmatists see "art" as a label that
different discourse communities use differently. Morris Weitz's influential essay "The Role of Theory in Aesthetics" argues against trying to
generate "a real definition of the nature of art" that correctly identifies
the "necessary and sufficient properties" of works of art (1956, 27).
Claiming that there are "no necessary and sufficient properties," Weitz
advocates a turn to studying the way the category "art" is used in ordinary language use. He suggests that learning what to call "art" is a linguistic skill that parallels the acquisition of other categories that include
varied items, such as "games": "The problem of the nature of art is like
that of the nature of games, at least in these respects: If we actually look
and see what it is that we call 'art,' we will find no common properties—
only strands of similarities. Knowing what art is is not apprehending
some manifest or latent essence but being able to recognize, describe,
and explain those things we call 'art' in virtue of these similarities" (31).
Rather than focus on the metaphysical qualities of art objects or the truth
conditions of statements about art, pragmatists are more likely to search
for "acceptance conditions" under which individual objects are entitled
as art (Tilghman 1984, 181). Art is an *aspect* of our experience that we
may or may not be induced to "see" in a given instance, and "the very
idea of a theory or definition" that applies to all works of art "is a confused one" (187).

In another of the early efforts to suggest that producing a univer-
salizable definition of art may be unnecessary as well as impossible, Paul
Ziff declares that "no one definition can mirror" the "manifold and

varying usage" of the phrase "work of art" (1953, 77). He points out that deciding whether the phrase "work of art" is being used in a reasonable manner "depends on the particular context in which the question is raised" and cannot be decided *in vacuo* (1953, 71; cf. Mothersill 1961, 197–98). Ziff continues: "To ask 'What are the consequences and implications of something's being considered a work of art?' is to ask an equivocal question to which there can be no univocal answer. We must first know in what context we are to suppose the phrase 'work of art' is being used" (1953, 72). Because new works of art are always being created, society is always changing, and the role of art in society is always changing as well, Ziff concludes that in the future it "will be necessary to revise our definition of a work of art" (78).

Ziff points out that such disputes are not "merely verbal," because the decision of whether to entitle a given work as art can have important consequences. Referring to controversies over various post-impressionist paintings in the first decades of the twentieth century, Ziff notes that "traditional critics explicitly and with great vehemence maintained that the post-impressionist works ought not to be placed in museums; that the public funds ought not to be spent on them; that the public would be ill-advised to spend its time looking at them or reading books about them; and so forth" (1953, 73). When the Society of Independent Artists decided that Marcel Duchamp's *Fountain*—a porcelain urinal hung at a 90-degree angle and signed with the pseudonym "R. Mutt"— was not art, they excluded it from the society's first exhibition in 1917. The controversy in Cincinnati over the Mapplethorpe photographs is similar to these controversies because there could have been consequences to the determination that the objects in question did not count as art. But they are different in that post-impressionism called into question the dominant definitions of art of the time in a way that Mapplethorpe's photographs did not.

Post-impressionist and cubist paintings by artists such as Gauguin, Matisse, van Gogh, and Picasso were attacked viciously by various art critics of the early twentieth century. Kenyon Cox in *Harper's Weekly* described the work of these "artistic anarchists" as "sickening," "revolting," and "defiling" (1913). Of work such as Picasso's he claimed, "[T]he real meaning of this Cubist movement is nothing else than the total destruction of the art of painting." He dismisses van Gogh as "a painter too unskilled to give quality to an evenly laid coat of pigment" and says of Matisse that "it is not madness that stares at you from his canvases, but leering effrontery." Cox is convinced that such "art" is only a passing fad: "I have no fear that this kind of art will prevail, or even that it can long endure." In an article originally published in the April 1913 issue of *Century Magazine* (1913b), republished in the same year in his book *Art and Common Sense* (1913a), Royal Cortissoz dismisses the art of the post-impressionist "movement" as an illusion and a farce. Of Cézanne, Cortissoz claims that many of his pictures "should have been discarded as crude attempts" (1913a, 130). Concerning van Gogh, he suggests the painter was too self-absorbed and, artistically, "the result was disastrous" (131). Van Gogh's later work is blasted as "immature, even childish," created by "incompetence suffused with egotism" (132). Cortissoz concludes his critique by quoting approvingly a statement by artist John Sargent, who claims to be "absolutely skeptical as to their [the post-impressionists' works] having any claim whatever to being works of art" (138).

Significantly new approaches to art often create a definitional rupture in which facts of essence (what art "really is") are in conflict with facts of usage (what some people call art). Most critics and theorists respond by arguing over the facts of art's essence and defend specific claims that "this is art" using arguments from definition. For example, Clive Bell's defense of post-impressionists could be reconstructed as:

(1) The visual enactment of Significant Form is art.
    Post-impressionists' paintings enact Significant Form.
    Therefore, post-impressionists' paintings are art.

Cortissoz's and Cox's critiques depend on the definition that art is aesthetically valuable representation. Based on such a definition, their argument for excluding nonrepresentational work that they do not find aesthetically valuable could be reconstructed as follows:

(2) That which is not aesthetically valuable representation is not art.
    Post-impressionists' works are not aesthetically valuable representations.
    Therefore, post-impressionists' works are not art.

As art history, the controversy over post-impressionism is significant for two reasons. First, the questioning of the "essential" quality of art-as-representation begun with impressionism was pushed even further. Subsequent efforts to produce a definition of art would be forced to find qualities that representational and nonrepresentational, "realistic" and completely "unrealistic" works of art had in common. The possible range of phenomena that could count as art was broadened significantly. Since the early decades of the twentieth century, various movements in art have stretched the category so far that one theorist claims art has gone through a process of "de-definition" (Rosenberg 1972). Second, because vilified artists such as Cézanne, van Gogh, Matisse, and Picasso eventually were vindicated and widely considered great artists, judgments about what works are aesthetically valuable are recognized to be malleable. Belief in the self-evident value of works of art was called into question; instead, critics recognized that viewers of new and provocative art "must be persuaded to respond to them" (Rosenberg 1972, 38). If we do not recognize something proffered *as* art, history tells us that we may have to be taught or coached to see it as art. Our "puzzlement in the face of a new kind of art" is marked by not knowing how to describe or to appreciate it, which amounts to saying we do not know "how to look at the new painting, read the new poetry, listen to the new music and so on" (Tilghman 1984, 79). Although we may recognize other aspects of the object, we may feel we suffer from a specific "aspect-blindness" if we do not perceive its artistic aspects (122–51).

The pivotal part of the arguments from definition reconstructed above from Cortissoz, Cox, and Bell is the middle step in which a specific claim is advanced about specific artifacts. The claims that "Post-impressionists' paintings enact Significant Form" and "Post-impressionists' works are not aesthetically valuable representations" are contentious descriptions. From the standpoint of an advocate of a broad definition of art, one's willingness to agree that post-impressionists' works contain significant form or that post-impressionists' works are aesthetically valuable depends on whether one has been adequately taught to see the works as art. Such "teaching"—which can be described also as the process of "curing" a specific aspect-blindness—is persuasive. In particular, our willingness to assent to such descriptions depends on the acquisition and acceptance of a specific set of similarity/difference relationships.

In chapter 2, I noted that a key to using linguistic categories successfully is learning the salient set of SDRs that other language users have learned. Just as teaching children what objects they ought to include in a given category depends on persuading them to attend to some features as opposed to others, teaching people what counts as art depends on whether those people will learn and accept certain SDRs. Benjamin R. Tilghman describes the pattern of assimilating new movements in art as one of learning to see the selected similarities and differences between new and old works of art:

This pattern is composed of four elements. (1) There is the culture of the period, the background of artistic life, traditions, and practices, the artworld, against which works of art are understood, described, and evaluated. (2) Something is offered as a work of art that apparently cannot be accommodated by the tradition and that cannot be described and evaluated in terms of familiar categories and standards, with the result that the critics as well as the general public are puzzled, if not outraged in addition. (3) The new work is defended by the demonstration of a connection, however unsuspected, with some aspect of the familiar tradition. The connection is established by showing the *likeness that is to be seen between the new and the already familiar.* The demonstration thus provides a way to understand and assess the new work. (4) The result of all this is that the relevant aspect of the tradition is given an importance it did not have previously and the tradition is thereby modified and enlarged. (1984, 77–78 emphasis added)

Critics of new art, such as the critics of post-impressionism, tend to emphasize the differences between new and old exemplars of artistic movements. Proponents may grant that there are important differences but also demonstrate similarities that entitle the new works to be called "art." Art historian and critic Roger Fry, who organized the first exhibition of post-impressionism in Great Britain in 1910, defended the artists against attacks by noting that the differences between the post-impressionists and currently popular artists were less important than the similarities between the post-impressionists and previous recognized artists who reacted against what they perceived as the excesses of realism (Tilghman 1984, 72–77). Clive Bell, as another example, argued that Significant Form is what all great art has in common, and he proceeded to try to show that post-impressionists' works manifest such form. Contending that simplification "is essential to all art," Bell claimed that "the contemporary movement has pushed simplification a great deal further" than the impressionists (1914, 220–22). If we are persuaded that controversial works are entitled to be called art, then we have been persuaded to understand those works in a new way. As Ziff noted over forty years ago with regard to the eventual acceptance of post-impressionist works as art: "In accepting the modern critics' decision, we are, in effect, accepting something of their view of what the present functions, purposes, and aims of a work of art are or ought to be in our society" (1953, 77).

Entitling Mapplethorpe's Photographs

Because the central issue in the Cincinnati obscenity trial was the artistic value of the photographs in question, each side had to present, implicitly or explicitly, an argument from definition that concluded either that "therefore, these photographs are art" or "therefore, these photographs are not art." The defense attorneys devoted considerable energy to advancing the conclusion that the photographs were entitled to count as art. In particular, the defense advanced arguments that implicate both an institutional and functional definition of art.

Perhaps the most persuasive argument advanced by the defense attorneys was that the disputed photographs were considered art by a variety of artists, critics, and historians—in short, the institutional art world. Art experts testifying for the defense included John Walsh, director of the Getty Art Museum in Los Angeles; Jacquelynn Baas, director of the University Art Museum at the University of California at Berkeley; Robert Sobieszek, chief curator at the International Museum of Photography at George Eastman House in Rochester, New York; and Janet Kardon, who had organized an exhibition of Mapplethorpe's photographs previously at Philadelphia's Institute of Contemporary Art. Two local art critics, Jerry Stein of the *Cincinnati Post* and Owen Findsen of the *Cincinnati Enquirer,* also testified for the defense. The prosecution did not provide one single witness with a connection to the art world to challenge the defense. Instead, prosecutor Prouty tried to make fun of the art experts: "Are they saying they're better than us?" (Siebert and Moores 1990). Interviews with the jurors after the trial indicate that the prosecution's strategy failed. The prosecution did nothing to challenge the defense attorney's efforts to draw the jury's attention to a key similarity between the controversial photographs and artwork like the *Mona Lisa*—they had been accepted as art by acknowledged art authorities and art institutions. Rightly or wrongly, in contemporary society art museums are perceived to be the "principle arbiter of what shall be considered art" (Rosenberg 1972, 235). As one juror put it, "[W]e had to decide whether the photographs were art or not. The prosecution didn't have witnesses to the contrary" (Cembalest 1990, 137). The defense's argument from definition, and in particular the pivotal middle step, went unscathed:

(3) All that is accepted by art institutions as art is art.
The Mapplethorpe photographs are accepted by art institutions as art.
Therefore, the Mapplethorpe photographs are art.

The defense also implicitly defended an argument from definition informed by a functional definition of art. Getty Art Museum director Walsh argued that an important function of contemporary art is to challenge the viewer; thus, good art is often controversial art (Cembalest 1990, 139). As a result, the defense led the jury to question the typical assumption that all art must be aesthetically pleasing. Although CAC director Barrie defended certain aspects of Mapplethorpe's photographic technique, other witnesses, such as art critic Findsen, admitted that the photographs were "repulsive" but claimed they were still art. Accordingly, another argument from definition was advanced successfully by the defense:

> (4) Good art includes controversial, nonaesthetically pleasing works.
> The Mapplethorpe photographs are controversial and nonaesthetically pleasing.
> Therefore, good art includes the Mapplethorpe photographs.

By itself, this argument would have been unpersuasive and is formally invalid, because the most worthless obscenity could also be described as controversial and nonaesthetically pleasing. By emphasizing that controversy and lack of a common aesthetic appeal were qualities that the Mapplethorpe photographs had in common with other accepted works of art, however, the defense articulated an important similarity relation that enhanced the plausibility of the jury expanding their category of art to include the photographs. Although the prosecution pointed to certain differences, such as by asking, "Are these van Goghs, these pictures?," the jury was given no reason to weight differences more heavily than similarities. The defense strategy was more persuasive. One juror noted after the trial, "We learned that art doesn't have to be pretty," while another described the photographs as "gross and lewd" but agreed that they were art (Cembalest 1990, 136–37).

The prosecution offered only one "expert" witness. Judith Reisman was described as a mass media expert who had worked as a consultant for the *Captain Kangaroo* show, the Meese commission on pornography, and the conservative American Family Association (Moores 1990). Reisman's testimony was the only effort the prosecution made to refute directly a definitional argument made by the defense. Specifically, another defining characteristic of art offered by the defense was that art is "emotionally expressive." The implicit argument from definition was:

(5) All emotionally expressive visual works are art.
     The Mapplethorpe photographs are emotionally expressive
     visual works.
     Therefore, the Mapplethorpe photographs are art.

Reisman challenged this definition of art provided by the defense, claiming that the works were not "expressive of human feeling." Unlike the previously described arguments from definition, there was direct clash on the crucial middle step:

(6) All visual works that are not emotionally expressive are not
     art.
     The Mapplethorpe photographs are not emotionally expressive visual works.
     Therefore, the Mapplethorpe photographs are not art.

Had Reisman been a more credible witness or been aided by witnesses considered part of the institution of art, her counterdescription might have had a chance to be persuasive, but such was not the case. Jurors said after the trial that Reisman's testimony "did not make a big impression" compared to the weight of testimony provided by the defense (Cembalest 1990, 140). Another juror complained that "the prosecution did not prove its case" (Siebert and Moores 1990). The jury foreperson volunteered that, "I think they could have brought in a sociologist or psychologist . . . somebody who could have said this is not art because . . ." (Siebert and Moores 1990).

Prosecutor Prouty told the jurors, "[Y]ou tell what is and is not art" and insisted repeatedly that the photographs "speak for themselves" (Cembalest 1990, 140). Prouty was following the typical strategy in obscenity cases that relies on the shock value of the material to persuade juries of their lack of value. The Supreme Court ruled in *Paris Adult Theatre I v. Slaton* (413 U.S. [1973] 49) that the prosecution is under no obligation to present expert testimony in obscenity trials. Chief Justice Burger ruled that potentially obscene films "are the best evidence of what they represent" and he quoted, approvingly, a lower court opinion that "hard core pornography . . . can and does speak for itself" (1973b, 56).

Prouty's strategy failed on two counts. First, he gave the jury no definitions or criteria with which to decide whether the photographs were or were not art, while the defense offered both institutional and functional criteria with which to categorize the photographs as art. Second, by insisting that the photographs "speak for themselves" and by somewhat snidely dismissing the experts, Prouty portrayed himself as blind to the artistic aspects of the photographs. By contrast, the jury perceived themselves, in effect, as being educated by the experts to overcome their "aspect-blindness" such that they could see, or at least acknowledge, the artistic merits of the photographs. A number of jurors described themselves as "learning" from the art experts. One credited the defense witnesses with helping her "to gain a new perspective on unfamiliar and disturbing images" (Cembalest 1990, 140). Although the jury decided that five of the photographs *did* meet the first two parts of the Miller test (appeal to prurient interests, depiction of sexual conduct in a "patently offensive" way), they decided that the photographs had serious artistic value and returned a "not guilty" verdict after deliberating for only two hours and ten minutes.

The prosecution's ineptitude should not imply that this was an open and shut case. Certainly each of the defense team's implicit or explicit definitions of art could have been challenged. Institutional and functional definitions each have their critics, so the first step in arguments (3) and (4) above could have been contested. The prosecution could have pointed out that the different definitions offered by the defense were inconsistent. Or the prosecution could have pursued a line of argument that suggested the net effect of the defense's definitions was to *un*-define "art," since once the aesthetic dimension is set aside and the functional aspect of being "controversial" is privileged, limiting what counts as art becomes almost impossible (Rosenberg 1972, 28–38; Adler 1990). Furthermore, the prosecution could have challenged the key middle step in which a description is offered and through which an important attribute is assigned to the object in question. Such a challenge occurred in arguments (5) and (6), but also could have occurred by challenging the middle step in arguments (3) and (4). Had these crucially important descriptions been challenged by credible witnesses, then the jury would have been in a position to decide for themselves "what is or is not art." There are art critics such as Robert Hughes who have challenged the "serious artistic value" of Mapplethorpe's work ("Body Politics" 1990).

Contrary to Chief Justice Burger's claim, phenomena do *not* "speak for themselves." It is *people* who make sense of their experience of the world. Through descriptions, people "entitle" tiny slices of reality from various points of view. Because such entitlements are inevitably partial and draw our attention to this aspect rather than that, they are never "neutral" or absolutely "objective"; rather, they are better understood as persuasive efforts that encourage intersubjective agreement about how to see the world. For a description to be accepted, people must be willing to "see" the similarity between the current phenomenon and a prototypical exemplar and be persuaded the similarities are more salient than the differences. In the case of the Mapplethorpe photographs, the question was whether to entitle the works as art or obscenity. The decision was not a "factual" determination in the sense that describing the photographs' size would be, but an arguable decision. As Weitz points out, "No 'is X a novel, painting, opera, work of art, etc.?' question allows of a definitive answer in the sense of a factual yes or no report." Rather, the question is whether to extend a preexisting category, such as artwork, "to cover this case" (1956, 32). To decide the matter, persuasive appeals are made to the SDRs that language users consider most salient to the situation. As Rosenberg notes, the classification of would-be art items "cannot avoid being interpreted in a partisan way" (1972, 235). If Burke's and Weaver's arguments are taken seriously, then what has been said about the Mapplethorpe photographs can be said about all phenomena: No neutral or purely objective descriptions are possible; all entitlements are persuasive.

8
Naming as Argument by Definition: The Case of "Nukespeak"

The previous chapter illustrated the idea that a given act of naming an object or situation can function in a persuasive manner. In many cases, the persuasion involved is merely to reinforce a widely shared or commonsense way of making sense of the world. These mundane cases, however, can be disrupted if there is disagreement about how a particular object or situation ought to be described and understood. In the case of a disputed entitlement, such as in the Mapplethorpe trial, the definitional rupture is explicit, and participants are compelled to come to terms with the process of definition itself. In most cases, the act of entitling a phenomenon goes unchallenged. It is only with hindsight that the persuasive function of a particular naming may become obvious. In such cases, the act of naming/entitling may have succeeded in enacting what David Zarefsky (1998) has called "argument by definition." According to Zarefsky, advocates often offer descriptions that function strategically by redefining phenomena without acknowledging that a redefinition is taking place and a new point of view is being promoted. Rather than explicitly advancing an argument *about* a definition (X should be defined as Y) or constructing an argument *from* definition (All X are Z; Y is an X; therefore Y is Z), advocates simply posit that X is Y and move on: "[T]he key definitional move is simply stipulated, as if it were a natural step along the way of justifying some other claim" (Zarefsky 1998, 5). Zarefsky offers a series of examples of advocates redefining a situation simply by naming it in a strategic manner:

> The ambiguous term "welfare reform," for which there has been widespread support for decades, has been used to describe a law that will end altogether the guarantees of welfare benefits. Supreme Court Justice Clarence Thomas was able to refocus his confirmation hearings by defining Professor Anita Hill's accusations as a "high-tech lynching for uppity blacks," thereby creating the conditions under which race trumped gender. President Kennedy's use of the term "quarantine" rather than "blockade" to define our response to the Cuban missile crisis made it easier to view our conduct as therapeutic and medical rather than as an act of war. Speaking of war, the use of military metaphors to define our campaigns against poverty and drug use helps to characterize those issues as crises requiring immediate action rather than sustained debate. (1998, 4)

Zarefsky's examples illustrate that the strategic use of naming can advance an advocate's values and beliefs without the advocate having to defend such values and beliefs explicitly. Arguments by definition "are not claims supported by reasons and intended to justify adherence by critical listeners. Instead they are simply proclaimed as if they were indisputable facts" (5).

To illustrate in more detail the notion that naming functions argumentatively by defining or redefining phenomena persuasively, I want to use the benefit of hindsight to examine the naming strategies employed by President Ronald Reagan with respect to aspects of his nuclear policy. Although my examples are drawn from what has come to be known as "nukespeak" (Hilgartner, Bell, and O'Connor 1982; Aubrey 1982), it will be evident to most readers that the strategic functions identified here—"domestication" and "bureaucratization"—can be found in advocates' naming strategies in many other political contexts as well. Furthermore, given that the current Bush administration is calling for a revival of national efforts to construct a defense against ballistic missiles, a recognition of the rhetorical strategies involved in the naming of nuclear weapons and policies may be particularly useful (Thomma 2001; cf. Mitchell 2000).

Description by Domestication

Domestication refers to the use of everyday language to describe the extraordinary in ordinary terms. Specifically, domestication is the use of "friendly" metaphors drawn from ordinary language to name otherwise objectionable nuclear weapons, strategy, and war. Domestication combines some of the most potent trivializing resources available in a culture and, hence, is a powerful rhetorical strategy.

The suggestive power of naming is magnified when it involves the use of metaphor. The significance of metaphor in shaping a community of language users' understanding of "reality" is well established (Burke 1984b; Edelman 1977, 16–17; Sapir and Crocker 1977). The use of metaphor becomes persuasive or argumentative when the speaker seeks adherence to a particular perspective on "reality" (Perelman and Olbrechts-Tyteca 1969, 167–71). To the extent that metaphor "brings out the thisness of a that," as Kenneth Burke puts it, the "character" of a "that" is largely determined by the "this" being used to describe it (1945, 503). A point of view or particular bias, then, is unavoidable when a phenomenon is named via metaphor. The most persuasive metaphors are those drawn from ordinary language. Ordinary language often exhibits a high degree of denotative conformity and thus embodies the common sense of a community of language users, which includes the judgments, attitudes, and feelings associated with certain words. Metaphors drawn from ordinary language help shape the "meaning" of a newly named phenomenon by eliciting relatively entrenched attitudes and feelings. The oft-repeated experience of ordinary language leads to a high degree of "fixity" or stability to the meaning ordinary language evokes (Gregg 1984, 87). Because "ordinary language is by itself the manifestation of agreements of a community of thought," the use of ordinary language helps to promote agreement between a speaker and audience (Perelman and Olbrechts-Tyteca 1969, 153). In sum, because domestication involves naming by metaphorically extending ordinary language, it is a very persuasive means by which to talk about nuclear phenomena.

Examples of domesticated nukespeak are plentiful. Domestication began at the birth of the nuclear age with the naming of the first atomic bombs dropped on Hiroshima and Nagasaki: "Little Boy" and "Fat Man" (Musil 1983, 28). Nuclear weapons as a class are less threatening when referred to as "nukes" (Cohn 1987, 710). The atomic bomb was originally described as a "super" conventional bomb. Later, the H-bomb was described as a "super" A-bomb (Hook 1985, 72–73; Musil

1983, 27). Bombs with less radiation fallout have been referred to as "clean" or "less dirty" than other classes of atomic bombs (Hilgartner, Bell, and O'Connor 1982, 218–19). The common sense reflected in ordinary language suggests that some weapons are preferable to others if they are "super," "clean," or "smart." Calling nuclear weapons "hardware" evokes "impressions of something familiar, useful, and available in a neighborhood store" (Nash 1980, 26). Of course, no nukespeak analysis would be complete without mentioning Reagan's failed attempt to name the MX missile "The Peacekeeper" (Kauffman 1989), which was awarded the National Council of Teachers of English "Doublespeak" award (Totten 1984, 44).

Many more examples of domestication are available. The rhetorical significance of domestication is that it normalizes and trivializes extraordinary technology. Albert Einstein once claimed that "the unleashed power of the atom has changed everything save our modes of thinking" (Nathan and Norden 1960, 376). Domestication perpetuates the use of conventional modes of thought concerning unconventional weapons, strategy, and war. For example, Hook has argued that the use of "metaphors of life" has obscured the deadly nature of nuclear weapons (1985, 69–71). The beginning of nuclear weapons development is called the "birth" of a new era, which has a number of patriarchs: Robert Oppenheimer, father of the atomic bomb; Edward Teller, father of the hydrogen bomb; and others. Two recent "parents" are Edward Teller as the father of Star Wars and S. T. Cohen as father of the neutron bomb. The use of life-cycle metaphors is used to describe nuclear weapons from beginning to end: "As members of weapons families, nuclear weapons, like other members of the military, have a 'useful life': they 'enter service,' are kept on 'active service' for a number of years, then 'retired' so as to give way to a new 'generation' of weapons, produced after a technological 'gestation' period, to replace the 'aging' weapons" (Hook 1985, 70).

Weapons are procured as the result of public policy decisions, which are made more acceptable to the political public through domestication. Calling the vast accumulation of nuclear weapons part of an "arms race" implies that we are involved in a contest that can be won if we are determined to be strong and fast enough. Additional nuclear weapons are seen as desirable when they give us a "wider" or "richer" "menu of options" (Cohn 1987, 699), strengthen our "nuclear umbrella" (Gray and Payne 1980, 16), protect us against bomber or missile "gaps" or a "window of vulnerability," or provide us with a "bargaining chip" (Rowny 1988, 21; Breslauer 1983, 85).

Nuclear war itself is made more palatable when represented through domesticated nukespeak. The mass destruction of two superpowers can seem manageable and even mildly pleasant when dubbed a "nuclear exchange," a phrase that "sounds something like mutual gift-giving" (Lifton and Falk 1982, 107). Fighting a nuclear war becomes a game when understood through such phrases as "competitive escalation" and "strategic superiority" (Breslauer 1983, 84–85). "Victory is possible" when the winner loses only 20 million lives or so—an "acceptable outcome" (Gray and Payne 1980, 14).

Description by Bureaucratization

Bureaucratization is the counterpart to domestication. If some aspect of nuclear weapons, nuclear strategy, or nuclear war cannot be conveyed persuasively through the use of friendly or trivializing metaphors, then the next best option is either to sanitize the concept so that it appears neutral and inoffensive or to technologize the concept by applying technical terms or acronyms that only insiders or "experts" can "really" understand. In either case, the effect is to mystify—to render nuclear policy irrelevant or inaccessible to public investigation and deliberation. As Burke observes, mystification is equated with class distinctions (1950, 122). One consequence of nukespeak is that the nuclear policy-making bureaucracy is granted a privileged status because the lower "class" (that is, the general public) is disenfranchised from the decision-making language. As documented by rhetorical critics Thomas B. Farrell and G. Thomas Goodnight's study of the discourse surrounding the accident at Three Mile Island, "insulated terminology" and "sanitized language" work at cross-purposes with the need for public deliberation (1981, 296). With respect to nuclear weapons policy, Scilla McLean claims: "As the jargon of strategic debate and the arcane acronyms of weapons systems drive discussion into more and more compartmentalized and specialist fora, these 'expert' analysts, wargamers and consultants are tending to set the parameters of the defense debate. 'These questions are too complicated for either politicians or the public,' said a former national security official in the Carter Administration; 'they need help'" (1986, 77).

As with domestication, examples of bureaucratization are plentiful. Reagan's runner-up for the Doublespeak award was an Air Force colonel who described the Titan 2 missile as a "very large, potentially disruptive re-entry system" (Totten 1984, 44). Because it has been sanitized (although in a transparent effort), the longer description actually tells the audience less than the original domesticated title. A more complicated instance of bureaucratization is that of the neutron bomb. While the name "neutron bomb" does not immediately inform the citizenry of the weapon's special characteristics, "neutron" implies a difference from other weapons, and "bomb" suggests it kills. The bureaucratized version of "neutron bomb" is "radiation enhancement weapon" (Van Cleave and Cohen 1987, 33–34). To the nuclearist, the phrase is more revealing, but to the "uninitiated," the concept is now bureaucratized because the key word—"enhancement"—is equivocal and thus mystifying.

Acronyms are particularly useful tools for the bureaucratization of nuclear concepts. The military establishment is infamous for its use of acronyms; hence, one of the effects of extending the use of acronyms to nuclear weapons, strategy, and war is to render such concepts part of the "normal" military order. The more significant effect, however, is the consequent disenfranchisement of the "laity" who do not know what the acronyms denote. The burden is on the hearer—the public—to understand what MIRV, MARV, ASW, ICBM, SLBM, GLCM, SLCM, LOW, LUA, ELF, EMP, ERW, PAL, MAD, SDI, SBKKV, SALT, BMD, START, and the like actually mean (examples from Department of Defense 1987; Semler 1987). It is arguably the case that many people assume that an ability to state what the acronym stands for is the equivalent of understanding the concept or strategy.

As in the case of domestication, nuclear war itself is made palatable through bureaucratization. When the Federal Emergency Management Agency refers to a "nuclear or radiological emergency," it makes what could be the end of the world on a par with less threatening disasters such as floods or tornadoes (Winter 1983, 16–17). Starting a nuclear war by launching missiles or dropping bombs before the enemy has the chance to launch or drop theirs has been called launching a "first strike," a "preemptive" or "preventive" strike, and even an "anticipatory counterattack" (Boyer 1985, 102; Colen 1988, 29; Shenfield 1985, 63–76). Aiming missiles to incinerate millions of men, women, and children is called "demographic" or "countervalue" targeting (Cohn 1987, 691; Hilgartner, Bell, and O'Connor 1982, 209–10; Totten 1984, 45). If one lives through a "protracted period" or a "subholocaust engagement" (a nuclear war) and is not part of the "collateral damage" (unintended death and destruction), then one "operates" in a "postattack environment" (like Hiroshima after August 6, 1945). In nukespeak, "survivability" most often refers to weapons, sometimes to military command and control centers, and least often to human beings.

Implications for "Nukespeakers"

Nukespeak influences speakers as well as hearers. Consequently, nukespeak is a potentially dangerous terministic screen for those in positions of policy making and in the military establishment. The risk is that nukespeakers will tend to understand nuclear weapons, strategy, and war as benign or beneficial rather than repulsive and horrifying. This hypothesized result is supported by reports of former members of the military establishment and by an observer of military "culture."

Herman Kahn's 1965 book, *On Escalation: Metaphors and Scenarios,* provides an excellent example of the bureaucratic tendencies fostered by nukespeak. Kahn maintained that certain metaphors were more appropriate than others to describe the escalation of nuclear war. Kahn rejected the "strike" and "chicken" metaphors as "misleading" and recommended reference to the "rungs of the escalation ladder" as a "useful" metaphor (1965, 37). In contrast to the image of a violent strike or the irrational and dangerous game of chicken, Kahn offered his own domesticated vision of an escalating nuclear war: "Another metaphor as useful as the escalation ladder would be that of an elevator stopping at various floors. We can think of a typical escalation situation between the United States and the Soviet Union in terms of a department store with seven floors, each offering a number of options of varying intensity but still appropriate to that floor, from which the decisionmakers on one side or the other may choose" (41). In J. C. Thomson's analysis of the Vietnam War, he insists that it is impossible to understand the decision-making process without reference to the role of language (1973, 275). From his own experience in the military establishment, Thomson provides examples of what have been described here as bureaucratization and domestication. Thomson states that use of such terms as "systematic pressure," "targets of opportunity," and "body count" bred a "bureaucratic" or "game-theory" detachment. Describing the intensity of a proposed bombing and strafing strategy, Thomson quotes an assistant secretary of state: "It seems to me that our orchestration should be mainly violins, but with periodic touches of brass" (274). Thomson concludes, not surprisingly, that such language led to "professional callousness" in the conduct of the Vietnam War.

H. T. Nash provides a similar report based on his experience as a former intelligence analyst for the Air Targets Division of the Air Force. He recounts a variety of maxims, acronyms, and loaded terms that "helped to obscure the reality of what the work was all about—to distract attention from the homicidal reality and give a brighter hue to the ominous" (1980, 26). His examples match the twin strategies of bureaucratization and domestication. Nash states that the use of such phrases as "power vacuum" and "power equilibrium" had "the ring of respected and predictable laws of the physical sciences that had nothing to do with such things as war and annihilation" (26). Nash also provides anecdotal evidence of the effects of domestication: "I recall the time in the late 1950s when the term 'baby H-bomb' was commonly used in referring to low yield, small tactical nuclear weapons suitable for use in limited wars. This image of the lovable 'baby' bomb helped to make a typical question in war planning such as 'Should we deliver 10 or 15 baby nukes on the Irkutsk Party headquarters?' seem like an innocent inquiry" (26). Conceived in the domesticated and bureaucratized language of nukespeak, nuclear war becomes far more than "thinkable"—it becomes the banal by-product of proper training. By domesticating the results of a nuclear attack through such "humanizing" metaphors as "crippling" and "disabling," nuclear war appears recoverable and limitable and, hence, contributes to "the underestimation of the risks involved in starting a nuclear war" (Hook 1985, 71). By bureaucratizing nuclear war through sanitized jargon and metaphors based on trade, games, and physics, military planners avoid the major moral considerations of nuclear war, because nukespeak "enables America's nuclear war planners to maintain a moral self-image, treat the extermination of millions as a 'job,' and obfuscate the value problem underlying the use of nuclear weapons" (72).

An ethnographic study by Carol Cohn (1987), senior research fellow of the Center for Psychological Studies in the Nuclear Age of the Harvard University Medical School, provides additional evidence of the incapacitating effects of nukespeak on users. Cohn spent a year as a participant and observer in a university "center on defense technology and arms control." The center was populated by "defense intellectuals"—persons who move between government positions, influential defense "think tanks," and academic institutions—who "create the theory that informs and legitimates American nuclear strategic practice." During Cohn's research, she "attended lectures, listened to arguments, conversed with defense analysts," and generally went "native" in an effort to understand the "rationality" of the "professional discourse" of nuclear theorists (1987, 687–88). Cohn reports that language patterns learned in her study had the overall effect of reconstructing the consciousness of nukespeak users. In terms of domestication, Cohn found that the use of abstraction and euphemism redirected attention away from the realities of a nuclear situation. The words were "so bland that they never forced the speaker or enabled the listener to touch the realities of nuclear holocaust that lay behind the words" (690). The reliance on harmless sounding metaphors such as "Christmas tree farm" for a line of submarine missiles ready for launch, "footprint" for the pattern in which missile warheads land, "BAMBI" for an early version of an antiballistic missile system, and "cookie cutter" for the neutron bomb "took away the emotional fallout that would result if it were clear one was talking about plans for mass murder, mangled bodies, and unspeakable human suffering" (691).

What has been described here as mystification by bureaucratization was also documented by Cohn. Early in her research, Cohn was reluctant to learn and use the "expert" language. This reluctance to communicate in the language of the nuclear strategists had the effect of disenfranchising Cohn. Her opinions were inferior: "No matter how informed or complex my questions were, if I spoke English rather then expert jargon, the men responded to me as though I were ignorant, simple minded, or both. It did not appear to occur to anyone that I might actually be choosing not to speak their language" (1987, 708). This attitude made it imperative for anyone who wished to contribute in the exchange to learn the technical language.

In short, nukespeak influences speakers in ways that separate the technical possibilities from related moral and ethical concerns. I recognize that specialized professional vocabularies are unavoidable. Their use is inevitable and even beneficial for the conceptual progress of intellectual disciplines. However, the uncritical use of nukespeak by "expert" speakers neglects the fact that nuclear policy involves issues of public concern. Moreover, there is a risk that nukespeak will use its speakers as much as they use it. Once the nukespeaker turns technician, the issue is no longer whether or not an action should be taken but simply a question of logistics. The use of nukespeak cognitively separates competing "technical" and "social" knowledge claims and renders the attendant moral concerns obsolete.

Implications for the Public

Farrell and Goodnight have suggested that the status of deliberative argument is constrained by "prevailing conceptions of the public" (1981, 299). It is clear that with regard to nuclear issues, the public has been and still is conceived as a crowd to be calmed rather than co-creators of public policy (cf. Park 1972). Demonstrating that the relationship between language and public attitudes has been recognized almost from the start, the 1950 book *How to Survive an Atomic Bomb* laments the fact that people have been scared by the words "radiation" and "radio-activity" and condemns the "loose talk" about the atomic bomb and the "rays" it makes (Gerstell 1950, 22). The public's fears concerning atomic war in the early 1950s are well known. Accordingly, it is hard to believe that it was an accident that in 1953 the Atomic Energy Commission named measured amounts of radiation as "Sunshine Units" (Hilgartner, Bell, and O'Connor 1982, 219). During the development and testing of the hydrogen bomb, President Dwight D. Eisenhower reportedly suggested to the chairman of the Atomic Energy Commission in May of 1953 that "we leave 'thermonuclear' out of press releases and speeches. Also 'fusion' and hydrogen.'" Eisenhower was reported to have said, "[K]eep them confused as to 'fission' and 'fusion'" (U.S. Congress 1979, 151). Domestication of nuclear issues renders them accessible to the public, but in a trivial manner. There is no need to deliberate over that which is not a problem or threat. Bureaucratization of nuclear issues insulates them from public inspection and critical appraisal; indeed, as rhetorical critic Rebecca S. Bjork notes, technological issues "are shielded from public debate due to the cult of expertise surrounding technology, the specialized language of technicians, and the sense of awe and wonder concerning technology" (1992, 116). The result of nukespeak is a further decline in the public sphere of argumentation. Nukespeak "covertly tends to quell citizen involvement and decision-making about the nuclear arms race" (Totten 1984, 44). Maxine Greene, in an essay advocating that peace education be critical of positivism and "technical talk and control," warned that "danger lies" in the public's acceptance of a reality defined by "official others" (1982, 130). In Greene's view, failure to critique self-confirming interpretations is disastrous: "The more people are drawn into technical talk and the belief that some Other has the right to define the world, the more likely a nuclear war will be" (134).

Once the question is put as to whether the nukespeak strategies of domestication and bureaucratization are beneficial or detrimental to the practice of deliberative argumentation, only diehard "nuclearists" would challenge a negative verdict.[1] No one disputes the horror nuclear war would produce. Language that masks this horror makes its avoidance more difficult. As Carl Sagan has put it, "If everyone had a profound and immediate sense of the actual consequences of nuclear war, we would be much more willing to confront and challenge national leaders of all nations when they present narrow and self-serving arguments for the continuation of mutual nuclear terror" (1983, 3).

It may seem paradoxical that nukespeak calms and pacifies the public, and yet researchers have documented widespread terror of nuclear war, anxiety so strong that Lifton and Falk describe it as "nuclear numbing" (1982), anxiety so acute that Sagan and others suggest that it triggers "denial"—"that makes us feel it's so horrible that we might as well not think about it" (Sagan 1983, 3). To resolve the paradox, a distinction must be made between the experience of anxiety and the experience of fear (Fisher 1984, 11–12; Hyde 1980, 140–54). Anxiety is a generalized existential dread that is associated, for example, with a highly uncertain future or death. Anxiety concerning nuclear war fits this description, for it is the threat of non-existence that "numbs" or brings about denial. Fear, on the other hand, is specific: "That which is feared always presents itself as something definite existing in a person's world" (Hyde 1980, 147). Nukespeak cannot completely eliminate awareness that nuclear war could annihilate the planet; hence, it does not prevent (though it may mask) nuclear anxiety. But nukespeak decreases the fear of the specific instruments of nuclear death, the weapons and policies whose deadly nature are clouded by domestication and bureaucratization. Understanding nukespeak is an important key to interpreting the paradoxical public sentiments concerning the issues of a nuclear age: nukespeak leaves people with general anxiety but without the appropriate motivation to evaluate and act toward the objects of nuclear war-making.

The preceding pages offer an explanation for the persuasive effects of strategic naming. Two cases of nukespeak strategies used by President Ronald Reagan are sketched here as illustrations of the implications of nukespeak for the public. Those examples are the term "CORRTEX" as an instance of bureaucratization and the use of domestication to describe the purpose of the Strategic Defense Initiative.

"CORRTEX" as Bureaucratization

CORRTEX stands for "Continuous Reflectometry for Radius versus Time Experiment."[2] According to the Department of State Bulletin, CORRTEX "is a hydrodynamic yield measurement technique that measures the propagation of the underground shock wave from an explosion" ("U.S. Policy" 1986, 15). Three claims are supported here with respect to the use of "CORRTEX" as an example of bureaucratization. First, in early 1986, pressure increased on President Reagan to respond positively to the Soviet Union's moratorium on nuclear test explosions and Soviet general secretary Mikhail Gorbachev's offer to negotiate a Comprehensive Test Ban Treaty (CTBT). Second, Reagan's response was to offer the Soviet Union "CORRTEX," a "verification" technology of uncertain value.[3] Third, because little was known or told of CORRTEX, its value was primarily symbolic. CORRTEX became "proof" of Reagan's cooperative and generous nature and of the "impracticality" of the Soviet Union's overtures. CORRTEX was a successful instance of bureaucratization because it appeared to respond to the Soviet initiatives (hence it quieted or sidetracked public debate), yet as a policy matter CORRTEX was irrelevant to the Soviet testing moratorium and to a comprehensive test ban.

With an eye toward ratification of a Comprehensive Test Ban Treaty, Gorbachev announced on July 29, 1985, that the Soviet Union would unilaterally cease nuclear testing until the end of the year. The moratorium began on August 6, 1985, and in December was extended by Gorbachev another three months. In early 1986, Gorbachev extended the moratorium a third time, claiming that the U.S.S.R. would continue to refrain from testing nuclear weapons until the U.S. conducted another nuclear test. He further pledged to meet President Reagan under any circumstances to begin negotiations for a CTBT. This offer to begin negotiations for a test ban treaty in the face of unilateral cessation of testing was significant given the consequences advocates have persistently claimed that a Comprehensive Test Ban Treaty would provide. The Soviet Union's nuclear testing moratorium and offer to negotiate a CTBT met with considerable support from arms control enthusiasts. Scientists, public interest groups, arms control experts, and members of Congress already had concluded that a comprehensive ban on the testing of nuclear weapons was vital (Epstein 1986). Hence, the moratorium was perceived by many as a golden opportunity to press for U.S. progress toward a test ban.

Pressure on President Reagan to respond positively to the Soviets' initiative came from a number of quarters. Congressional support for a CTBT "had been mounting" ("U.S. Conducts Test" 1986, 1), and a joint resolution from the House calling on the administration to resume negotiations for a complete nuclear testing ban passed on February 26. A similar resolution already had passed the Senate. International pressure for positive movement toward the CTBT was building as well. Between September of 1985 and February of 1986, 121 countries passed four resolutions in the United Nations General Assembly calling for the conversion of the Partial Test Ban Treaty to a Comprehensive Test Ban

Treaty: "No measure of disarmament has been pursued so long and so persistently [in the U.N.] as a ban on all nuclear testing" (Epstein 1986, 29). In August of 1985, the leaders of six non-aligned nations, the "New Delhi Group," reported that they were "convinced that no issue is more urgent and crucial" than ending nuclear tests. Early in March 1986, these leaders called on Washington to "conduct no more tests" (Atlas 1986, 4) and to "proceed to negotiate a comprehensive treaty that would ban all nuclear tests" ("Reagan Sends," 1986).[4]

Consequently, the Reagan administration faced significant pressure both to participate in the moratorium and to begin negotiations for a test ban treaty. The Associated Press reported on March 15, 1986, that "the Soviets have put international pressure on the Reagan administration" ("Reagan Sends," 1986), and Reuters News Service on March 23, 1986, reported that in Congress, "pressure has been mounting on President Reagan to resume negotiations with Moscow for a comprehensive test ban treaty" ("U.S. Conducts Test," 1986). Summarizing the climate that Gorbachev's offer created, William Arkin, director of the national security program at the Institute for Policy Studies, claimed, "[T]he Soviet Union has demonstrated a keen understanding of the American debate, shrewdly dangling a few more months of their unilateral test moratorium in front of American noses in every quarter to feed outside political pressures on the U.S. government. These offers are becoming more and more difficult to refuse" (1986, 4). The U.S. response to the Soviet invitation was described by one congressperson as crucial, sending "signals of governmental importance to the world at large" (Gingrich 1986).

Reagan's response to the pressure to respond positively to the Soviet initiatives was to offer the Soviets CORRTEX. Gorbachev's March 13 offer to extend the testing moratorium prompted Reagan to offer the Soviets CORRTEX the next day (Gerstenzang 1986, 1). A White House official admitted that the CORRTEX announcement was made earlier than originally planned because of Gorbachev's offer (Robinson 1986). In a written statement issued by the White House, the president acknowledged "correspondence which I have had recently with Soviet General Secretary Gorbachev, the leaders of six nations known as the New Delhi Group, and Senate Majority Leader Dole" (1986b, 364). Reagan's offer was described as part of a "new, very specific, and far-reaching proposal concerning nuclear testing limitations." The "specific new technical method," CORRTEX, was "unique" in its "specificity and concreteness." He referred to CORRTEX as a signal of his "resolve to make tangible progress" and urged that the Soviet Union engage with the

United States "in this first practical step" to solve "verification" uncertainties (1986b, 364–65).

As a rhetorical strategy, CORRTEX was unquestionably a success in directing attention away from Soviet CTBT initiatives. The CORRTEX offer was characterized as representing "the latest American rejoinder to a Soviet nuclear arms initiative" (Robinson 1986, 1). It was depicted in various newspaper headlines on March 15 as "Reagan Sends Soviet Leader Plan to Detect Nuclear Blasts," "U.S. Offers New Plan on A-Tests" (Gerstenzang 1986), "Reagan Gives Nuclear Plan to Soviets," "Reagan Offers Soviets New System to Monitor Underground Arms Tests" (Robinson 1986), and "U.S. Offers Nuclear Test Plan." Opponents of a nuclear test ban used CORRTEX as a means of downgrading the Soviet efforts. Conservative members of Congress and the administration lauded the president's "specific, concrete proposal" (Garn 1986, S5240; Wilson 1986, S5049) as a "realistic approach" (Goldwater 1986, S6625), suggesting that the Soviet moratorium and offer to negotiate a CTBT were "a ploy" and "outrageous hypocrisy" not to be treated seriously (Wilson 1986, S5049). A number of Republican senators argued that the Soviets had rejected all U.S. initiatives in this area and failed "to address these concerns in a constructive manner" (Adelman 1986). Senator Jake Garn suggested that "it is incumbent upon the Soviet leaders to take the President up on his offer" (1986, S5240). CORRTEX also was used to gain congressional support for the president. Robert B. Barker, deputy assistant director for verification and intelligence at the Arms Control and Disarmament Agency, argued that "[c]ongressional support for the President's proposal can only enhance the prospects for a positive Soviet response" (1986, S5244), and Senator Barry Goldwater said that the president "should be commended for his efforts" and that "Congress should stand behind him on this issue" (1986, S6625).

Because the name CORRTEX was unfamiliar—even the meaning of the letters was not explained in the White House statement—and because the concrete details and specifics of the proposal were not revealed to the press in the president's statement of March 14, most news accounts were able initially only to report that the president was generously giving CORRTEX to the Soviets. The Associated Press account of the president's statement reported that an arms control expert outside of the administration had never heard of CORRTEX. Only the *Los Angeles Times* initially reported that CORRTEX was not a "new technology" as portrayed by the president. An administration official, speaking anonymously, said that "it has been used in monitoring about 100 nuclear tests in the last decade" (Gerstenzang 1986, 1). The *New York Times* reported that the superpowers discussed a similar technology during 1976 treaty negotiations (Gwertzman 1986). The Los Alamos National Laboratory, which developed CORRTEX, was using it to measure test yields at the time Reagan called the technology "new" (Kerr 1986, S6627).

As "verification" technology, the necessity and value of CORRTEX is debatable since few people outside of the Reagan administration have any doubt about the verifiability of a Comprehensive Test Ban Treaty (Evernden and Archambeau 1986). As a rhetorical strategy, CORRTEX was unquestionably successful as an example of bureaucratized nuke-speak. The obscurity of CORRTEX muffled public debate and allowed Reagan to portray himself as cooperative and generous. In effect, Reagan hoped that by tossing a ball to the Soviets, he could deflect attention away from the Soviet ball that had been sitting on the U.S. court for almost a year. The president packaged CORRTEX as a sophisticated technological solution to problems between the superpowers. Reagan symbolized his offer as "new," "specific," "detailed," "tangible," "concrete," "far-reaching," "practical," and a "first step." The implication was that Gorbachev's proposal, a CTBT, was old, general, vague, short-term, and impractical. Reagan's offer was "real," but Mikhail Gorbachev's was merely a "ploy."

In short, Reagan was able to camouflage his rejection of the CTBT through the strategic use of an unfamiliar name: CORRTEX. His offer did not deal with the merits of ceasing testing and did not explain why the administration insisted on further tests. Reagan's chief claim in his opposition to a CTBT was that limits on testing were not "verifiable" (Arkin 1986, 5). Muchkind Dubey, India's representative to the United Nations Conference on Disarmament, claimed that "verification has now become a political ploy . . . an excuse not to engage in meaningful and serious discussions. The Western nuclear powers use the red herring of verifiability to justify their rejection of all proposals" (1985, 29). Critic Alexander Cockburn concurred in harsher language: "The whole verification ploy, as now being operated by the Reagan Administration, is a gigantic non-issue, designed to bamboozle the sheep and sidetrack discussion away from arms control" (1986, 39). The symbolic offer of CORRTEX allowed Reagan to appear active and cooperative toward the Soviet Union and permitted him to invoke another well-known bureaucratization: "verification." The Soviet Union, for the moment, was left with the moratorium—a vague symbol of inaction.

When faced with a losing battle for positive public opinion in the period between July 1985 and the spring of 1986, Reagan's response was not to reject a CTBT directly. Rather, Reagan chose to mystify the matter through the use of a bureaucratization—CORRTEX—that was rhetorically successful in deflecting public pressure until new symbols were required.

The Domestication of the Strategic Defense Initiative

Two claims are supported here concerning Reagan's use of language employed in the defense of the Strategic Defense Initiative (SDI).[5] First, during the period of March 1983 until he left office in January 1989, President Reagan consistently described the goals of SDI to the public with the use of domesticated language implying that SDI's purpose was to protect the civilian population. Second, the president's use of domesticated language was misleading, since the programmatic goals of SDI shifted from the purpose of population defense to missile protection soon after 1983. Reagan's misleading defense of the project helped maintain SDI's support by the public throughout the elections of 1984, during key arms control discussions at Reykjavic, and throughout the remainder of his occupation of the White House.

On March 23, 1983, Reagan broadcast an address to the nation that, in its closing minutes, introduced a "new idea," a "threshold" in "changing the course of human history": the Strategic Defense Initiative (1983a, 447–48). Although the speech has come to be known as the "Star Wars" address, the administration insisted on calling the program the "Strategic Defense Initiative," a more favorable and arguably less descriptive phrase. The name SDI had the virtues of "strategy, defense and initiative . . . rolled into one" (Galtung 1987, 248). The address gave the clear impression to the public that Reagan's project would render nuclear weapons "impotent and obsolete." In the transition to his discussion of SDI in the address, Reagan posed the question of whether it would not be better to "save lives than avenge them." Incoming hostile missiles would be destroyed before they "reached our soil" (1983a, 447). John Pike of the Federation of American Scientists commented on Reagan's imagery when he asserted that many Americans "have the idea that with SDI, during a nuclear attack they simply run out to the backyard, pull up a lawnchair and watch this terrific laser light show" (in Coney 1986).

The metaphors employed by Reagan to name and describe SDI over the last six years of his administration did nothing to change the perception of SDI as population defense. Responding to questions asked by the West German magazine *Bunte* soon after the introductory address, Reagan said the system would "free our populations from serving as hostages underwriting the peace" (1983b, 687). The 1985 State of the Union address portrayed SDI as saving "millions of lives" and possibly "humanity itself" (1985a, 145). During a radio address in the summer of 1985 dedicated exclusively to the subject, SDI became a "security shield" (1985c, 902)—an obvious use of domestication designed to comfort the public and make SDI appear "defensive." Reagan told the General Assembly of the United Nations that the goal of SDI was to make nuclear missiles "obsolete" (1985d, 1293), and in a radio address to the world he claimed this "security shield" would make nuclear weapons "obsolete" (1985e, 1376). Another metaphor Reagan employed was that of the gas mask. In November of 1985, Reagan referred back to Geneva of 1925 when all nations banned poison gas but "kept their gasmasks. . . . [SDI] is kind of the gasmask thing" (1985f, 1387). Reagan's 1986 State of the Union address echoed the theme of a "shield" for security that protects against nuclear attacks (1986a, 138). A textbook case of domestication was achieved before a high school commencement audience in which SDI became a "roof" protecting a family from "rain" (1986c, 839). Even in the context of population defense, the implied logical inference was that even a leaky roof is better than none. Later in 1986, Reagan described SDI as a "vital insurance policy" for the "security" of the United States (1986e, 1556).

The metaphor of a shield was dropped for the next State of the Union address, and the connection of SDI defending "human life" was made directly (1987a, 62). The end of the year was marked by a statement in response to questions submitted by *Izvestiya* when Reagan said SDI will "protect people instead of target them" (1987b, 1442). As the project reached its fifth-year anniversary in 1988, Reagan still described SDI as true to its original goals. In a speech at Notre Dame University, the choice of Americans to erect a "shield" rather than a "sharper sword" was a chance to raise the "moral standards of mankind" (1988a, 318). On March 14, 1988, at a "birthday party" for the project, Reagan confirmed that his goal remained a "fully comprehensive defense system" (1988b, 342). A new domesticated metaphor was introduced to secure the president the moral high ground against critics of SDI: "Isn't it time to begin curing the world of this nuclear threat? If we have the medicine, can we in good conscience hold out on the patients?" (1988b, 342). On March 23, 1988, in a statement on the anniversary of SDI, it was described as a system to "protect American people" (1988c, 381). During the summer, Reagan described SDI as a "defensive weapon" that can "just make it impossible for missiles to get through the screen" (1988d, 729). Reagan continued his use of the "shield" metaphor as long as he was in office (1988e, 1209).

During this time, in contrast to what Reagan was saying about the project, SDI was undergoing what some have called a "covert reorientation" from the vision of the Star Wars address (Waller and Bruce 1987). Rather than existing for *population* defense, the system's objective was *missile* defense (Union of Concerned Scientists 1986, 1–5). The distinction between SDI as population or missile defense is extremely important. To protect the U.S. population, SDI would have to be virtually 100 percent effective, or "leak-proof," as even a tiny fraction of Soviet missiles would wipe out the U.S. population. As missile defense to "enhance" the ability to "retaliate" against a Soviet strike, SDI could be less effective, although precise estimates of "minimal" protection needs vary. The two visions of SDI are dramatically different. Population defense was billed by Reagan as a way to *eliminate* the doctrine of "mutually assured destruction" (or "MAD"), while missile defense was seen as *augmenting* "MAD." Despite the inconsistency, the Reagan administration defended SDI on both levels. Arms control expert William Broad's research documented that as early as May of 1984, SDI researchers were acknowledging the impossibility of population defense yet advocating SDI as missile defense (1985, 206–20). A year later, news of the shift in program objectives began to surface publicly (albeit rarely). Mike Heylin, editor of *Chemical and Engineering News,* noted in June 1985 that some in the defense establishment felt a "leaky" shield would be useful to maintain our "retaliatory posture" (1985, 3). The Union of Concerned Scientists noted in 1986 that SDI officials were now speaking of "radically different objectives" than the "astrodome" shield. The "real" strategy of military planners who controlled SDI was to defend the "targets" of the United States' retaliatory force ballistic missiles (Paine 1985, 7). Late in the Reagan tenure, the priority of the SDI project was the "early deployment" of ballistic missile defenses: "This reorientation is not awaiting a publicly announced presidential decision to commit to near term deployment" (Bunn 1988, 20–21; Waller and Bruce 1987, 2).

In his book, *Strategic Deception,* Gordon R. Mitchell puts the matter bluntly: "Reagan's argument for SDI was based on a lie" (2000, 278). It is not difficult to understand the motives for Reagan's misleading description of the purpose of SDI. Public opinion concerning SDI has been ambivalent, with survey results varying widely according to the wording of the questions asked (Graham and Kramer 1986). Some surveys showed opposition to SDI from the start. The Harris Survey reported a 58 percent majority opposed "spending billions of dollars for the U.S. to develop a laser-beam and particle-beam outer space defense system" (Harris 1983). Two years later, nearly identical results were found (Harris 1985); however, public opinion research indicated that there was considerably more support for population defense than for missile defense. In a 1987 study by the Cambridge Reports, Americans supported population defense by a margin of 81 percent to 17 percent but opposed "point" defense—missiles, military bases, and Washington, D.C.—by 83 percent to 15 percent (cited by Council for a Livable World 1987). An almost identical study by Martilia and Kiley, Inc., in 1985 yielded similar results: population defense was favored by 86 percent to 9 percent, while "point" defense was opposed by 73 percent to 21 percent (Council for a Livable World 1987; Graham and Kramer 1986). Hence, research toward Reagan's dream of a "leak-proof" population defense was the least likely to succeed but the most likely to maintain political support for SDI.

An exemplary test of SDI popularity came after the summit meeting between Reagan and Gorbachev in Reykjavik, Iceland, in October 1986. When Reagan spoke on nationwide television to defend his unwillingness to trade SDI for large reductions in, or total elimination of, nuclear weapons, he compared SDI to "gas masks" and described SDI as "America's insurance policy" (1986d, 1376–77). Reagan portrayed his motive for launching SDI as the belief that "a policy of mutual destruction and slaughter of their citizens and ours was uncivilized." Reagan claimed he would not limit SDI research because "there was no way I could tell our people their government would not protect them against nuclear destruction." Although administration figures already had acknowledged the reorientation of SDI to missile defense, Reagan's myth of SDI as population defense brought him a surge of public approval for his Reykjavik "performance" (Hoffman 1985, 37).

SDI has been accessible to the general public primarily in domesticated and misleading terms. One critic claimed that by selling SDI as making nuclear weapons "obsolete," the administration "brainwashed" the public with the dream of a "leak-proof" shield (Galtung 1987. Significantly, there is evidence that Reagan was aware of the deceptiveness of his word choice. When pressed on the feasibility of a "leak-proof"

SDI during a 1985 press conference, Reagan stated that 100 percent effectiveness would be unnecessary for SDI to protect missiles. He quickly added, "[N]ow, that isn't really the goal of the Strategic Defense Initiative." Caught with the inconsistency of admitting a 100 percent effective defense was not feasible and yet defending SDI's goal of population defense, Reagan shifted to a defense of SDI as a means to disarmament. He added, "[T]his is what I mean by making nuclear weapons obsolete" (1985b, 154–55). Such a reinterpretation is hard to reconcile with his public speeches. Nonetheless, one might infer from the exchange that Reagan understood the difference between the objectives of population and missile defense, and that he may have been aware that his words could be misleading.

SDI was reoriented to a defense for ballistic missiles without significant public debate and without a "publicly announced presidential decision." The *Bulletin of the Atomic Scientists* asked "what kind of public resonance" the president would have received if SDI had been explained as a component of existing "deterrence" policy (Paine 1985, 7). Portrayed as just another option to enhance "deterrence," SDI's comparison to cheaper and less destabilizing strategic choices or even arms control would have helped to clarify the public debate over U.S. defense policy (Union of Concerned Scientists 1987, 5). An enhanced debate would be desirable because SDI was and remains an extremely costly and potentially dangerous program.[6] As Mitchell points out, the basic elements of ballistic missile defense policy and the arguments used to defend it "have not only persisted but flourished in the post-cold war milieu" (2000, 279).

With the demise of the Cold War, most Americans are no longer worried about the risk of a full-scale nuclear war with the former Soviet Union. Looking back, I confess that I find it remarkable how much danger U.S. citizens were willing to let Cold War nuclear policy put them in. Part of the explanation, I believe, lies in the way such policies were named and described to them by those in positions of authority. The nuclear threat was "fundamentally a textual problem," posed in part by linguistic strategies that concealed their persuasive attributes (Williams 1988, 193). Accordingly, an important part of critically evaluating public discourse is prompting new ways of seeing familiar descriptive practices. Two practices have been identified and named in such a way as to emphasize that their use constitutes strategic action: one casts nuclear weapons, strategy, and war in a positive light (domestication), and one sanitizes or technologizes nuclear concepts (bureaucratization). Nukespeak is an illustrative case study because it clearly demonstrates the persuasiveness of naming and description. Nukespeak consists of symbols that are, in Goodnight's words, designed to keep us watching as opposed to inviting us to participate in the construction of a future (1982, 225).

9
Defining the Situation or Framing as Social Influence: "Public," "Personal," and "Technical"

When we define a situation, that definition becomes a form of social influence by implying what are or are not appropriate responses to it. Sociologists Gregory Bateson (1972) and Erving Goffman (1974) describe the ways that language "frames" our understanding of the world in the same way a picture frame marks off the picture from the surrounding background. That is, when a given phenomenon is named or labeled *as* ecological destruction or *as* economic development, our expectations and evaluations are framed accordingly. Goffman considers competing frames as competing "definitions of a situation" that influence our understanding and involvement with a given event (1974, 10). For my purposes, there is no significant difference between "defining" or "framing" a situation. In either case, we sum up a complex set of stimuli with a name we can make sense of. In chapter 7, what was at stake was how a series of very specific objects, seven photographs, were to be understood and described—as art or as obscenity. In chapter 8, the analysis focused on how classes of objects, practices, and events can be entitled in a persuasive manner. In this chapter, I want to pull back the lens another step to examine how we make sense of whole situations through the use of framing terms.

If I have been at all successful so far in this book, then the reader will understand that definitions are socially constructed and why definitional disputes ought to be considered in ethical and pragmatic terms. When we define objects or things, we participate in a process of socially constructing an understanding of reality. In this particular chapter, I want to call attention not only to the idea that we define whole situations through the use of framing language but also to the ways in which this can be done quite subtly through the use of rather familiar and commonsense adjectives, in particular with the adjectives "public," "personal," and "technical."

To support my case, I want to emphasize the sometimes neglected role of the audience. Richard Weaver claims that all language use is evocative; thus, language can be described as sermonic: "[E]very use of speech, oral and written, exhibits an attitude, and an attitude implies an act" (1970, 222). Psychologist Roger W. Brown observed that "[t]he dime in pocket is not only a *dime*. It is also *money,* a *metal object,* a *thing*" (1958, 14). Yet there is no question that using one name rather than another can invoke quite different attitudes and responses.

The "dime" example refers to an object, so an example of defining a situation may be more useful here. Perhaps on my way to the office today I notice a particular phenomenon occurring outside the building in which I work. I ask each person I meet what he or she sees outside the building, and I receive the following answers:

1. A mean old man is cutting down that nice shady oak tree.
2. They are finally clearing off more land to develop for a new parking lot we need.
3. A tree is being murdered.
4. A cylindrical organic object is being rotated from a vertical to a horizontal position.
5. A tree is being cut down.

The theoretical point I wish to illustrate is that each of these definitions of the situation is persuasive not only in the sense of being "partial" (abstractive and selective) but also because each one implies or encourages a somewhat different set of attitudes and actions among its hearers/readers.[1] The persuasive aspects of the first three descriptions are readily apparent. The first statement, "A mean old man is cutting down that nice shady oak tree," clearly involves an interpretation of the person cutting down the tree, the tree's desirability, and the undesirability of the tree being cut down. Whether we are persuaded or not does not matter; the point is that the framing of the event "exhibits an attitude," that this is not a good thing. The implied action on our part is to disapprove of the event and perhaps even to take steps to stop it.

Presumably the second sentence, "They are finally clearing off more land to develop for a new parking lot we need," is uttered with a sense of approval. The attitude of approval encourages our support or at least our tacit agreement. So far the two statements are about the "same" event but express two very different attitudes and valuations of it. Notice that each statement is partial in the sense that it frames and directs our attention to certain aspects of the event but not to others. The first statement directs our attention to an inference about the personality of the person cutting the tree down and to the shade that the tree provides. It deflects our attention from the possible purposes and advantages of the event. This is not a flaw or criticism of the statement, because all descriptions are abstractive and simultaneously direct and deflect our attention in a selective manner. The second statement frames and directs our attention to the potential social gain from the event (more parking space), but deflects our attention from the ecological aspects of the event.

"A tree is being murdered," the third statement listed, will strike many people as more extreme than the others, but the ways in which the statement functions persuasively are the same as in the earlier statements, even if our reaction may be stronger. It is partial in a sense similar to the first statement in that it omits the possible social advantages of the tree's removal, but it calls our attention to the biological aspects of the act in a way that encourages us to think of the tree as a fellow living being that is having its life ended involuntarily. Conceivably, a member of the Earth First! movement might define or frame the event in such a manner so as to encourage us to protest such actions.

But what of the fourth statement, "A cylindrical organic object is being rotated from a vertical to a horizontal position"? Some would find the statement the most "objective" and the least persuasive because it is devoid of what most people would consider value-laden or emotional language. I contend that the utterance is persuasive for two reasons. First, the statement is still partial in the sense of being abstractive and selective. A virtually foolproof way to assess the persuasive aspects of any given description is to consider what *choices* were made in producing the statement. *What point of view is being privileged, and what is being left out?* All descriptions highlight some aspects while downplaying or hiding others (Lakoff and Johnson 1980, 163). Which aspects of the phenomenon are we being encouraged to consider, and which aspects are being neglected? I recognize that the word "choice" implies to many a conscious decision, whereas most of the time we generate discourse at such a rapid pace that we probably would say we did not stop to think about our language choices. Nonetheless, our discourse always displays preferences, whether by habit or by choice, and it is those preferences that are of importance here. The acts of framing and naming always serve preferred interests, even if those interests are not noticed or are uncontroversial. "A cylindrical organic object is being rotated from a vertical to a horizontal position" represents a preference of one way of defining the event to the neglect of other ways. The statement does not remind us of the biological, ecological, or social aspects of it. Instead, the event is sized up, or evaluated, using a vocabulary that privileges the chemical and physical characteristics of the event—constituting what some might call a scientific or technical framing of the event. The statement represents the event from a particular point of view, and in that sense it is every bit as partial (selective and abstractive) as the first three statements. As the illustrations that I examine below will suggest, such a "technical" framing can have significant persuasive implications.

The fourth statement is persuasive also because it elicits a response different from the first three statements. Each description implies or encourages a somewhat different set of attitudes and actions among its hearers/reader, and this description does as well. That response may be one of confusion or lack of understanding if the hearer/reader does not follow the quasi-technical vocabulary. For that reason, Kenneth Burke and other language theorists talk of the "mystification" that sometimes accompanies the use of technical vocabularies (1950). If one is mystified, one may either seek additional information or, more often, simply neglect the description and the event as being beyond one's understanding. In either case, one is still being influenced. One is not being encouraged to approve of the action (as in statement two) or to disapprove (as in statements one and three). We are being encouraged not to think of the event in a particularly action-oriented way, in which case we are being encouraged *not* to evaluate or act toward the event. Although the event is being acknowledged, it is acknowledged in such a way as to discourage us from developing clear attitudes toward it. Such a description, if unchallenged, would be a particularly effective way of discouraging further thought about the matter.

If, on the other hand, a technical vocabulary that emphasizes the chemical/physical aspects of the event is understood, the description reaffirms a particular way of understanding the world. I cannot help but recall the first *Star Trek* movie, in which humans are described consistently by a deadly and powerful computerized mechanism as "carbon-based units." From the perspective of "V'ger" (the mechanism's name in the movie), that is all we are—merely a type of "unit" among many that has (initially, at least) no particular interest or value. Imagine your daily newspaper reporting the intentional taking of human life not as "murder" but as "the conversion of carbon-based units to an inactive state." I am not arguing that all technical descriptions are ethically suspect. I am arguing that any and all descriptions are selective and function to serve certain interests as opposed to others, and it behooves us to be aware of those interests particularly when technical framings and descriptions are advanced in public discourse.

The last description, "A tree is being cut down," at first blush also seems unpersuasive. Once again, however, by comparing this description to the previous ones, we can quickly discern what is being left out. No agent is identified as responsible for the action. No particular advantages or disadvantages of the event are mentioned. In short, the event is framed as relatively trivial and unimportant. But to trivialize an event is still a persuasive act, because it amounts to saying, "[T]his event is not worth noticing, let alone developing an opinion of approval or disapproval." For example, communication scholar Robin Clair describes trivialization as a key way that an organization may try to deny or sequester allegations of sexual harassment. She notes that many women within organizations may adapt to harassing environments by trivializing harassing acts in order to reduce the anxiety associated with assertively challenging those in authority (1993, 127). By framing an event as a meaningless joke or harmless entertainment, the offensive, discriminatory, or painful aspects of the event are neglected. As Catherine MacKinnon notes, "[T]rivialization of sexual harassment has been a major means through which its invisibility has been enforced" (1979, 52).

Different definitions of a situation function in a manner that is analogous to the way different maps work (Dorling 1997). The same domain can be mapped in a variety of ways—meteorological, demographic, economic, biological, topographical, transportational, geological, hydrological, bathymetric, historical, political, and so on. It is pointless to ask which sort of map depicts reality as it "really is." Maps are necessarily selective, "partial," and are constructed for specific interests and purposes (Wood 1992). Maps can be judged for their usefulness only with respect to such interests and purposes. Even such notions as "accuracy" only make sense relative to the specific purpose of a map (Monmonier 1991). Similarly, different definitions of a situation must be judged according to our particular needs and interests. The value of a definition (or map) will vary considerably depending on those needs and interests, but there is no idealized language that captures all our possible needs and interests at once, just as no single map can serve simultaneously all the possible uses to which maps can be put. Once a map is presented to us, or a situation defined, social influence is exerted in the sense that we either must behave appropriately or provide an alternative mapping/definition.

Political scientists David A. Rochefort and Roger C. Cobb contend that social issues often are framed through "problem definitions" and that such definitions have "major import for an issue's political standing and for the design of public solutions" (1994, 4). Indeed, whether a problem is even defined *as* a "public" issue plays a significant role in the attention and treatment it receives: "By dramatizing or downplaying the problem and by declaring what is at stake . . . descriptions help to push an issue onto the front burners of policymaking or result in officials' stubborn inaction and neglect" (3). Similarly, communication scholar J. Robert Cox argues that definition of a situation functions "pragmatically" to limit what factors are relevant to making decisions, what counts as appropriate evidence or grounds for action, and ultimately what choices are "rational, reasonable, or justified" (1981, 200–202). In sum, the act of defining a situation, especially in public discourse, simultaneously identifies a competent audience for the contested issue, specifies a type of knowledge being sought, and suggests appropriate modes of analysis.

To understand how descriptions function persuasively, I propose that we think of the act of defining a situation as *invoking an exemplar.* When a situation is defined by someone, especially someone in authority, we are encouraged to "see" the similarity between the current situation and a prototypical exemplar and to behave accordingly. To define a situation as a "crisis" encourages us to act how we have been taught is appropriate for a crisis, which is quite different from how we have been taught to behave in a "normal situation." To define a situation as a "private matter" urges us to consider it "none of our business." It is my hope that this chapter illustrates that even the most banal description, label, or name can function persuasively to define a situation so as to direct our attention in one direction rather than another.

In the remainder of this chapter, I examine some of the ways we use the terms "public," "personal," and "technical" to define and frame our experiences. My particular interest is in how these terms are used to include or exclude people from participating in public conversation. I then briefly describe examples of the ways that public discourse can be shaped by how specific situations are defined by those in positions of authority.

The Politics of the Personal

According to Goodnight, discourse is typically grounded in the personal, technical, or public "sphere of argument" (1982; 1987). Argument in the personal sphere is relatively unrestricted and often unsophisticated by normative standards of argument. Technical argument brings with it the formal expectations of a scholarly community bent on advancing a "special kind of understanding." Public debate ensues when an argument reaches beyond the boundaries of a specialized community or group of private individuals and engages a larger group of people known as "the public." Goodnight's own critical focus is on the public sphere, described as the forum in which citizens share in the construction of the future and which is being eroded by certain communicative practices.

A good example of a typically taken-for-granted framing using these notions of human spheres of activity is to define a situation as "personal" or "private" rather than "political" or "public." Although not all uses of these distinctions are problematic, it is worth noting that the distinction between the personal and public spheres has been one of the most persistent dichotomies used throughout the history of Western civilization to oppress women (Jay 1981). Although the current conception of the public/private split has its origins in the advent of the industrial revolution, one can trace the notion that only men are fit for public life back to the time of Homeric Greece (Elshtain 1981; Jaquette 1984). Philosopher Jean Grimshaw argues that "the public sphere is seen as paradigmatically the province of males and the private one that of females" (1986, 198). The world of home and family is conceptualized as "personal, particularistic, based on emotion and on care and nurturance for others" (197), while the public sphere, at least in Western capitalist societies, is typically characterized as the polar opposite, dominated by impersonal instrumental rationality and self-interest (Poole 1985). The more entrenched the public/personal dichotomy becomes, the more the distinctions drawn typically perpetuate gendered differences (cf. Jay 1981). According to anthropologist Michelle Zimbalist Rosaldo's synthesis of various studies, "universal asymmetries in the actual activities and cultural evaluations of men and women" are directly related to "a universal, structural opposition between domestic and public spheres" (1974, 41). Rosaldo's conclusion is that "women's status will be lowest in those societies where there is a firm differentiation between domestic and public spheres of activity" (36; cf. Eisenstein 1983, 15–26; Rosaldo 1980).

Defining our appropriate "place" in the world as public or private tends to continue power relations that limit options for both men and women. In particular, women's participation in public discourse has been discouraged through violence, ridicule, and societal commonplaces. Although women are no longer threatened with ducking stools and gossip's bridles, there is no doubt that women engaged in public discourse continue to be, more often than not, considered suspect (Jamieson 1988, 67–89). One result has been that women continue to be socialized to avoid participation in the public sphere. According to a study by political scientist Ivy Ellen Deutchman (1985), different "power orientations" influence the "form and degree or political participation" by men and women. Women demonstrate less interest in the "public realm" in part because "women, reading the 'men only' signs, sense that they cannot participate" (1985, 89). It is not surprising, therefore, that the current dominant political language, including the public/personal dichotomy, functions to "silence particular persons or groups" and "proscribe particular topics and spheres of life from discourse" (Elshtain 1982, 620). Precisely how different public discourse would be if women were not implicitly and explicitly discouraged from the "male sandbox" of the public sphere is an open question (Jaquette 1984, 24), but the potential contributions of a feminist perspective have been claimed to be considerable (Ruddick 1984, Hartsock 1983, Tabak 1984). Carol Gilligan (1982) suggests that women's ethical reasoning differs from men's because "women understand people as connected, as having responsibilities toward each other, as anxious to avoid doing harm" (Stiehm 1984, 222). Such depictions of an innate female pacifism or "ethic of care" have been critiqued for reproducing stereotypes of men and women and for assuming the outdated philosophy of essentialism (Grant 1987; Richards 1982; Tronto 1987). But even if male/female value differences are a result of socialization rather than biology, a case can still be made that greater participation by women can make a constructive difference. The success of widespread feminist participation in Scandinavian politics (Edgar 1988) and studies of the impact of greater female participation in legislative policymaking suggest that there are desirable values to be advanced by "feminizing" public discourse (Kathlene 1995). Grimshaw, who is openly skeptical about the notion of an inherent or intrinsic "female ethic," nonetheless suggests that social change can be advanced by questioning the public/personal dichotomy: "[T]he life experiences and activities of women, centred as they have tended to be, more than those of men, around the 'microcosm' of household, family and the physical and emotional care of others, may provide space more easily than those of men for questioning some dominant social priorities. In particular, they may provide space for questioning the split between a 'public' world whose concerns or constraints tend to exclude the personal, and a 'private' world of care for others whose constraints are not suppose to impinge on the 'public' realm" (1986, 224–25).

The well-known feminist phrases "The personal is political" and "The politics of the personal" are examples of discourse strategies aimed at breaking down reified gender-based distinctions between the personal and public spheres. Space does not permit an exhaustive review of all the uses to which such phrases have been put, but one line of thinking is particularly noteworthy from the perspective of the study of defining situations and social control. To say that the personal is political is to draw attention to the power relations that take place out of public view. All power relations are political, even those treated as nonpolitical because they exist in the personal sphere (Deutchman 1985, 83). To claim that the personal is political draws attention to the various forms of domination and violence that have traditionally been regarded as "private matters" (such as marital or date rape and child abuse) and that can be addressed only when they are redefined as public problems. According to activist Jane Meyerding, the violence associated with sexism will continue as long as the dominant communicative strategies perpetuate the personal/public sphere distinction precisely because of the way such framing functions as a form of social control:

> Integrating nonviolence into feminism requires us to really believe that the personal is political and there is no dividing line between them, no hierarchy of which is more important. This is necessary because from the beginning of history, no method of hiding, disguising, excusing, or rationalizing violence has ever been as successful as the trivialization of violence against womyn [author's spelling]. And this violence has been trivialized precisely by the creation of the dichotomy between personal and political, with "political" defined as important and male, and "personal" defined as unimportant and female. (Meyerding 1982, 9–10)

One key to the success of feminism, according to Meyerding, is a rhetoric of empowerment—"the process by which people realize their personal power" (10). Because the personal versus public sphere dichotomy has been used literally for centuries to perpetuate the repression of women (Elshtain 1981; 1982; Jamieson 1988, 67–76; Janeway 1971), most discourse practices (though not all) that subvert the dichotomy are more likely to be politically liberating than those that reproduce it.

In short, defining a situation or issue as a matter for the personal as opposed to the public sphere is usually a matter either of trivializing the significance of the issue or of removing the issue from public consideration. In this latter category belong assertions of privacy rights that attempt to declare some actions beyond the state's authority to regulate. But such "private" actions virtually always have political implications, as evidenced by the fact that privacy rights must be negotiated in the public sphere. "The personal is political" is not only an important declaration aimed at personal empowerment but also a useful description of the ever-present power relations that operate in and through "personal" relations, communication, and actions. Accordingly, when arguments are grounded in such a way as to oppose personal and public spheres, we are well advised to examine how power relations are being transformed or obfuscated.

On Spheres and Roles: The *Challenger* Disaster

On January 28, 1986, the space shuttle *Challenger* blasted off from the Kennedy Space Center in Florida. Seventy-three seconds later, millions watched on television as the rocket disintegrated in an explosion. The deaths of all seven crew members, particularly teacher Christa McAuliffe, shocked the nation. A presidential commission identified the primary cause of the accident as a failure in the joint between two stages of the rocket that allowed hot gases to escape during the burn (*Report* 1986). Volatile rocket fuel spewed out when a rubber O-ring failed to seal the joint. The lesson of the *Challenger* disaster has less to do with engineering than it does with failed decision making (Vaughan 1996). The day before the launch, engineers from Morton Thiokol (hereafter Thiokol), the company that produced the rocket booster that failed, warned that the flight might be risky. The engineers expressed concern that the O-ring had never been tested at the freezing temperature forecast for the launch, and there was reason to believe they would not function properly. In part because the flight already had been postponed several times, managers from the National Aeronautics and Space Administration (NASA) and Thiokol overruled the engineers and approved the disastrous launch.

Argument critic Robert C. Rowland (1986) contends that the decision-making failures leading up to the *Challenger* disaster were a result of undue interference by the public sphere in matters better determined in the technical sphere. Rowland distinguishes between the public and technical spheres in terms very similar to those I have described as typifying a realist stance (1986, 139):

Sphere	*Audience*	*Mode of Discourse*	*Knowledge Created*
public	general public	value/policy	public decisions
technical	technicians/scientists	fact	science

According to Rowland, "[T]he NASA managers erred primarily by ignoring the warnings of their own experts and technicians from Thiokol and Rockwell. They ignored those warnings largely because of perceived pressure from the public" (1986, 139–40). Rowland suggests that "when it comes to deciding on the safety of a shuttle launch, there may be a need for less, not more, public input" (141). Rowland's analysis generalizes beyond the particulars of the shuttle accident in a manner that clashes directly with Goodnight's position that the public sphere is being unduly eroded. There are "costs associated with increasing public participation in a technical area," Rowland declares, because the "technical issues are so complex" (144). A "decision to ignore the experts" is "fraught with danger" because the "careful consideration" of issues "required in a technical assessment" is "by its very nature" difficult to accomplish in the public sphere (140–41, 144). Rowland's analytical framework perpetuates a series of dichotomies that are at the heart of the assault on public discourse. The sort of social control advocated by Rowland is that the public is better off leaving technical matters to "experts" whose integrity is assured by intraspherical disputation (see 143–44).

A very different picture of the *Challenger* accident emerges if we look for discourse practices that promote or discourage particular power relations. Communication scholar Dennis Gouran's analysis of the decision-making processes involved with the accident identifies five problems (1987; Gouran, Hirokawa, and Martz 1986). Three of the factors identified by Gouran, "unwillingness by several parties to violate perceived role boundaries," "ambiguous and misleading use of language that minimized the perception of risk," and a "frequent failure to ask important questions relevant to the final decision," can be interpreted as evidence of dysfunctional communicative practices that reflect precisely the sort of power and knowledge relations advocated by Rowland. For example, the engineers most concerned with the possibility of an O-ring failure had repeated opportunities to "veto" the launch decision. The engineers, after initially recommending against launching, agreed to revise their recommendation because they could not "prove" the launch was unsafe. During the teleconference in which the revised recommendation was communicated to NASA managers, the engineers and managers of Thiokol were asked collectively if there was any disagreement with the recommendation to launch. Gouran, Hirokawa, and Martz argue that none was expressed because the engineers "apparently felt at this point that it was not their place to do so" (1986, 124). Because their job was to ascertain the "facts" and the decision to launch was defined as outside their purview (a "management decision"), the engineers' definition of their "place" created an unwillingness "to cross role boundaries" (124–25). Gouran, Hirokawa, and Martz cite statements by the engineers indicating that they did not fear punishment for vocalizing dissent, hence role propriety "appears to have been the standard by which role conflicts were managed" (125). Defined as "engineers" and not as "management," the parties involved felt that further objection to the launch would have been inappropriate. Put another way, when power becomes "naturalized" into established roles and social practices, "norms" emerge that make challenges of such power abnormal and irrational (McKerrow 1989, 99; see also Vaughan 1996). In this way, well-worn definitional terms such as public, personal, or technical act as forms of social control.

Representatives from Thiokol had the opportunity to state unambiguously that they opposed the launch. Instead, such statements as "[T]emperature data not conclusive on predicting primary O-ring blow-by" and "[W]e did not have a sufficient data base to absolutely assure that nothing would strike the vehicle" were made (Gouran, Hirokawa, and Martz 1986, 130). The problem with these statements is not so much their ambiguity or abundance of technical jargon but rather their formation as statements of "fact" rather than of "policy." As discussed in some detail previously, all descriptions encourage a particular point of view and invite some reactions as opposed to others. The relevant critical question is about what *choices* were made in producing the description: What point of view is being privileged, and what is being left out? Which aspects of the phenomenon are we being encouraged to consider, and which aspects are being neglected? In the case of the *Challenger* disaster, by preferring the language of facticity and pseudo-objectivity, the statements quoted above obscure the value-laden knowledge that a safe launch could not be assumed. Just as perpetuating a technical/public contrast through patterns of self-definition (engineers versus managers) disenfranchised those best in a position to stop the launch, so too the language of distinct communicative domains (fact versus policy) created statements about data rather than warnings. It is worth noting that launch decisions now require input from diverse groups including the astronaut crew, engineers, and operations crews, and the final decision to launch is made by one of the astronauts.

Gouran, Hirokawa, and Martz also identify the failure to ask important relevant questions about the decision to launch as a factor leading to the accident. Although some questions were not asked because the "person in a position to raise the question may have anticipated receiving a response he would prefer not have," an additional reason was that "there may have been a reluctance to ask a question based on the individual's sense of propriety" (1986, 132). Asking questions, particularly questions that violate the constraints of defined roles and prevailing assumptions, may be one of the best communicative strategies for making problematic dominant power and knowledge relations (Mills 1940; cf. Graesser and Black 1985, chapters 8 and 9). That important questions were not asked in this case is further evidence for the dangerous implications of taking a definition of a situation for granted.

The final two factors identified by Gouran, Hirokawa, and Martz are "questionable patterns of reasoning" by key personnel and "perceived pressure to produce a desired recommendation." The errors in reasoning can be grouped into two categories: a presumption that success in the past meant success in the future, and underestimating the cost of error. There are two notable themes identifiable in published critiques of the errors in reasoning involved in the launch decision (Ice 1987; Gouran 1987). The first is that there is nothing unique about the errors that points to different spheres having distinct modes of reasoning. Although the specific materials of argument may vary, arguments based on precedent, analogy, example, and definition (for example) as well as the fallacies associated with them appear whenever and wherever humans engage in shared reasoning. Careful analysis of the arguments involved in the *Challenger* launch supports the position advanced by sociologists of science that reasoning processes by scientists (or "experts") do not differ in kind from those of nonscientists (Gilbert and Mulkay 1984; Latour and Woolgar 1979).

Rowland suggests that the "perceived pressure" to launch originated in the public sphere. Because the source of Rowland's evidence for such a claim is testimony from those who made the faulty decisions, it is prudent to characterize such claims as stated "reasons" rather than "causes" (Buss 1978, 1979; Toulmin 1970). As C. Wright Mills put it, "When an agent vocalizes or imputes motives, he is not trying to describe his experienced social action. He is not merely stating 'reasons.' He is influencing others and himself. Often he is finding new 'reasons' which will mediate action" (1940, 907). One could equally well attribute the "cause" of the perceived pressure on NASA to (1) bureaucratic momentum and habituated ways of thinking, (2) the pressure to develop the military capability of the shuttle, (3) pressure from President Reagan to launch in order to divert attention from problems in his administration, or (4) Thiokol's concern that they could lose future NASA contracts. Blaming the public for the pressure scapegoats participatory democracy in order to sustain NASA's autonomy: "NASA officials, of course, should be immune from such petty anxieties and pressures. . . . They should ignore public opinion" (Ignatius 1986, 20). By blaming "the public" for unfairly creating a pressured atmosphere in which "the experts" had to operate, faulty reasoning is excused, and the basis for perpetuating status quo power relations is bolstered.

The previous two illustrations demonstrate how dominant, commonsense understandings of spheres can perpetuate potentially undesirable forms of social control. In both cases, discourse strategies that emphasize inclusion rather than exclusion would have facilitated a productive empowerment of otherwise disenfranchised groups or individuals. In the case of sexism, almost all feminist analysts "share at least one overriding imperative: they would redefine the boundaries of the public and the private, the personal and the political, in a manner that opens up certain questions for inquiry" (Elshstain 1981, 202). In the case of the *Challenger* disaster, at least part of the problem was the unwillingness or inability of key participants to see themselves as personally involved with the fate of other human beings or as responsible members of a specified community. In short, once reified, some situation definitions can become the source of individual and collective incapacities. We need not eliminate the words "personal," "public," and "technical" from the vocabulary. Rather, the task is to question the oppositions implied by certain definitions of situations; in particular, we need to inspect the implicit and explicit strategic use of "spherestalk" to redirect or shut down public debate.

There is widespread agreement that a primary cause for the decline of political discourse is the rise of the technical expert associated with specialized and complex modern technology: "Mainstream technical experts are alleged to be in a better position to make [policy] decisions for the common good because of their knowledge base and risk-assessment capabilities than the general public or its elected representatives" (Walsh 1988, 12). The issues with the most importance for global survival, such as nuclear arms and environmental degradation, which "should present live possibilities for argumentation and public choice, disappear into the government technocracy or private hands" (Goodnight 1982, 225). If one questions the "givenness" of how real the distinction among spheres is and we see such framing as competing definitions of the situation, then it can be argued that technical expertise, per se, is not the culprit; rather, it is when issues are defined as matters of purely nonpolitical technical specialization that problems arise. The myth of value-free science was literally exploded decades ago, but many scientists and technical experts still believe that "it is not their job" to consider the social and political implications of their work. Alternatively, some technical experts recognize that their work has social significance but believe that they are the only ones competent to evaluate important policy arguments. As a former national security official concerned with nuclear weapons policy in the Carter administration put it, "[T]hese questions are too complicated for either politicians or the public" (in McLean 1986, 77). Specific discourse strategies are often employed that reinforce the power of technical elites over the rest of us. Communication scholars George N. Dionisopoulos and Richard E. Crable note that the rhetorical strategy of the nuclear power industry after the Three Mile Island accident was to exert "definitional hegemony," that is, to dominate the framing of the emergent issues and define the situation in a manner consistent with their interests (1988). In a democracy, no one should have complete or absolute definitional hegemony. Given the mass media's dependence on "official sources" that typically represent the government or corporate interests—sources also likely to frame matters as too "technical" for public deliberation—the risks posed by efforts to exert definitional hegemony are ongoing.

The argument of this chapter is that framing or defining situations is a form of social influence. I have discussed the rhetorical uses of the terms "public, "personal," and "technical" to illustrate the argument, but an almost endless supply of other examples is available. David Zarefsky has devoted an entire volume to documenting how President Lyndon B. Johnson's choice of the metaphor of declaring "war on poverty" influenced citizens and elected officials alike in the 1960s (1986). Denise M.

Bostdorff has documented with a series of case studies that U.S. presidents use their ability to frame a situation as a "crisis" in order to justify the exercise of their military authority (1994). William N. Elwood has traced some of the more unfortunate influences of U.S. politicians declaring a "war on drugs" in the 1980s (1994). Rochefort and Cobb's collection contains a series of studies of how various social problems are defined and how those definitions influence public policy, including competing definitions of plant closings, air transportation, sexual harassment, drug use, tax policy, agriculture, and AIDS (1994). Philip Eubanks details the prevalence and significance of defining international trade as "war" (2000). In each of these studies, the scholar has documented in some detail that the defining or framing of a particular historical situation acted as a form of social coordination and control. Furthermore, important studies have documented that citizens' perceptions of political issues are significantly shaped and influenced by the way they are reported in news coverage (Iyengar 1991). The social influences of framing are not limited to politicians and the news media, however. As the examples of "public," "personal," and "technical" suggest, the use of "commonsense" ways of defining the situations in which we find ourselves every day can have significant consequences.

10
Conclusion: Toward a Pragmatic Approach to Definition

In this final chapter, I wish to summarize the case for a pragmatic approach to definition advanced throughout this book and point to questions that ought to be asked in contexts in which participants find themselves engaging in arguments about, from, or by definition.

I began by noting that definitions constitute a form of rhetorically induced social knowledge. That is, definitions are the result of a shared understanding of the world and are both the product of past persuasion and a resource for future persuasion. Particularly when definitions become part of law or public policy, they can have rather significant consequences. In short, definitions *matter*. The "natural attitude" toward definitions takes their mundane status for granted. That is, established definitions are assumed to represent the way things "really are" (facts of essence) as well as current linguistic practices (facts of usage). It is only in a context in which we can identify what I have called a "definitional rupture" that the question of how we define words becomes particularly relevant. Because defining words is a relatively sophisticated linguistic practice that must be learned and refined, it is a practice that is also open to analysis and improvement.

To learn a category is to learn a salient set of similarity/difference relationships. The key difference between the social constructionist approach of this book and various forms of essentialism and realism is the belief that SDRs are learned and not simply "given" by the world. We make sense of the world by sorting its objects into what philosopher Nelson Goodman describes as socially "relevant" kinds, not "natural" kinds (1978). Definitions are one way that social groups try to formalize and stabilize categories, whether that group is made up of scientists defining entities like "planets" or "wetlands," academics trying to define key theoretical concepts, or public policy makers defining legally enforceable categories such as "death" or "rape." Typically, the goal of persuading members of a social group to accept a definition of any particular X is to promote what I have described as denotative conformity, such that there is wide agreement on what sorts of phenomena should count as X and, often, an attempt to secure agreement about what sorts of behavior toward/with X are appropriate.

Definitional questions in the form of "What is X?" are problematic because they encourage a search for so-called real definitions—articulations of what X really and truly is. Such an approach to definitions is problematic because the idea of identifying the unchanging essence or nature of things is doubly vexed. First, all we have access to are things-as-experienced (phenomena); things-in-themselves (noumena) are inaccessible. Second, definitions are linguistic, and there is no way to escape the historical contingency of any particular definitional proposition. The "realness" of any proposed definition is theory bound; that is, the belief that a particular definition captures the "real" nature of any given X is inextricably linked to a number of related beliefs that are held in a particular historical context and subject to possible revision. Furthermore, an emphasis on real definition often risks a deflection of important ethical and practical questions involved in acts of definition. Once we abandon metaphysical absolutism, then we must acknowledge that any act of definition is purposeful within a given social group and historical context. And if we set aside essentialism, it follows that we should abandon the "language of essentialism" (Barnes 1982, 79–83). We thus recognize that "[d]efinitions are symbolic constructions, involving a host of value judgments, designed to serve particular social ends and are therefore assessed for their utility in carrying out social programs" (Chesebro 1985, 14). Accordingly, the "What is X?" question needs to be replaced with such questions as, "How ought we use the word X given our needs and interests?," "What is the purpose of defining X?," and "What should count as X in context C?"

In taking such a pragmatic approach to definition, we can reverse the age-old definitional practice that can be described as "valorization of essence" and replace it with the pragmatic essentializing of values.[1] Instead of presuming to be able to identify metaphysical "essences" in definitions, we should acknowledge that definitions emphasize aspects of social realities that serve particular interests. We should embrace William James's redescription of essentialism in pragmatic terms that treats "the idea of essence" as involving "the idea of value" (Wilshire 1968, 201). For James, what counts as "essential" about a given definiendum is an evaluative question of *importance,* not metaphysics. The question is, *What are the appropriate values that we want to make "essential" to particular definitions?* With respect to "death," brain activity is most valued by proponents of various "brain death" definitions; with respect to "wetlands," one definition suggests the wetter the better, while another values the specific ecological functions of various sorts of "wet" lands. Common to all these definitions is a close relationship between what is valued of the definiendum (X) and what is counted as "essential" to identify as the definiens (is Y). As the analysis below of *PGA Tour, Inc. v. Martin* suggests, our definitional debates will be more honest, direct, and productive if our values are discussed more openly and not obscured by metaphysical posturing.

Definitions describe the world, but they do so prescriptively. That is, definitions prescribe language use (how term X ought to be used) and influence our attitudes and behaviors relevant to X. Accordingly, we can characterize definitions as political, both because definitions serve particular interests and because definitions involve issues of power and influence. As Douglas Walton notes, once definitions "are lodged into place, in law, government regulations, or otherwise enshrined in public policies and regulations, then they are coercive and they do serve particular interests" (2001, 129).

Although the prescriptive and political dimensions of the act of defining are typically visible in arguments *about* a definition, particularly when a definitional rupture occurs and the process of definition itself becomes an issue, the persuasive dimensions of arguments *from* and *by* definition are equally important—especially because such arguments may do their work relatively unobtrusively. Whenever we name or describe a phenomenon or class of objects or define a situation, we entitle that phenomenon, class of objects, or situation to a specific status that invites appropriate attitudes and behaviors in response. In short, we are engaging in a persuasive act. As noted earlier, rhetorical critic Richard Weaver describes language as *sermonic:* "[E]very use of speech, oral and written, exhibits an attitude, and an attitude implies an act" (1970, 222).

To offer predicates about any given X is to advocate or "preach" a way to think and act toward X: "Language, which is thus predicative, is for the same cause sermonic. . . . We are all of us preachers in private or public capacities. Thus caught up in a great web of inter-communication and inter-influence, we speak as rhetoricians affecting one another for good or ill" (1970, 224).[2]

Such a sermonic function of language can be obvious in cases of disputed entitlements. Whether a *particular* object is entitled as "art" or "obscenity," each description advocates the way we are to understand and treat that object. Similarly, how a *class* of objects, such as nuclear weapons, is understood (or not understood, if the language used is obscure or overly technical) is profoundly influenced by the language we use to make sense of that class. Finally, how we define *situations* can give meaning to a complex set of phenomena, practices, and experiences. Such language use can invite our participation, or encourage our exclusion, as in the case of defining a situation or set of issues as "public," "private," or "technical."

In sum, *all* language use is persuasive and, once scrutinized, reveals a nontrivial political and ethical dimension. Even statements intended by a speaker to represent a "realistic" assessment of some event or phenomenon are efforts to persuade us about "reality" as the speaker understands it. All definitions and descriptions are persuasive, and all function to advance certain interests and not others.

The social constructionist account of language is messy. That is, without a God or the secular equivalent belief in metaphysical absolutism, there are no nonhuman, ahistorical criteria that can be stipulated for judging the usefulness of definitions and descriptions. All such judgments must be made given the needs and interests of particular groups of language users occupying a particular historical situation. Even within a given moment of history, the needs and interests of different groups can result in quite different purposes for definition and description. As Walton notes, "The rules for putting forward, challenging and accepting definitions clearly vary with the type of conversational exchange an argument is supposed to be part of. So there are no easy or pat solutions to the problems of when definitions should be judged to be proper and when not" (2001, 130).

The purpose of this book is to urge us to ponder our definitions and descriptions as argumentative claims rather than a revelation of "the real." As Walton says with respect to persuasive definitions, an attempt to define reality "should be treated as an argument. It should be regarded as open to critical questioning and to the posing of counterdefinitions" (2001, 130). Accordingly, I wish to end this project by providing a brief description of certain definitional arguments in the Supreme Court decision of *PGA Tour, Inc. v. Martin* (532 U.S. [2001]). The case is an interesting one because the philosophical concept of "essentialism" and its relevance to legal definitions are addressed by the Court's opinion, written by Justice John Paul Stevens, and by a dissent, by Justice Antonin Scalia. I then identify normative implications for definitional argument evaluation. Although a priori criteria for the evaluation of any and all definitional proposals are not possible, *PGA Tour, Inc. v. Martin* helps to illustrate the usefulness of the *topoi* of history, values, and power relations for analyzing such proposals.

Definitional Argument in *PGA Tour, Inc. v. Martin*

On May 29, 2001, the U.S. Supreme Court announced its decision in *PGA Tour, Inc. v. Martin*. In this case, golfer Casey Martin sought protection under the Americans with Disabilities Act (ADA) in order to compete in Professional Golfers Association (PGA) events with the assistance of a golf cart. Martin has been afflicted since birth with a progressive case of Klippel-Trenaunay-Weber syndrome, "a degenerative circulatory disorder that obstructs the flow of blood from his right leg back to his heart" (Stevens 2001, 5). Martin argued that the ADA forbids the PGA from preventing his participation in their events through the use of a rule that requires all golfers to walk the course. Martin claimed that such a rule constitutes discrimination in his case due to his disability-related need for a golf cart. By a 7–2 majority, the Court agreed.

There are two main questions involved in *PGA Tour, Inc. v. Martin*. The first is whether a professional golf tour should be considered a "public accommodation" within the meaning of the ADA. As controversial (and occasionally convoluted) as this part of the decision may be, I will omit it from this analysis in order to concentrate on the second question: Would Martin's use of a golf cart change the "fundamental nature" of the event? The question is crucial because the ADA requires "reasonable modifications" in public accommodations *unless* making such modifications "would fundamentally alter the nature of such . . . accommodations" (42 U.S.C. §12182-b-2-A-ii).

Two appellate courts reached opposite conclusions about whether allowing the use of a golf cart would change the fundamental nature of PGA tournaments. The Ninth Circuit Court of Appeals had ruled in

Martin's case that his use of a cart would not fundamentally alter the nature of the game (204 F. 3d 994 [2000]), but the Seventh Circuit came to a contrary conclusion in a case involving another disabled golfer, ruling that "the nature of the competition would be fundamentally altered if the walking rule were eliminated" (*Olinger v. U.S. Golf Association,* 205 F. 3d 1001 [2000]). Given that the ADA makes explicit reference to the "fundamental nature" of public activities and accommodations, it is understandable that Justice Stevens approached his analysis of the case through a discussion of the fundamental nature of golf and golf tournaments (see Stevens 2001, 28n).

Stevens argues that "the use of carts is not itself inconsistent with the fundamental character of the game of golf. From early on, the essence of the game has been shot-making—using clubs to cause a ball to progress from the teeing ground to a hole some distance away with as few strikes as possible" (21). Stevens's argument is, in part, historical, as he supports his description of golf by quoting the earliest surviving rules of golf, published in 1744. He also notes that the use of golf carts is widespread today, including in various professional-level tournaments such as the Senior PGA Tour, lower-level PGA qualifying tournaments, and, under certain conditions, parts of regular PGA Tour events. He concludes that the so-called walking rule is "not an essential attribute of the game itself" (23).

If one were taking a strictly metaphysical approach to defining the essence of golf, Stevens's task would be done. But he goes further to make the argument that waiving the walking rule in Martin's case would not give him an unfair advantage over players who are required to walk. Stevens documents that PGA representatives contend that the purpose of the rule is to add to the physical and mental challenge of the game "at its highest level" by inducing stress and fatigue. Stevens's approach to this issue is empirical: he notes that the physical exertion involved is negligible, that most professional golfers do not use a cart even when it is allowed, and that Martin's own physical condition is far more fatiguing and stress-inducing to him than walking is for nondisabled competitors. Stevens concludes that the *purpose* of the walking rule is "not compromised in the slightest by allowing Martin to use a cart"; thus, it cannot be said to "fundamentally alter" the tournaments in which he competes (2001, 28).

Justice Scalia disagreed. He makes fun of the idea of "essential" golf and initially appears to take what philosophers call a nominalistic approach: "the rules are the rules" (2001, 10). Now, I say "appears" because at no point does Scalia directly reject the idea that golf might have an "essence"; rather, he argues that even if there is something he calls "classic, Platonic golf," the PGA does not have to play it. They can promote something slightly different. His opinion continues, dripping with sarcasm, arguing it should not be up to the Supreme Court to make a metaphysical determination of "What Is Golf" (2001, 10): "I am sure that the Framers of the Constitution, aware of the 1457 edict of King James II of Scotland prohibiting golf because it interfered with the practice of archery, fully expected that sooner or later the paths of golf and government, the law and the links, would once again cross, and that the judges of this august Court would some day have to wrestle with that age-old jurisprudential question for which their years of study in the law have so well prepared them: Is someone riding around a golf course from shot to shot *really* a golfer?" (10–11).

Scalia's approach might be more specifically described as institution-dependent essentialism rather than nominalist. As Steve Schwarze notes, one argumentative tactic in legal definitional disputes is to shift the terms of the debate to *which institution* should have the authority to define (2002). Scalia points out that, for example, *all* rules for games are "arbitrary and none is essential" (2001, 11). Accordingly, it should be left up to the "ruling body of the sport" to decide what is or is not golf. Scalia's wording elsewhere in the same opinion suggests that he is not a nominalist—he refers to "the very nature of" game and sports (11, 13), and he has referred to the essence of gifts, islands, and compassion (Safire 2001). Although Scalia appears committed to essences, he is quite adamant that the Supreme Court is not the institution to try to discern them in this case. He sneers at the decision as an "Alice in Wonderland determination that there are such things as judicially determinable 'essential' and 'nonessential' rules of a made-up game" (2001, 15).

Scalia has every right to question Stevens's apparent reliance on essentialism in the Court's opinion, and Stevens is wrong to describe Scalia's position as a "postmodern view" (2001, 28n). Philosophical critiques of essentialism have been around as long as essentialism's beginnings, which can be dated to Plato and Aristotle. Nominalism, the position that says there are no essences but only particular instances that we group based on resemblances, can be dated to the middle ages. William of Ockham (who gave us "Ockham's razor") has a thorough critique of essentialism now over six centuries old (Moody, 1967).

In chapter 3, I described William James's critique of essentialism, which can be summed up as arguing that a thing may have as many "essences" as we have interests: "The essence of a thing is that one of its properties which is so *important for my interests* that in comparison with it I may neglect the rest" (James 1981, 961). I will return to James's analysis below because he provides a key with which to approach definitional disputes, but for the moment I need to explain why I think Scalia's position is problematic. I think he is wrong because if we take his apparently institution-dependent essentialist approach, it would vitiate the ADA. Keep in mind that the ADA uses the "language of essentialism" by referring to the fundamental nature of services, facilities, privileges, advantages, or accommodations. Given such language, the Court has little choice but to decide what modifications are "fundamental" or not. Indeed, in the arguments leading up to the Supreme Court's decision—found in the original trial court decisions, the opinions issued from the appellate decisions in *PGA Tour, Inc. v. Martin* and in *Olinger v. U.S. Golf Association,* the briefs filed with the Supreme Court by the petitioner and respondent in *PGA Tour, Inc. v. Martin,* and in the oral arguments before the Supreme Court—at no point was there a serious effort to avoid essentialism. Indeed, the arguments offered by both sides are rife with the language of essentialism.

Scalia takes the position in this case that "the rules are the rules" and PGA golf is what the PGA says it is (2001, 10). Scalia insists that "there is no basis on which anyone—not even the Supreme Court—can pronounce" one rule or another "to be 'nonessential' if the rulemaker (here the PGA Tour) deems it to be essential" (28). Such an institution-dependent approach is thus willing to grant what has been called "definitional hegemony" (Dionisopoulos and Crable, 1988) to whomever controls the contested services, facilities, privileges, advantages, or accommodations. As Stevens notes, Scalia's dissent ignores the statutory language because Congress did not give "organizations carte-blanche authority to exempt themselves" from the provisions of the ADA by allowing them to decide for themselves what is or is not "fundamental" (2001, 28n). As the attorney for Casey Martin, Roy L. Reardon, noted in oral argument before the Court, "[I]f you roll over and let them make a rule and say it's substantive, and that's the end of the game, then you are basically giving them a free pass out of the ADA, which would be improper" (Oral Argument 2001, 34).

Scalia's opinion would support the following chain of reasoning. *Step 1:* The ADA requires reasonable modifications except where such modifications would fundamentally alter the nature of the activity. *Step 2:* The Court is not in a position to determine "essences" or "fundamental" attributes. Scalia attacks the Court's ability to determine the essential nature of sporting events only, but it is unclear how he could grant the Court an ability to determine essence in *any* case involving social institutions or activities. *Step 3:* Deciding what is the fundamental nature of activities should be left to those in authority in those activities. It is noteworthy that Scalia's position in the Martin case is consistent with his dissent in *United States v. Virginia et al.* (518 U.S. 515 [1996]), when he argued that the administrators of the Virginia Military Institute should decide for themselves whether allowing women to attend would require the education offered there to be "fundamentally altered."

If one takes these steps along with Scalia, then it is difficult to see any role for the courts with respect to enforcing the ADA, because it would be up to the PGA (or whomever is charged with discrimination) to decide what is or is not fundamental to its activity and thus what modifications are required. As Stevens notes (2001, 28n), Scalia's "reading of the statute renders the word 'fundamentally' largely superfluous," which is odd given Scalia's stated commitment to a strict textualist approach to statutory interpretation (Scalia 1997) and his "reverence for the plain meaning of texts" (Brisbin 1997, 326). In short, while I agree with Scalia's apparent distrust of essentialism, I am not willing to follow him down a path that gives the power to define to the very institutions asked to comply with the provisions of the ADA.

Normative Implications of a Pragmatic Approach to Definition

Although it is impossible to set forth specific, a priori criteria that can distinguish unequivocally between "good" and "bad" definitions, the brief description of *PGA Tour, Inc. v. Martin,* in concert with the previous chapters and case studies, underscores several normative beliefs salient to the critical evaluation of public definitional arguments. I conclude by attempting to describe these normative implications through a series of suggestions and questions for engaging such disputes.

First, at the risk of repeating myself, we should avoid questions of the form "What is X?" As Robinson notes, "[T]his question-form flourishes precisely because it is vague. It saves us the trouble of thinking out and saying exactly what it is that we want to know about *x*" (1950, 190). Posed as a metaphysical inquiry, such questions have proved to be impossible to answer. James's critique strikes me as fatal: What is "essential" to *anything* depends on our needs and interests in a given historical situation.

Fortunately, we can replace metaphysics with a judicious combination of history and values. As James points out, when we define an attribute of X as "essential," we are declaring what we think is important about X given our particular needs and interests. When appealing for a particular definitional interpretation, reference to "the nature of X" is problematic. A more productive approach would utilize careful historical accounts that document what has been constant and what has changed about X and would give reasons when changes have occurred. For example, it is not a matter of metaphysics that has led the Supreme Court to count wiretaps, urine tests, or the use of thermal imaging as a form of "search and seizure"; rather, it is a sensitivity to the *history* of search and seizure and the *values* of personal privacy that the 4th Amendment has protected. Guided by such history and values, the Court has "pragmatically essentialized" what it considers to be the most important purposes served by the 4th Amendment and has (arguably) protected those purposes in the face of changing technologies.

The "What is golf?" example nicely illustrates the point: We may not be able to divine the metaphysical essence of golf coherently, but we *can* talk about golf's history and what it is that we value about it. Justice Stevens's opinion would require relatively little tweaking to have its implicit Platonism replaced with Jamesian pragmatism. Notice that Stevens says, "[T]he essence of the game has been shot-making." Now, a diehard Platonist would never say "has been" but would say "is," because essences are supposed to be forever, like the three-sidedness of triangles. That Stevens relies heavily on history and emphasizes the pragmatic purpose of the ADA and the purpose underlying the walking rule (to induce stress and fatigue) show how easily one could strip his opinion of the language of essentialism.

The concept of pragmatic essentializing can be understood more clearly if one thinks about certain rhetorical uses of the word "real." Often in locutions such as "*Real* food for *real* people," "This is a *real* crisis," "It's time to make a *real* change," "Get a *real* job," or "My radio station plays *real* rock," what "real" means is "the kind I think is important" or "the kind I value" (cf. Clair 1996). Thus, it is a simple matter to "translate" the ADA's notion of "fundamental nature" of X to "what we have historically valued about X." When Justice Stevens says that "the essence of the game has been shot-making" and that the "walking rule" is "not an essential attribute of the game itself," we can translate this as, "The most important part of the game that we value most is shot-making; thus, the walking rule is not so valuable to the game as to allow Martin's access to be denied." Scalia mostly makes fun of Stevens's effort to describe what is "essential" about professional golf. But given that Stevens provides a reasonably thorough historical and contemporary argument for the pragmatic essentializing of shot-making over the walking rule, his opinion does not deserve the sort of venomous comments made by Scalia. In fact, given the language of essentialism enacted in the ADA, it is difficult to imagine how one could decide such a case without some sort of pragmatic essentializing. The alternative, as Scalia's dissent demonstrates, is simply to walk away.

I have argued that definitions are always political. That is, definitions always serve interests and advance values, and they always require the exercise of power to be efficacious. The Supreme Court is sometimes described as a nonpolitical body, but we all know better. As Jeffrey Rosen, professor at George Washington University Law School, nicely documents (2001), even the current conservative justices of the Court are not shy about imposing their values through their decisions; indeed, that has been the role of the Court ever since *Marbury v. Madison.* Despite Scalia's posturing in *PGA Tour, Inc. v. Martin,* he is not about to give all definitional power away in the name of judicial restraint. His dissent strikes me as having less to do with golf or metaphysics or definitions than it is symptomatic of his assessment of the values associated with the ADA. Scalia describes the Court's decision as an "Animal Farm determination that fairness and the ADA mean that everyone gets to play by individualized rules which will assure that no one's lack of ability (or at least no one's lack of ability so pronounced that it amounts to a disability) will be a handicap" (2001, 15). For Scalia and the PGA, Martin's malady is simply a *pronounced lack of ability* (cf. Titsworth 1999). The ADA provides a judicial check on such pronouncements. By prompting the question of what the most important ("fundamental") aspects of given activities and institutions are and requiring reasonable modifications to promote access, the ADA pursues the goal of *solidarity* "by increasing our sensitivity to the particular details . . . of other, unfamiliar sorts of people," which "makes it more difficult to marginalize people different from ourselves" (Rorty 1989, xvi).

There are at least two sorts of questions that citizens interested in definitional arguments should consider. First, we should consider questions of *purpose* and *interest:* What are our shared purposes in defining X? What interests and values are advanced by competing definitions? *Whose* interests are being served by a particular definition, and do we want to identify with those interests? What are the practical consequences of the "essential" characteristics promoted by a definition, given that every category "valorizes some point of view and silences another" (Bowker and Star 1999, 5)? Competing definitions need to be assessed according to the needs and interests of the particular community of language users involved with the dispute. This "relativized" aspect of a pragmatic approach to definition does not mean, as Walton points out, "that the term in question can freely be redefined by another interest group simply to meet the rhetorical needs of the moment" (2001, 124), as one might do, say, by ignoring the history and values associated with a particular phenomenon. In *PGA Tour, Inc. v. Martin,* what Stevens's opinion accomplishes is to broaden the community of professional golfers by one while maintaining respect for the history and value of shot-making to the game. Although Scalia (2001, 16) may consider this on par with the nightmarish dystopia of Kurt Vonnegut's "Harrison Bergeron," obviously most of the justices found the purposes and interests of the ADA to be reasonable in this case.

Second, we should ponder questions of *power:* Who has the power to define? Who *should* have such authority? A proposed definition is a request for institutional norms: When should X count as Y in context C? In the Martin case, the question is not "Should the walking rule count as an essential part of golf?" but "Should the walking rule count as an essential part of golf in the context of the ADA?" Stevens claims that it is up to the courts to answer such a question, while Scalia contends that it should be left up to the PGA. Who should have the power to define or decide what counts as what? How much coercion—if any—is acceptable to further the end of denotative conformity? Such questions, of course, cannot be answered in a vacuum, which is precisely why I have endeavored to illustrate my general claims about definitions with case studies. But it is important to ask questions about power relations because our lives can be profoundly affected by such decisions; indeed, the question of who should have the authority to make definitional decisions amounts literally to who has the power to delineate what counts as Real.

Philosopher Hilary Putnam has suggested that the belief in "natural kinds" thrives best in an environment where deference to authority flourishes (attributed by Fodor 1998, 154). I take this to suggest that metaphysical absolutism implies a potentially dangerous ideology in which it is appropriate to concede the power to define only to the official experts. In the long run, therefore, one can hope that the Court and other institutions concerned with public definitions will move away from essentialism and be more candid in its "pragmatic adjudication" (cf. Posner 1999, 240–42).

If we reject the notions of natural kinds and real definitions in favor of relevant kinds and pragmatic definitions, then we are encouraged not to take the definitional interests of those in power for granted. The question in *PGA Tour, Inc. v. Martin* was not *whether* an institution would decide what is golf but *which* institution has the power to make such a determination. If one agrees with the outcome of the case, one need not conclude that it is safe to count on the U.S. Supreme Court's sense of metaphysics; rather, agreement results from a sense of solidarity with the majority's understanding of the interests and values of the ADA and with their pragmatic essentializing of the purposes of the rules of professional golf.

Lastly, I hope that this book encourages the consideration of questions of *definitional practice:* How should new definitions be worded? How can a particular group of language users achieve denotative conformity with a definition (new or old)? Is denotative conformity an appropriate goal? Can we identify prototypical exemplars and appropriate SDRs that can teach the relevant language users how to use a definition "correctly"? Our best bet in formulating new definitions in most contexts would be the sort of stipulative, constitutive approach often used in writing public legislation, since that approach comes closest to the formula "X counts as Y in context C." However, attention needs to be paid to how people learn definitions and how to apply categories. It is relatively easy to learn a category based on perceptual similarities, for example, while it may be more complicated to learn a set of functional similarities. With respect to "wetlands," it is easier to argue that "wetter is better" based on a visually encouraged intuition that wetlands are wet most of the time, but for biologists, the ecological *functions* associated with wetlands are far more complex—and important. The way we stereotypically envision "rape" occurring tends to stress force and violence rather than the more abstract concept of "lack of consent," yet it is consent or lack thereof that is at the heart of what legally counts as rape. In the case of "wetlands," "rape," and many others, we need to recognize that teaching a community of language users a new definition is the same as teaching them a new way of understanding the world. Accordingly, the more prototypical exemplars the better, because it is only through exposure to such exemplars that the newly relevant SDRs will be assimilated.

Much of what I have said in this book about language has been articulated previously by philosophers of language and theorists of rhetoric. What I hope to have added, by focusing on definitional disputes, is a sense of urgency about the need for *public engagement* with the definitional arguments that shape our world. As Zarefsky has noted, "Public argument revitalizes a political community by coaching public judgment. Engaging in the argument changes the participants and the listeners. They engage in the act of shaping their world as they shape their language—even though, paradoxically, they are constrained by the very culture they create" (1990, 245).

The process of defining and describing our world to make sense of it and to cope with it has been a part of human culture for a long time. As Quine suggests, "Our patterns of thought or language have been evolving, under pressure of inherent inadequacies and changing needs, since the dawn of language; and, whether we help guide it or not, we may confidently look forward to more of the same" (1969, 24). As technology and politics grow increasingly complex, the temptation to surrender the authority to define our world to those who claim to be in touch with Reality in ways that we are not will increase. If it is agreed that definitions are made, not found, then we are encouraged to resist that temptation and face the responsibility of knowing that the process of definition is social through and through.

Notes
Bibliography
Index

Notes

1. Definitions Matter

1. As Robinson (1950) notes in general, and Greg Bayer (1997) argues with respect to Aristotle's *Posterior Analytics,* the point of "What is X?" questions can vary more than I imply, but I think it is safe to assume that most contemporary language users have the sort of simple and straightforward objective described here.

3. Moving Beyond "Real" Definitions: The Case of "Death"

1. With one odd exception (Benardete 1993), I cannot find a defense of the classical notion of real definitions by philosophers writing in recent collections devoted to definitions. See David 1993; Fetzer, Shatz, and Schlesinger 1991; Matthews 1998.

2. For a defense of a position opposing mine, see Bernat 1999.

4. Definitions as Prescriptive and Theory Bound: The Case of "Rape"

1. My objective here is not to evaluate such arguments in detail. For more extensive analysis, see Augustine 1991, 570–78; Coonan 1980, 42–44; Estrich 1986; "To Have" 1986, 1268–70; Sallmann 1980, 84.

2. As Quine points out, the theory that every idea "must either originate in sense experience or else be compounded of ideas thus originating" can be traced back to John Locke and David Hume (1980, 38). The move to make direct experience and direct observation the criterion of *meaning,* however, helped to ignite philosophy's twentieth-century "linguistic turn" (Rorty 1967).

5. When Are Definitions Political? Always: The Case of "Wetlands"

1. There is more involved in the dispute over federal regulations regarding wetlands than the issue of definition. For example: Does a ban of development on a privately owned wetland constitute an uncompensated "taking" by the federal government? Are the costs and delays involved in obtaining a development permit reasonable? I set aside such issues in this chapter; though they are important, they are not directly relevant to the question of how wetlands ought to be defined.

2. These claims are challenged explicitly by members of the Georgia Conservancy (see U.S. Congress 1992, 398–402).

6. Reformulating the "What Is X?" Question: The Case of "Person" vis-à-vis the Abortion Debate

1. The Court officially broke from the trimester approach in *Webster v. Reproductive Health Services* (492 U.S. (1989) 490).

2. O'Connor's opinion in *Planned Parenthood* in 1992 was, by no means, universally applauded by abortion rights advocates. The primary target of criticism was the ruling that several restrictions imposed by the Pennsylvania law, such as a twenty-four-hour waiting period, did not constitute an "undue burden" or "substantial obstacle" to obtaining an abortion. Much of O'Connor's opinion in *Planned Parenthood* provides a strong endorsement of women's right to decide for themselves the meaning of the act of abortion. In theory, the government is limited to the option of persuading pregnant women to consider alternatives to abortion rather than coercing a particular point of view. However, in practice, the cumulative impact of a series of Court decisions denies many women the option of an abortion; the government's power to "discourage" has grown to such a point that it could be classified as effectively coercive. The Court in *Harris v. McRae* (488 U.S. [1980] 297) upheld a congressional ban on the use of Medicaid funds to pay for almost all abortions, a decision that makes a legal abortion out of reach for many impoverished women. In several cases, the Court has upheld parental notification laws that require pregnant minors to obtain their parents', or a court's, permission to receive an abortion. In *Webster v. Reproductive Health Services,* the Court expanded its holding in *Harris* and upheld Missouri's ban on the use of public facilities, employees, and public funds for performing abortions. In *Planned Parenthood,* the Court upheld, among other things, a requirement by the State of Pennsylvania that women seeking an abortion must be informed by a physician about the gestational age of the fetus and about alternatives to abortion at least twenty-four hours prior to the abortion procedure. Critics argue that such a twenty-four-hour waiting period creates an enormous burden on many women who must travel long distances and take off additional time from work in order to obtain an abortion.

Part Three: Naming and Describing as Entitlements

1. Weaver was committed to a philosophical essentialism, drawn largely from Plato, that I obviously do not share. His faith in argument from definition as a metaphysically and morally superior form of argument has been nicely challenged by Brian R. McGee (1999). Accordingly, I treat argument from definition as a form of reasoning, the content of which is socially variable and open to ethical appraisal.

7. Description as Persuasive Entitlement: The Mapplethorpe "Obscenity" Trial

1. For the argument that Whorf's position is not deterministic, see Lucy and Wertsch (1987) and Stam (1980).

2. See the discussion of encoding specificity in Smith et al. (1987, 228–29). Compare the evidence of a relationship implied between vocabulary and learning in Chiesi, Spilich, and Voss (1979). Most recent studies tend to presume a relationship between categorical representation in thought and the availability of names for categories. See, for example, Harnad (1987, 535–65). Although cognitive psychologists stress the autonomy of language and thought, most acknowledge that there are learning contexts in which a change in the lexicon corresponds to a change in "underlying conceptual structure" (Keil 1989, 148).

8. Naming as Argument by Definition: The Case of "Nukespeak"

1. I am aware of the claim that the nuclear arms race, and SDI in particular, put a huge burden on the Soviet Union's economy and hastened the economic and political collapse of the Soviet Union. For a devastating critique of this claim that includes testimony from historians and former U.S. and Soviet scientists and military leaders, see Mitchell (2000, 87–93). The weight of the evidence supports an opposite conclusion; namely, that the fall of the Berlin Wall and the end of Soviet hegemony in Eastern Europe would have happened *earlier* had it not been for the perceived threat of Reagan's SDI initiative.

2. The CORRTEX case study was originally co-written with Mary Keehner.

3. CORRTEX technology is useful only for measuring the "yield" of large, nearby explosions—it is useless for the purposes of a CTBT. Scientists argue that CORRTEX is equally useless for the Threshold Test Ban Treaty—the use to which the Reagan administration wanted to put it (Guldin 1987).

4. How sincere were the members of the New Delhi Group? It depends on who one asks. A ban on nuclear testing has been argued to be the key to stopping nuclear proliferation. Supporters of a CTBT see the subsequent nuclear testing in India and Pakistan as a direct consequence of the U.S. refusal to support the CTBT, while opponents argue such tests prove the CTBT would have never worked.

5. The SDI case study was originally co-written with Steven Woods.

6. For detailed assessments of SDI, see Donohue 1994; Office of Technology Assessment 1985; Union of Concerned Scientists 1986; Boffey et al. 1988; and Smith 1987.

9. Defining the Situation or Framing as Social Influence: "Public," "Personal," and "Technical"

1. My examples, I should note, pale in comparison with Raymond Queneau's ninety-nine different descriptions of the "same" situation offered as an exercise in style (1981).

10. Conclusion: Toward a Pragmatic Approach to Definition

1. Obviously, my notion of "pragmatic essentializing" denotes a practice similar to what Gayatri C. Spivak advocates as "a strategic use of positivist essentialism in a scrupulously visible political interest" (1988, 205). Although there are conceptual parallels between defining cultural identities and defining

legal concepts, I use the phrase "pragmatic essentializing" because I respect the differences enough to want to avoid (mis)appropriating Spivak's label.

2. Weaver probably was aware of the fact that the word "predicate" is derived from the Latin *prædico,* which in classical Latin means "to declare" or "to proclaim" and in medieval Latin meant "to preach."

Bibliography

Abelson, Raziel. 1967. "Definition." In *The Encyclopedia of Philosophy*, edited by Paul Edwards, 2: 314–24. New York: Macmillan.

Adelman, K. L. 1986. "Statement Before the Senate Armed Services Committee." 99th Cong., 2nd sess. *Congressional Record*, May 1, vol. 132: S5241.

Adler, Amy. 1990. "Post Modern Art and the Death of Obscenity Law." *Yale Law Journal* 99: 1359–70.

Allan, Keith. 1977. "Classifiers." *Language* 53: 285–311.

Alston, William P. 1964. *Philosophy of Language*. Englewood Cliffs, NJ: Prentice.

———. 1996. *A Realist Conception of Truth*. Ithaca: Cornell UP.

Archer, Margaret, Roy Bhaskar, Andrew Collier, and Tony Lawson, eds. 1998. *Critical Realism: Essential Readings*. London: Routledge.

Arkin, William M. 1986. "Test Ban Fever." *Bulletin of the Atomic Scientists* 42 (Oct.): 4–5.

Armstrong, D. M. 1978a. *Nominalism and Realism*. Cambridge: Cambridge UP.

———. 1978b. *A Theory of Universals*. Cambridge: Cambridge UP.

Atlas, T. 1986. "Reagan Offers Soviets a Peek at Nuclear Test." *Chicago Tribune*, Mar. 15, 1, 4.

Aubrey, C. 1982. *Nukespeak: The Media and the Bomb*. London: Comedia.

Augustine, Rene I. 1991. "Marriage: The Safe Haven for Rapists." *Journal of Family Law* 29: 559–90.

Ayer, Alfred Jules. 1936. *Language, Truth, and Logic*. London: Victor Gollantz.

"Back in the Bog on Wetlands." 1991. *New York Times*, Nov. 26, A20.

Barbour, Ian G. 1974. *Myths, Models, and Paradigms*. New York: Harper.

Barker, R. B. 1986. "Testimony Before the Senate Armed Services Committee." 99th Cong., 2nd sess. *Congressional Record*, May 1, vol. 132: S5241–S5244.

Barnes, Barry. 1982. *T. S. Kuhn and Social Science*. New York: Columbia UP.

Bateson, Gregory. 1972. *Steps to an Ecology of the Mind*. New York: Ballantine.

Bayer, Greg. 1997. "The What-Is-X? Question in the Posterior Analytics." *Ancient Philosophy* 17: 317–35.

Beardsley, Monroe C. 1961. "The Definitions of the Arts." *Journal of Aesthetics and Art Criticism* 20: 175–87.

Bell, Clive. 1914. *Art*. New York: Stokes.

Benardete, José A. 1993. "Real Definitions: Quine and Aristotle." *Philosophical Studies* 72: 265–82.

Bernat, James L. 1999. "Refinements in the Definition and Criterion of Death." In *The Definition of Death: Contemporary Controversies*, edited by Stuart J. Youngner, Robert M. Arnold, and Renie Schapiro, 83–92. Baltimore: Johns Hopkins UP.

Bessmer, Sue. 1984. *The Laws of Rape*. New York: Praeger.

Best, Steven, and Douglas Kellner. 1991. *Postmodern Theory: Critical Interrogations*. New York: Guilford.

Bett, Richard. 1989. "The Sophists and Relativism." *Phronesis* 34: 139–69.

Bhaskar, Roy. 1997. *A Realist Theory of Science*. 2nd ed. London: Verso.

Bjork, Rebecca S. 1992. *The Strategic Defense Initiative: Symbolic Containment of the Nuclear Threat*. Albany: State U of New York P.

Black, Henry Campbell. 1999. *Black's Law Dictionary*. 7th ed. St. Paul: West.

Blackmun, Justice H. 1973. *Opinion of the Court, Roe v. Wade*, 410 U.S. 113–78.

Blackstone, William. [1765] 1859. *Commentaries on the Laws of England*. Philadelphia: Lippincott.

"Body Politics." 1990. *Commonweal* 107 (Nov. 9): 627–28.

Boffey, P. M., W. J. Broad, L. H. Gelb, C. Mohr, and H. B. Noble. 1988. *Claiming the Heavens: The "New York Times" Complete Guide to the Star Wars Debate*. New York: Random.

Bornstein, M. H., W. Kessen, and S. Weiskopf. 1976. "The Categories of Hue in Infancy." *Science* 191: 201–2.

Bostdorff, Denise M. 1994. *The Presidency and the Rhetoric of Foreign Crisis*. Columbia: U of South Carolina P.

Bowerman, Melissa. 1976. "Semantic Factors in the Acquisition of Rules for Word Use and Sentence Construction." In *Normal and Deficient Child Language*, edited by Donald M. Morehead and Ann E. Morehead, 99–179. Baltimore: University Park P.

———. 1981. "Language Development." In *Handbook of Cross-Cultural Psychology*, edited by Harry C. Triandis and Alastair Heron, 4: 93–185. Boston: Allyn.

Bowker, Geoffrey C., and Susan Leigh Star. 1999. *Sorting Things Out: Classification and Its Consequences*. Cambridge: MIT P.

Boyer, P. 1985. *By the Bomb's Early Light*. New York: Pantheon.

Braithwaite, Richard. 1953. *Scientific Explanation*. Cambridge: Cambridge UP.

Breslauer, G. W. 1983. "Soviet Aggression Is No Excuse for the Arms Buildup." In *Nuclear Arms: Opposing Viewpoints*, edited by D. L. Bender, 84–87. St. Paul: Greenhaven.

Brisbin, R. A. 1997. *Justice Antonin Scalia and the Conservative Revival*. Baltimore: Johns Hopkins UP.

Broackes, Justin. 1987. "Thoughts and Definitions." *Analysis* 47: 95–100.

Broad, W. J. 1985. *Star Warriors*. New York: Simon.

Brock, Dan W. 1999. "The Role of the Public in Public Policy on the Definition of Death." In *The Definition of Death: Contemporary Controversies*, edited by Stuart J. Youngner, Robert M. Arnold, and Renie Schapiro, 293–307. Baltimore: Johns Hopkins UP.

Bronowski, Jacob. 1965. *Science and Human Values*. New York: Harper.

———. 1978. *The Origins of Knowledge and Imagination*. New Haven: Yale UP.

Brown, Emily. 1995. "Changing the Marital Rape Exemption: I Am Chattel (?!); Hear Me Roar." *American Journal of Trial Advocacy* 18: 657–71.

Brown, Roger W. 1956. "Language and Categories." In *A Study in Thinking*, edited by J. S. Bruner, J. J. Goodnow, and G. A. Austin, 247–310. New York: Wiley.

———. 1958. "How Shall a Thing Be Called?" *Psychological Review* 65: 14–21.

Brown, Roger W., and E. H. Lenneberg. 1954. "A Study in Language and Cognition." *Journal of Abnormal Psychology* 59: 452–62.

Browne, Alister. 1987. "Defining Death." *Journal of Applied Philosophy* 4: 155–64.

Brownmiller, Susan. 1975. *Against Our Will: Men, Women, and Rape*. New York: Simon.

Bunn, M. 1988. "SDI Focus on Near-Term Deployment Continues." *Arms Control Today* (May): 18, 20–21.

Burger, Chief Justice W. E. 1973a. *Opinion of the Court, Miller v. California*, 413 U.S. 15.

———. 1973b. *Opinion of the Court, Paris Adult Theatre I v. Slaton*, 413 U.S. 49.

Burke, Kenneth. 1945. *A Grammar of Motives*. New York: Prentice.

———. 1950. *A Rhetoric of Motives*. New York: Prentice.

———. 1966. *Language as Symbolic Action*. Berkeley: U of California P.

———. 1973. *The Philosophy of Literary Form*. 3rd ed. Berkeley: U of California P.

———. 1984a. *Attitudes Towards History*. 3rd rev. ed. Berkeley: U of California P.

———. 1984b. *Permanence and Change*. 3rd rev. ed. Berkeley: U of California P.

Bush, George H. W. 1989. "Remarks to Members of Ducks Unlimited at the Sixth International Waterfowl Symposium." *Weekly Compilation of Presidential Documents* 25: 860–63.

———. 1990a. "Remarks and a Question-and-Answer Session with the National Association of Agriculture Journalists." *Weekly Compilation of Presidential Documents* 26: 630–35.

———. 1990b. "Statement by Press Secretary Fitzwater on the Development of Wetlands Conservation Policy." *Weekly Compilation of Presidential Documents* 26: 73.

———. 1992a. "Remarks and a Question-and-Answer Session with the Agricultural Community in Fresno, California." *Weekly Compilation of Presidential Documents* 28: 968–72.

———. 1992b. "Remarks and a Question-and-Answer Session with the Agriculture Communicators Congress." *Weekly Compilation of Presidential Documents* 28: 1172–79.

———. 1992c. "Remarks to the American Farm Bureau Federation in Kansas City, Missouri." *Weekly Compilation of Presidential Documents* 28: 81–84.

Buss, Allan R. 1978. "Causes and Reasons in Attribution Theory: A Conceptual Critique." *Journal of Personality and Social Psychology* 36: 1311–21.

———. 1979. "On the Relationship Between Causes and Reasons." *Journal of Personality and Social Psychology* 37: 1458–61.

Calabresi, Guido. 1985. *Ideals, Beliefs, Attitudes, and the Law.* Syracuse: Syracuse UP.

Capron, Alexander Morgan, and Leon R. Kass. 1972. "A Statutory Definition of the Standards for Determining Human Death: An Appraisal and a Proposal." *University of Pennsylvania Law Review* 121: 87–118.

Carnap, Rudolf. 1936. "Testability and Meaning." *Philosophy of Science* 3: 419–71.

———. 1937. "Testability and Meaning." *Philosophy of Science* 4: 1–40.

Caron, Rose F., Albert J. Caron, and Rose S. Myers. 1982. "Abstraction of Invariant Face Expressions in Infancy." *Child Development* 53: 1008–15.

Carroll, Noël. 1988. "Art, Practice, and Narrative." *Monist* 71: 140–56.

Cavell, Stanley. 1969. *Must We Mean What We Say?* Cambridge: Cambridge UP.

Cembalest, Robin. 1990. "The Obscenity Trial: How They Voted to Acquit." *Art News* 89 (Dec.): 136–41.

Center for Defense Information. 1988. "Star Wars Reality: The Emperor Has No Clothes." *Defense Monitor* 17: 1–8.

Charo, R. Alta. 1999. "Dusk, Dawn, and Defining Death: Legal Classifications and Biological Categories." In *The Definition of Death: Contemporary Controversies,* edited by Stuart J. Youngner, Robert M. Arnold, and Renie Schapiro, 277–92. Baltimore: Johns Hopkins UP.

Chemerinsky, Erwin. 1982. "Rationalizing the Abortion Debate: Legal Rhetoric and the Abortion Controversy." *Buffalo Law Review* 31: 107–64.

———. 1987. *Interpreting the Constitution.* New York: Praeger.

Chesebro, James W. 1985. "Definition as a Rhetorical Strategy." *Pennsylvania State Communication Annual* 41: 5–15.

Chiesi, H. L., G. J. Spilich, and J. F. Voss. 1979. "Acquisition of Domain-Related Information in Relation to High and Low Domain Knowledge." *Journal of Verbal Learning and Verbal Behavior* 18: 257–73.

Chomsky, Noam. 1965. *Aspects of the Theory of Syntax.* Cambridge: MIT P.

———. 1968. *Language and Mind.* New York: Harcourt.

Clair, Robin Patric. 1993. "The Use of Framing Devices to Sequester Organizational Narratives: Hegemony and Harassment." *Communication Monographs* 60: 113–36.

———. 1996. "The Political Nature of the Colloquialism 'A Real Job': Implications for Organizational Socialization." *Communication Monographs* 63: 249–67.

Clark, Eve V. 1977. "Universal Categories: On the Semantics of Classifiers and Children's Early Word Meanings." In *Linguistic Studies Offered to Joseph Greenberg,* edited by A. Juilland, 449–62. Saratoga, CA: Anma Libri.

———. 1981. "Lexical Innovations: How Children Learn to Create New Words." In *The Child's Construction of Language,* edited by Werner Deutsch, 299–328. New York: Academic.

Cockburn, Alexander. 1986. "Beat the Devil." *Nation* (Jan. 18): 38–39, 52.

Cohen, Leslie B., and Mark S. Strauss. 1979. "Concept Acquisition in the Human Infant." *Child Development* 50: 419–24.

Cohn, C. 1987. "Sex and Death in the Rational World of Defense Intellectuals." *Signs: Journal of Women in Culture and Society* 12: 687–718.

Colen, D. J. 1988. *The ABC's of Armageddon: The Language of the Nuclear Age.* New York: Pharos.

Collingwood, R. G. 1938. *The Principles of Art.* Oxford: Clarendon.

Condit, Celeste Michelle. 1990. *Decoding Abortion Rhetoric: Communicating and Social Change.* Urbana: U of Illinois P.

Coney, C. 1986. "Reagan Snake Oil Not Selling Well on Campus." *Guardian,* May 14, 5.

Connerton, Kelly C. 1997. "The Resurgence of the Marital Rape Exemption: The Victimization of Teens by Their Statutory Rapists." *Albany Law Review* 61: 237–84.

Converse, R. 1975. "But When Did He Die?: *Tucker v. Lower* and the Brain-Death Concept." *San Diego Law Review* 12: 424–35.

Coonan, Helen. 1980. "Rape Law Reform: Proposals for Reforming the Substantive Law." In *Rape Law Reform,* edited by Jocelynne A. Scutt, 37–47. Canberra: Australian Institute of Criminology.

Corrigan, Roberta. 1978. "Language Development as Related to Stage 6 Object Permanence Development." *Journal of Child Language* 5: 173–89.

———. 1989. "Introduction." In *Linguistic Categorization,* edited by Roberta Corrigan, Fred Eckman, and Michael Noonan, 1–28. Philadelphia: John Benjamin.

Cortissoz, Royal. 1913a. *Art and Common Sense.* New York: Scribner's.

———. 1913b. "The Post-Impressionist Illusion." *Century Magazine* 85 (Apr.): 805–15.

Council for a Livable World. 1987. *Recent Public Opinion Findings on Nuclear Arms Control Issues.* Apr. 7. (Press release available from the Council for a Livable World, 100 Maryland Ave., NE, Washington, DC 20002.)

Courtright, Jeffrey L. 1995. "'I Respectfully Dissent': The Ethics of Dissent in Justice O'Connor's *Metro Broadcasting, Inc. v. FCC* Opinion." In *Warranting Assent: Case Studies in Argument Evaluation,* edited by Edward Schiappa, 125–52. Albany: State U of New York P.

Cowardin, L. M., V. Carter, F. C. Golet, and E. T. LaRoe. 1979. *Classification of Wetlands and Deepwater Habitats of the United States.* Washington, DC: U.S. Fish and Wildlife Service.

Cox, J. Robert. 1981. "Argument and the 'Definition of the Situation.'" *Central States Speech Journal* [now *Communication Studies*] 37: 197–205.

Cox, Kenyon. 1913. "The 'Modern' Spirit in Art." *Harper's Weekly* 57 (Mar. 15): 10.

Crain, Stephen, and Diane Lillo-Martin. 1999. *An Introduction to Linguistic Theory and Language Acquisition.* Maldin, MA: Blackwell.

Croce, Benedetto. 1922. *Aesthetic: As Science of Expression and General Linguistic.* 2nd rev. ed. Translated by Douglas Ainslie. New York: Macmillan.

Culver, C. M., and B. Gert. 1982. *Philosophy in Medicine.* Oxford: Oxford UP.

Currie, Bethia S. 1978. "The Redefinition of Death." In *Organism, Medicine, and Metaphysics,* edited by Stuart F. Spicker, 177–97. Dordrecht, The Netherlands: Reidel.

Dahl, Thomas E. 1990. *Wetland Losses in the United States, 1780s to 1980s.* Washington, DC: U.S. Fish and Wildlife Service.

David, Marian A., ed. 1993. "Definitions." *Special Issue of Philosophical Studies* 72: 111–282.

Department of Defense. 1987. *Soviet Military Power.* Washington, DC: GPO.

Deutchman, Iva Ellen. 1985. "Socialization to Power: Questions about Women and Politics." *Women and Politics* 5: 79–91.

Devitt, Michael. 1996. *Realism and Truth.* 2nd ed. Princeton: Princeton UP.

Dickie, George. 1974. *Art and the Aesthetic: An Institutional Analysis.* Ithaca, NY: Cornell UP.

Dieter, O. A. L. 1994. "Stasis." In *Landmark Essays on Classical Greek Rhetoric,* edited by Edward Schiappa, 211–41. Hillsdale, NJ: Erlbaum.

Dionisopoulos, George N., and Richard E. Crable. 1988. "Definitional Hegemony as a Public Relations Strategy: The Rhetoric of the Nuclear Power Industry after Three Mile Island." *Central States Speech Journal* 39: 134–45.

Donohue, George L. 1994. *Star Wars: A Case Study of Marginal Cost Analysis and Weapon System Technology.* Santa Monica: Rand.

Dorling, Daniel. 1997. *Mapping: Ways of Representing the World.* London: Longman.

Dubey, M. 1985. "Deterrence Masks Superpowers Hegemony." *Bulletin of the Atomic Scientists* 41 (Feb.): 28–31.

Duhem, Pierre. [1906] 1954. *The Aim and Structure of Physical Theory.* Translated by Philip P. Wiener. Princeton: Princeton UP.

Dworetzky, Tom. 1992. "Promises, Promises: What Did Bush Say? What Did He Do?" *Omni* 14: 9.

Edelman, Murray. 1977. *Political Language: Words That Succeed and Policies That Fail.* New York: Academic.

Edgar, J. 1988. "Political Miracle in Iceland?" *Ms.* 17 (Aug.): 84.

Eisenstein, Hester. 1983. *Contemporary Feminist Thought.* Boston: Hall.

Eldridge, Richard. 1985. "Form and Content: An Aesthetic Theory of Art." *British Journal of Aesthetics* 25: 303–16.

Elshtain, Jean B. 1981. *Public Man, Private Woman: Women in Social and Political Thought.* Princeton: Princeton UP.

———. 1982. "Feminist Discourse and Its Discontents: Language, Power, and Meaning." *Signs: Journal of Women in Culture and Society* 7: 603–21.

Elwood, William N. 1994. *Rhetoric in the War on Drugs.* Westport, CT: Praeger.

Ely, John Hart. 1973. "The Wages of Crying Wolf: A Comment on *Roe v. Wade.*" *Yale Law Journal* 82: 920–49.

Environmental Defense Fund. 1992. *How Wet Is a Wetland?: The Impact of the Proposed Revisions to the Federal Wetlands Delineation Manual.* New York/Washington, DC: Environmental Defense Fund/World Wildlife Fund.

Environmental Protection Agency (EPA) et al. 1991. "'Federal Manual for Identifying and Delineating Jurisdictional Wetlands'; Proposed Revisions." *Federal Register* 56 (Aug. 14): 404445–80.

Epstein, W. 1986. "New Hope for a Comprehensive Test Ban." *Bulletin of the Atomic Scientists* 42 (Feb.): 29–30.

Estrich, Susan. 1986. "Rape." *Yale Law Journal* 95: 1087–184.

Eubanks, Philip. 2000. *War of Words in the Discourse of Trade: The Rhetorical Constitution of Metaphor.* Carbondale: Southern Illinois UP.

Evernden, J. F., and C. B. Archambeau. 1986. "Some Seismological Aspects of Monitoring a CTBT." In *Arms Control Verification,* edited by K. Tsipis, D. W. Hafemeister, and P. Janeway, 223–63. Washington, DC: Pergamon-Brassey's International Defense.

Fagan, J. F. 1976. "Infants' Recognition of Invariant Features of Faces." *Child Development* 47: 627–38.

Faludi, Susan. 1991. *Backlash: The Undeclared War Against American Women.* New York: Crown.

Farrell, Thomas B., and G. Thomas Goodnight. 1981. "Accidental Rhetoric: The Root Metaphors of Three Mile Island." *Communication Monographs* 48: 271–300.

Faux, Marian. 1988. *Roe v. Wade.* New York: Macmillan.

Federal Interagency Committee for Wetland Delineation. 1989. *Federal Manual for Identifying and Delineating Jurisdictional Wetlands.* Washington, DC: Cooperative Technical Publication.

Feild, Hubert S. 1980. *Jurors and Rape: A Study in Psychology and Law.* Lexington, MA: Heath.

Feinman, Saul, ed. 1992. *Social Referencing and the Social Construction of Reality in Infancy.* New York: Plenum.

Fetzer, James H., David Shatz, and George Schlesinger, eds. 1991. *Definitions and Definability: Philosophical Perspectives.* Dordrecht, The Netherlands: Kluwer.

Fine, Arthur. 1984. "The Natural Ontological Attitude." In *Scientific Realism,* edited by J. Leplin, 83–107. Berkeley: U of California P.

Finnegan, Ruth. 1988. *Orality and Literacy: Studies in the Technology of Communication.* Oxford: Blackwell.

Fisher, D. F. 1984. "Fear." In *Encyclopedia of Psychology,* edited by R. J. Corsini, 2: 11–12. New York: Wiley.

Fodor, Jerry A. 1998. *Concepts.* Oxford: Clarendon.

Fraser, Nancy. 1989. *Unruly Practices: Power, Discourse, and Gender in Contemporary Social Theory.* Minneapolis: U of Minnesota P.

Frye, Marilyn. 1983. *The Politics of Reality.* Freedom, CA: Crossing.

Gallie, W. B. 1964. *Philosophy and the Historical Understanding.* New York: Schocken.

Galtung, J. 1987. "The Real Star Wars Threat." *Nation* (Feb. 28): 248–50.

Garn, J. 1986. "Nuclear Testing and Arms Control." 99th Cong., 2nd sess. *Congressional Record,* May 1, vol. 132: S5240–S5241.

Gerstell, R. 1950. *How to Survive an Atomic Bomb.* Washington, DC: Combat Forces.

Gerstenzang, J. 1986. "U.S. Offers New Plan on A-Tests." *Los Angeles Times,* Mar. 15, 1, 26.

Gervais, K. G. 1986. *Redefining Death.* New Haven: Yale UP.

Gilbert, G. Nigel, and Michael Mulkay. 1984. *Opening Pandora's Box: A Sociological Analysis of Scientists' Discourse.* New York: Cambridge UP.

Gilligan, Carol. 1982. *In a Different Voice: Psychological Theory and Women's Development*. Cambridge: Harvard UP.

Gingrich, Newt. 1986. "Preventing Nuclear Explosive Testing." 99th Cong., 2nd sess. *Congressional Record*, Mar. 3, vol. 132: E572.

Goffman, Erving. 1974. *Frame Analysis: An Essay on the Organization of Experience*. Cambridge: Harvard UP.

Goldwater, Barry. 1986. "Nuclear Testing." 99th Cong., 2nd sess. *Congressional Record*, June 3, vol. 132: S6624-S6625.

Golet, Francis C. 1991. "A Critical Review of the Proposed Revisions to the 1989 Federal Manual for Identifying and Delineating Jurisdictional Wetlands." In *Wetlands Conservation*, by U.S. Congress (1992), 633-60. Washington, DC: GPO.

Goodman, Nelson. 1978. *Ways of Worldmaking*. Indianapolis: Hackett.

Goodnight, G. Thomas. 1982. "The Personal, Technical, and Public Spheres of Argument: A Speculative Inquiry into the Art of Public Deliberation." *Journal of the American Forensic Association* 18: 214-27.

———. 1987. "Public Discourse." *Critical Studies in Mass Communication* 4: 428-32.

Gopnik, Alison, and Soonja Choi. 1990. "Do Linguistic Differences Lead to Cognitive Differences? A Cross-Linguistic Study of Semantic and Cognitive Development." *First Language* 10: 199-215.

Gouran, Dennis S. 1987. "The Failure of Argument in Decisions Leading to the 'Challenger Disaster': A Two Level Analysis." In *Argument and Critical Practices: Proceedings of the Fifth SCA/AFA Conference on Argumentation*, edited by J. W. Wenzel, 439-47. Annandale, VA: SCA.

Gouran, Dennis S., R. Y. Hirokawa, and A. E. Martz. 1986. "A Critical Analysis of Factors Related to Decisional Processes Involved in the *Challenger* Disaster." *Central States Speech Journal* 37: 119-35.

Graesser, Arthur C., and John B. Black. 1985. *The Psychology of Questions*. Hillsdale, NJ: Erlbaum.

Graham, T. W., and B. M. Kramer. 1986. "ABM and Star Wars: Attitudes Toward Nuclear Defense, 1945-85." *Public Opinion Quarterly* 50: 125-34.

Grandy, R. E. 1973. *Theories and Observation in Science*. Englewood Cliffs, NJ: Prentice.

Grant, Judith. 1987. "I Feel Therefore I Am: A Critique of Female Experience as the Basis for a Feminist Epistemology." *Women and Politics* 7: 99-114.

Gray, C. S., and K. Payne. 1980. "Victory Is Possible." *Foreign Policy* 39: 14-27.

Green, M. B., and D. Wikler. 1982. "Brain Death and Personal Identity." In *Medicine and Moral Philosophy*, edited by D. J. Horan and D. Mall, 49-77. Princeton: Princeton UP.

Greene, M. 1982. "Education and Disarmament." *Teacher's College Record* 84: 128-36.

Gregg, Richard B. 1984. *Symbolic Inducement and Knowing*. Columbia: U of South Carolina P.

Grimshaw, Jean. 1986. *Feminist Philosophers: Women's Perspectives on Philosophical Traditions*. Minneapolis: U of Minnesota P.

Gross, Alan G. 1996. *The Rhetoric of Science.* 2nd ed. Cambridge: Harvard UP.

Guldin, B. 1987. "Glasnost Prevails Among Pioneers of Nuclear Monitoring." *Guardian,* Sept. 23, 10–11.

Guthrie, W. K. C. 1971. *Socrates.* Cambridge: Cambridge UP.

Gwertzman, B. 1986. "U.S. Aides Say Hope of Summit Talks in 1986 Is Fading." *New York Times,* Mar. 15, 1, 3.

Hacking, Ian. 1999. *The Social Construction of What?* Cambridge: MIT P.

Hale, Matthew. 1778. *Historia Placitorum Coronae: History of the Pleas of the Crown.* Edited by Sollom Emlyn. London: Payne.

Hanson, Norwood Russell. 1958. *Patterns of Discovery.* Cambridge: Cambridge UP.

Harnad, Stevan. 1987. *Categorical Perception.* Cambridge: Cambridge UP.

Harré, Rom. 1986. *Varieties of Realism.* Oxford: Blackwell.

Harris, L. 1983. "'Star Wars' Proposal Backfires on Reagan." *Harris Survey* (Apr. 14): 1–3.

———. 1985. "Public Opposed Star Wars Defense by 56 to 39 Percent." *Harris Survey* (Mar. 11): 1–3.

Harris, William V. 1989. *Ancient Literacy.* Cambridge: Harvard UP.

Hart, Alan. 1983. *Spinoza's Ethics: Part I and II.* Leiden: Brill.

Hartsock, Nancy C. M. 1983. *Money, Sex, and Power: Toward a Feminist Historical Materialism.* New York: Longman.

Havelock, Eric A. 1963. *Preface to Plato.* Cambridge: Harvard UP.

———. 1978. *The Greek Concept of Justice.* Cambridge: Harvard UP.

Heffernan, James M. 1975. "An Analytical Framework for Planning and Research in Higher Education." *Liberal Education* 61: 493–503.

Hempel, Carl. 1965. *Aspects of Scientific Explanation.* New York: Free.

Hesse, Mary. 1974. *The Structure of Scientific Inference.* Berkeley: U of California P.

Heylin, M. 1985. "Nuclear Strikes." *Chemical and Engineering News* (June 10): 3.

Hilgartner, S., R. C. Bell, and R. O'Connor. 1982. *Nukespeak: Nuclear Language, Visions, and Mindset.* San Francisco: Sierra Club.

Hilts, Philip J. 1991. "U.S. Aides Retreat on Wetlands Rule." *New York Times,* Nov. 23, A1, A10.

Hoffman, D. 1985. "Reagan's Handling of Foreign Policy Gets High Marks." *Washington Post National Weekly Edition,* Nov. 11, 37.

Hook, G. D. 1985. "Making Nuclear Weapons Easier to Live With: The Political Role of Language in Nuclearization." *Bulletin of Peace Proposals* 16: 67–77.

Hull, D. L. 1973. "Charles Darwin and Nineteenth-Century Philosophies of Science." In *Foundations of Scientific Method: The Nineteenth Century,* edited by R. N. Giere and R. S. Westfall, 115–32. Bloomington: U of Indiana P.

Humphrey, D., and A. Wickett. 1986. *The Right to Die.* New York: Harper.

Hyde, Michael J. 1980. "The Experience of Anxiety: A Phenomenological Investigation." *Quarterly Journal of Speech* 66: 140–54.

Ice, R. 1987. "Presumption as Problematic in Group Decision Making: The Case of the Space Shuttle." In *Argument and Critical Practices: Proceedings of the*

Fifth SCA/AFA Conference on Argumentation, edited by J. W. Wenzel, 411–18. Annandale, VA: SCA.

Ignatius, David. 1986. "Maybe the Media Did Push NASA to Launch *Challenger.*" *Washington Post National Weekly Edition,* Apr. 14, 19–20.

Iyengar, Shanto. 1991. *Is Anyone Responsible?: How Television Frames Political Issues.* Chicago: U of Chicago P.

James, William. [1890] 1981. *The Principles of Psychology.* Cambridge: Harvard UP.

Jamieson, Kathleen Hall. 1988. *Eloquence in an Electronic Age: The Transformation of Political Speechmaking.* New York: Oxford UP.

Janeway, Elizabeth. 1971. *Man's World, Woman's Place: A Study in Social Mythology.* New York: Morris.

Jaquette, Jane S. 1984. "Power as Ideology: A Feminist Analysis." In *Women's Views of the Political World of Men,* edited by J. H. Stiehm, 7–30. Dobbs Ferry, NY: Transnational.

Jay, N. 1981. "Gender and Dichotomy." *Feminist Studies* 7: 38–56.

Johnstone, Henry W., Jr. 1978. *Categories: A Colloquium.* University Park: Pennsylvania State UP.

Kahn, Charles H. 1973. *The Verb "Be" and Its Synonyms: Vol. 6, The Verb "Be" in Ancient Greek.* Dordrecht, The Netherlands: Reidel.

Kahn, Herman. 1965. *On Escalation: Metaphors and Scenarios.* New York: Praeger.

Kamhi, Alan G. 1982. "Overextensions and Underextensions: How Different Are They?" *Journal of Child Language* 9: 243–47.

Kant, Immanuel. [1787] 1965. *The Critique of Pure Reason.* 2nd ed. Translated by N. Kemp Smith. New York: St. Martin's.

Kathlene, Lyn. 1995. "Alternative Views of Crime: Legislative Policymaking in Gendered Terms." *Journal of Politics* 57: 696–723.

Kauffman, C. 1989. "Names and Weapons." *Communication Monographs* 56: 273–85.

Keil, Frank C. 1989. *Concepts, Kinds, and Cognitive Development.* Cambridge: MIT P.

Kekes, John. 1977. "Essentially Contested Concepts: A Reconsideration." *Philosophy and Rhetoric* 10: 71–89.

Kennedy, George A. 1991. *Aristotle, on Rhetoric: A Theory of Civic Discourse.* New York: Oxford UP.

Kerferd, George B. 1954. "The 'Relativism' of Prodicus." *Bulletin of the John Rylands Library* 37: 249–56.

———. 1981. *The Sophistic Movement.* Cambridge: Cambridge UP.

Kerr, D. M. 1986. "Statement Before the Senate Armed Services Committee." 99th Cong., 2nd sess. *Congressional Record,* June 3, vol. 132: S6625–S6628.

King, Geoff. 1996. *Mapping Reality: An Exploration of Cultural Cartography.* London: Macmillan.

Koons, Robert C. 2000. *Realism Regained.* New York: Oxford UP.

Kripke, Saul A. 1980. *Naming and Necessity.* Cambridge: Harvard UP.

Kuhn, Thomas S. 1963. "The Function of Dogma in Scientific Research." In *Scientific Change,* edited by A. C. Crombie, 347–69. London: Heineman.

———. 1970. *The Structure of Scientific Revolutions.* 2nd ed. Chicago: U of Chicago P.

———. 1977. *The Essential Tension.* Chicago: U of Chicago P.

———. 1983. "Commensurability, Comparability, Communicability." In *PSA 1982* [proceedings of the biennial meeting of the Philosophy of Science Association], edited by P. D. Asquith and T. Nickles, 669–88. East Lansing: Philosophy of Science Association.

———. 1989. "Possible Worlds in History of Science." In *Possible Worlds in Humanities, Arts and Sciences,* edited by Sture Allen, 9–32. Berlin: de Gruyter.

———. 1990. "Dubbing and Redubbing: The Vulnerability of Rigid Designation." *Minnesota Studies in the Philosophy of Science* 14: 298–318.

———. 2000. *The Road Since Structure.* Chicago: U of Chicago P.

Kurland, Philip B., and Gerhard Casper. 1975. *Landmark Briefs and Arguments of the Supreme Court of the United States: Constitutional Law.* Vol. 75. Arlington, VA: University Publications of America.

Lakoff, George. 1987. *Women, Fire, and Dangerous Things: What Categories Reveal about the Mind.* Chicago: U of Chicago P.

Lakoff, George, and Mark Johnson. 1980. *Metaphors We Live By.* Chicago: U of Chicago P.

Lamb, David. 1985. *Death, Brain Death, and Ethics.* Albany: State U of New York P.

Latour, Bruno, and Steve Woolgar. 1979. *Laboratory Life: The Social Construction of Scientific Facts.* Beverly Hills: Sage.

Le Blond, J. M. 1979. "Aristotle on Definition." In *Articles on Aristotle,* edited by J. Barnes, M. Schofield, and Richard Sorabji, 3: 63–79. New York: St. Martin's.

Lemonick, Michael D. 1991. "War over the Wetlands." *Time,* Aug. 26, 53.

Levinson, Jerrold. 1979. "Defining Art Historically." *British Journal of Aesthetics* 19: 232–50.

———. 1989. "Refining Art Historically." *Journal of Aesthetics and Art Criticism* 47: 21–33.

Lewis, David. 1970. "How to Define Theoretical Terms." *Journal of Philosophy* 67: 427–46.

Lifton, R. J., and R. Falk. 1982. *Indefensible Weapons.* New York: Basic.

Litowitz, Bonnie. 1977. "Learning to Make Definitions." *Journal of Child Language* 4: 289–304.

Longino, Helen E. 1990. *Science as Social Knowledge.* Princeton: Princeton UP.

Lucy, John A., and James V. Wertsch. 1987. "Vygotsky and Whorf: A Comparative Analysis." In *Social and Functional Approaches to Language and Thought,* edited by Maya Hickman, 67–86. Orlando: Academic.

Luria, Aleksandr R. 1976. *Cognitive Development: Its Cultural and Social Foundations.* Translated by M. Lopez-Morillas and L. Solotaroff. Cambridge: Harvard UP.

MacIntyre, Alasdair. 1967. "Ontology." In *The Encyclopedia of Philosophy,* edited by Paul Edwards, 5: 542–43. New York: Macmillan.

MacKinnon, Catherine A. 1979. *Sexual Harassment of Working Women.* New Haven: Yale UP.

Macklin, Ruth. 1984. "Personhood and the Abortion Debate." In *Abortion: Moral and Legal Perspectives,* edited by Jay L. Garfield and Patricia Hennessey, 87–102. Amherst: U of Massachusetts P.

MacNamara, J. 1972. "Cognitive Basis of Language Learning in Infants." *Psychological Review* 79: 1–13.

Marchant, E. C. 1923. *Xenophon.* Vol. 4. Cambridge: Harvard UP.

Margolis, Joseph. 1986. *Pragmatism Without Foundations: Reconciling Realism and Relativism.* Oxford: Blackwell.

Marsh, Jeanne C., Alison Geist, and Nathan Caplan. 1982. *Rape and the Limits of Law Reform.* Boston: Auburn.

Matthews, Alexander. 1998. *A Diagram of Definition: The Defining of Definition.* Assen, The Netherlands: Van Gorcum.

McGee, Brian R. 1999. "The Argument from Definition Revisited: Race and Definition in the Progressive Era." *Argumentation and Advocacy* 35: 141–58.

McGhee-Bidlack, Betty. 1991. "The Development of Noun Definitions: A Metalinguistic Analysis." *Journal of Child Language* 18: 417–34.

McKerrow, Raymie. 1989. "Critical Rhetoric: Theory and Praxis." *Communication Monographs* 56: 91–111.

McLean, Scilla. 1986. *How Nuclear Weapons Decisions Are Made.* London: Macmillan.

Merriman, William E., Joneen M. Schuster, and LaurieBeth Hager. 1991. "Are Names Ever Mapped onto Preexisting Categories?" *Journal of Experimental Psychology* 120: 288–300.

Mervis, Carolyn B., and John R. Pani. 1980. "Acquisition of Basic Object Categories." *Cognitive Psychology* 12: 496–522.

Mervis, Carolyn B., and Eleanor Rosch. 1981. "Categorization of Natural Objects." *Annual Review of Psychology* 32: 89–115.

Meyerding, J. 1982. "Reclaiming Nonviolence." In *Reweaving the Web of Life: Feminism and Nonviolence,* edited by Pam McAllister, 5–15. Philadelphia: New Society.

Miller, George A., and Patricia M. Gildea. 1987. "How Children Learn Words." *Scientific American* 257.3: 94–99.

Mills, C. Wright. 1940. "Situated Actions and Vocabularies of Motive." *American Sociological Review* 5: 904–13.

Mitchell, Gordon R. 2000. *Strategic Deception: Rhetoric, Science, and Politics in Missile Defense Advocacy.* East Lansing: Michigan State UP.

Monmonier, Mark. 1991. *How to Lie with Maps.* Chicago: U of Chicago P.

Moody, E. A. 1967. "William of Ockham." In *The Encyclopedia of Philosophy,* edited by Paul Edwards, 8: 306–17. New York: Macmillan.

Moore, G. E. 1903. *Principia Ethica.* Cambridge: Cambridge UP.

Moores, Lew. 1990. "Rally Against Mapplethorpe Trial." *Cincinnati Enquirer,* Oct. 5, 1.

Morgan, Douglas N. 1961. "Art Pure and Simple." *Journal of Aesthetics and Art Criticism* 20: 187–95.

Mothersill, Mary. 1961. "Critical Comments." *Journal of Aesthetics and Art Criticism* 20: 195–98.

Mulkay, Michael. 1979. *Science and the Sociology of Knowledge.* London: Allen.

Musil, R. K. 1983. "On Calling a Bomb a Bomb." *Nuclear Times* (Mar.): 26–28.

Nash, H. T. 1980. "The Bureaucratization of Homicide." *Bulletin of the Atomic Scientists* 36 (Apr.): 22–27.

Nathan, O., and H. Norden. 1960. *Einstein on Peace.* New York: Simon.

National Wildlife Federation. 1991. *Proposed Revisions to Federal Wetlands Manual* [press release]. Washington, DC: National Wildlife Federation.

Nelson, K. 1974. "Concept, Word, and Sentence: Interrelations in Acquisition and Development." *Psychological Review* 81: 267–85.

Ninio, Anat, and Jerome Bruner. 1978. "The Achievement and Antecedents of Labelling." *Journal of Child Language* 5: 1–15.

Nippold, Marilyn A. 1988. "The Literate Lexicon." In *Later Language Development: Ages 9 through 19,* edited by Marilyn A. Nippold, 29–47. Austin, TX: Pro-Ed.

Noonan, John T. 1984. "The Root and Branch of *Roe v. Wade.*" *Nebraska Law Review* 63: 668–79.

Norris, Christopher. 1997. *Resources of Realism.* New York: St. Martin's.

O'Connor, Justice Sandra Day. 1983. *Dissenting Opinion, Akron v. Akron Center for Reproductive Health,* 462 U.S. 452–75.

———. 1992. *Opinion of the Court, Planned Parenthood of Southeastern Pennsylvania et al. v. Robert P. Casey et al.,* 505 U.S. 833, 843–901.

Office of Technology Assessment. 1985. *Ballistic Missile Defense Technologies.* Washington, DC: GPO.

Official Transcript: Proceedings Before the Supreme Court of the United States. 1992. Washington, DC: Alderson Reporting.

Olsen, Frances. 1989. "Unraveling Compromise." *Harvard Law Review* 103: 105–35.

Oral Argument. 2001. *Transcript of the Oral Argument Before the Supreme Court in PGA Tour, Inc. v. Casey Martin, January 17, 2001.* Available online at: www.supremecourtus.gov/oral_arguments/argument_transcripts/00-24.pdf.

Paine, C. 1985. "The Low Road to Arms Control." *Bulletin of the Atomic Scientists* 41 (Dec.): 6–7.

"Papers Chastise Bush's Wetland Proposal." 1991. *Daily Collegian* [Pennsylvania State U], Nov. 22, 7.

Park, R. E. 1972. *The Crowd and the Public.* Chicago: U of Chicago P.

Paugh, Tom. 1988. "Sports Afield and the Candidates." *Sports Afield* (Oct.): 13–17.

Peckham, Morse. 1969. *Art and Pornography: An Experiment in Explanation.* New York: Harper.

Peetz, Dieter. 1987. "On Attempting to Define Abstract Art." In *Philosophy and the Visual Arts,* edited by Andrew Harrison, 135–45. Dordrecht, The Netherlands: Reidel.

Perelman, Chaïm, and Lucie Olbrechts-Tyteca. 1969. *The New Rhetoric: A Treatise on Argumentation.* Translated by J. Wilkinson and P. Weaver. Notre

Dame: Notre Dame UP. Original edition, *La Nouvelle Rhétorique: Traité de l'Argumentation*. Paris: Presses Universitaires de France, 1958.

Perry, William G. 1970. *Forms of Intellectual and Ethical Development in the College Years*. New York: Holt.

Phillips, Derek L. 1977. *Wittgenstein and Scientific Knowledge*. Totowa, NJ: Rowman.

Polanyi, Michael. 1958. *Personal Knowledge*. Chicago: U of Chicago P.

"Policy Regarding Limitations on Nuclear Testing." 1986. *Department of State Bulletin* 86 (Oct.): 14–18.

Poole, R. 1985. "Morality, Masculinity and the Market." *Radical Philosophy* 39: 16–23.

Pope, Carl. 1991. "That Question of Balance." *Sierra*, Nov./Dec., 22–23.

Posner, Richard. 1999. *The Problematics of Moral and Legal Theory*. Cambridge: Harvard UP.

Putnam, Hilary. 1981. *Reason, Truth, and History*. Cambridge: Cambridge UP.

———. 1990. *Realism with a Human Face*. Cambridge: Harvard UP.

Queneau, Raymond. 1981. *Exercises in Style*. Translated by Barbara Wright. London: John Calder. Original edition, *Exercises de Style*. Paris: Editions Gallimard, 1947.

Quine, Willard V. O. 1960. *Word and Object*. Cambridge: MIT P.

———. 1969. *Ontological Relativity and Other Essays*. New York: Columbia UP.

———. 1980. *From a Logical Point of View*. 2nd ed. Cambridge: Harvard UP.

"Rape." 1918. *Ruling Case Law*. Northport, NY: Thompson.

———. 1992. *American Jurisprudence*. 2nd ed. Vol. 65 [cumulative supplement], 88–149. Rochester, NY: Lawyers Cooperative.

"Rape and Battery Between Husband and Wife." 1954. *Stanford Law Review* 6: 719–28.

Reagan, Ronald. 1983a. "National Security." *Weekly Compilation of Presidential Documents* 19: 442–48.

———. 1983b. "Foreign Issues: Responses to Questions Submitted by *Bunte* Magazine." *Weekly Compilation of Presidential Documents* 19: 683–89.

———. 1985a. "The State of the Union." *Weekly Compilation of Presidential Documents* 21: 140–46.

———. 1985b. "Domestic and Foreign Issues." *Weekly Compilation of Presidential Documents* 21: 150–56.

———. 1985c. "Strategic Defense Initiative [radio address]." *Weekly Compilation of Presidential Documents* 21: 901–2.

———. 1985d. "Address Before the 40th Session of the General Assembly." *Weekly Compilation of Presidential Documents* 21: 1291–96.

———. 1985e. "United States–Soviet Summit in Geneva [radio address]." *Weekly Compilation of Presidential Documents* 21: 1375–77.

———. 1985f. "United States–Soviet Summit in Geneva." *Weekly Compilation of Presidential Documents* 21: 1382–87.

———. 1986a. "The State of the Union." *Weekly Compilation of Presidential Documents* 22: 135–40.

———. 1986b. "Nuclear Testing Limitations." *Weekly Compilation of Presidential Documents* 22: 364–65.

———. 1986c. "Remarks to the Graduating Class of Glassboro High School." *Weekly Compilation of Presidential Documents* 22: 835–40.

———. 1986d. "Meeting with Soviet General Secretary Gorbachev in Reykjavik, Iceland." *Weekly Compilation of Presidential Documents* 22: 1375–79.

———. 1986e. "Soviet Union–United States Nuclear and Space Arms Negotiations." *Weekly Compilation of Presidential Documents* 22: 1555–56.

———. 1987a. "The State of the Union." *Weekly Compilation of Presidential Documents* 23: 59–65.

———. 1987b. "Responses to Questions Submitted by *Izvestiya* of the Soviet Union." *Weekly Compilation of Presidential Documents* 23: 1441–45.

———. 1988a. "Remarks at the Dedication Ceremony for the Knute Rockne Commemorative Stamp at the University of Notre Dame, Indiana." *Weekly Compilation of Presidential Documents* 24: 313–19.

———. 1988b. "Remarks to Members of the Institute for Foreign Policy Analysis During a Conference on the Strategic Defense Initiative." *Weekly Compilation of Presidential Documents* 24: 340–43.

———. 1988c. "Statement on the Strategic Defense Initiative." *Weekly Compilation of Presidential Documents* 24: 381–82.

———. 1988d. "The President's News Conference at the Close of the Soviet–United States Summit in Moscow." *Weekly Compilation of Presidential Documents* 24: 725–32.

———. 1988e. "Address Before the 43d Session of the United Nations General Assembly." *Weekly Compilation of Presidential Documents* 24: 1205–12.

"Reagan Gives Nuclear Plan to Soviets." 1986. *Rocky Mountain News,* Mar. 15, 3.

"Reagan Offers Nuclear Test Plan." 1986. *Kansas City Times,* Mar. 15, 1.

"Reagan Sends Soviet Leader Plan to Detect Nuclear Blasts." 1986. *Denver Post,* Mar. 15, 3A.

Reichenbach, Hans. 1953. "The Verifiability Theory of Meaning." In *Readings in the Philosophy of Science,* edited by Herbert Feigl and May Brodbeck, 93–102. New York: Appleton.

Report of the Presidential Commission on the Space Shuttle "Challenger" Accident. 1986. Washington, DC: GPO.

Rescher, Nicholas. 1977. *Dialectics: A Controversy-Oriented Approach to the Theory of Knowledge.* Albany: State U of New York P.

———. 1987. *Scientific Realism: A Critical Reappraisal.* Dordrecht, The Netherlands: Reidel.

Rice, Mabel. 1984. "Cognitive Aspects of Communicative Development." In *The Acquisition of Communicative Competence,* edited by Richard L. Schiefelbusch, 141–89. Baltimore: University Park.

Richards. Janet. 1982. *The Skeptical Feminist.* London: Penguin.

Roberts, Kenneth, and Frances Degen Horowitz. 1986. "Basic Level Categorization in Seven- and Nine-Month-Old Infants." *Journal of Child Language* 13: 191–208.

Robinson, Richard. 1950. *Definition.* Oxford: Clarendon.

———. 1953. *Plato's Earlier Dialectic.* 2nd ed. Oxford: Clarendon.

Robinson, W. V. 1986. "Reagan Offers Soviets New System to Monitor Underground Arms Tests." *Boston Globe,* Mar. 15, 1, 12.

Rochefort, David A., and Roger C. Cobb. 1994. "Problem Definition: An Emerging Perspective." In *The Politics of Problem Definition: Shaping the Public Agenda,* edited by D. A. Rochefort and R. C. Cobb, 1–31. Lawrence: UP of Kansas.

Romanos, George D. 1983. *Quine and Analytic Philosophy.* Cambridge: MIT P.

Rorty, Richard. 1979. *Philosophy and the Mirror of Nature.* Princeton: Princeton UP.

———. 1989. *Contingency, Irony, and Solidarity.* Cambridge: Cambridge UP.

———. 1991. *Objectivity, Relativism, and Truth: Philosophical Papers, Volume 1.* Cambridge: Cambridge UP.

———. 1999. *Philosophy and Social Hope.* London: Penguin.

———, ed. 1967. *The Linguistic Turn.* Chicago: U of Chicago P.

Rosaldo, Michelle Zimbalist. 1974. *Woman, Culture, and Society.* Stanford: Stanford UP.

———. 1980. "The Use and Abuse of Anthropology: Reflections on Feminism and Crosscultural Understanding." *Signs: Journal of Women in Culture and Society* 5: 389–417.

Rosch, Eleanor. 1973. "On the Internal Structure of Perceptual and Semantic Categories." In *Cognitive Development and the Acquisition of Language,* edited by T. E. Moore, 111–44. New York: Academic.

———. 1974. "Linguistic Relativity." In *Human Communication: Theoretical Explorations,* edited by A. Silverstein, 95–121. Hillsdale, NJ: Erlbaum.

———. 1975. "Universals and Cultural Specifics in Human Categorization." In *Cross-Cultural Perspectives on Learning,* edited by R. Brislin, S. Bochner, and W. Lonner, 177–206. New York: Halstead.

———. 1988. "Coherences and Categorization: A Historical View." In *The Development of Language and Language Researchers,* edited by Frank S. Kessell, 373–92. Hillsdale, NJ: Erlbaum.

Rosen, Jeffrey. 2001. "The O'Connor Court." *New York Times Magazine,* June 3, 32.

Rosenberg, Harold. 1972. *The De-definition of Art.* New York: Horizon.

Rowe, M. W. 1991. "The Definition of Art." *Philosophical Quarterly* 41: 271–86.

Rowland, Robert C. 1986. "The Relationship Between the Public and the Technical Spheres of Argument: A Case Study of the *Challenger Seven* Disaster." *Central States Speech Journal* 37: 136–46.

Rowny, E. L. 1988. "Hard Work Ahead in Arms Control." *Department of State Bulletin* 88 (Jan.): 20–22.

Ruddick, Sara. 1984. "Preservative Love and Military Destruction: Some Reflections on Mothering and Peace." In *Mothering: Essays in Feminist Theory,* edited by Joyce Trebilcot, 213–63. Totowa, NJ: Rowman.

Russell, Bertrand. 1921. *The Analysis of Mind.* London: Allen.

Russell, Diana E. H. 1982. *Rape in Marriage.* New York: Macmillan.

Ryan, Rebecca M. 1995. "The Sex Right: A Legal History of the Marital Rape Exemption." *Law and Social Inquiry* 20: 941–99.

Saad, Lydia. 1992. "Bush Stance on Environment Unpopular." *Gallup Poll News Service,* June 10, 1–2.

Safire, William. 2001. "Compassion: In Which Justice Scalia Rises to a Linguistic Challenge." *New York Times Magazine,* July 15, 22–24.

Sagal, Paul T. 1973. "Implicit Definition." *Monist* 57: 443–50.

Sagan, Carl. 1983. "To Preserve a World Graced by Life." *Bulletin of the Atomic Scientists* 39 (Jan.): 2–3.

Sallmann, Peter A. 1980. "Rape in Marriage and the South Australian Law." In *Rape Law Reform,* edited by Jocelynne A. Scutt, 79–86. Canberra: Australian Institute of Criminology.

Sapir, J. D., and J. C. Crocker. 1977. *The Social Use of Metaphor: Essays on the Anthropology of Rhetoric.* Philadelphia: U of Pennsylvania P.

Sayers, Sean. 1985. *Reality and Reason.* Oxford: Blackwell.

Scalia, Justice Antonin. 1989. *Concurring Opinion in Webster v. Reproductive Health Services,* 492 U.S. 532–37.

———. 1997. *A Matter of Interpretation.* Princeton: Princeton UP.

———. 2001. *Dissenting Opinion, PGA Tour, Inc. v. Martin,* 532 U.S., slip opinion.

Schön, Donald A., and Martin Rein. 1994. *Frame Reflection: Toward the Resolution of Intractable Policy Controversies.* New York: Basic.

Schrag, Calvin O. 1980. *Radical Reflection and the Origin of the Human Sciences.* West Lafayette: Purdue UP.

Schutz, Alfred, and Thomas Luckmann. 1973. *The Structures of the Lifeworld.* Translated by R. M. Zaner and H. T. Englehardt. Evanston: Northwestern UP.

Schwarze, Steve. 2002. "Rhetorical Traction: Definitions, Institutional Arguments, and Hegemony in Judicial Rhetoric about Wilderness Access." *Argumentation and Advocacy* 38: 131–50.

Scinto, Leonard F. M. 1986. *Written Language and Psychological Development.* Orlando: Academic.

Searle, John R. 1969. *Speech Acts.* Cambridge: Cambridge UP.

———. 1995. *The Construction of Social Reality.* New York: Free.

Sederberg, Peter C. 1984. *The Politics of Meaning: Power and Explanation in the Construction of Social Reality.* Tucson: U of Arizona P.

Seligmann, Jean. 1991. "What on Earth Is a Wetland?" *Newsweek,* Aug. 26, 48–49.

Semler, E. 1987. *The Language of Nuclear War: An Intelligent Citizen's Dictionary.* New York: Perennial Library.

Senft, Gunter, ed. 2000. *Systems of Nominal Classification.* Cambridge: Cambridge UP.

Sera, Maria D., Eric L. Reittinger, and Javier del Castillo Pintado. 1991. "Developing Definitions of Objects and Events in English and Spanish Speakers." *Cognitive Development* 6: 119–42.

Shenfield, S. 1985. "Assertive and Reactive Threats." In *Avoiding Nuclear War,* edited by S. Windass, 63–76. London: Brassey's Defence.

Siebert, Mark, and Lew Moores. 1990. "Lewd, but Art, Jurors Say." *Cincinnati Enquirer,* Oct. 7, 1.

Silberstang, Edwin. 1972. "Rape." In *American Jurisprudence,* 2nd ed. Vol. 65, 757–838. Rochester: Lawyers Cooperative.

Skinner, B. F. 1957. *Verbal Behavior.* New York: Appleton.

Smith, Mary M., Peter E. Morris, Philip Levy, and Andrew W. Ellis. 1987. *Cognition in Action.* Hillsdale, NJ: Erlbaum.

Smith, Michael D. 1988. "The Meaning of Reference in Emergent Lexicons." In *The Emergent Lexicon: The Child's Development of a Linguistic Vocabulary,* edited by M. D. Smith and J. L. Locke, 23–48. New York: Academic.

Smith, S. 1987. "SDI and the New Cold War." In *The Cold War Past and Present,* edited by R. Crockatt and S. Smith, 149–70. London: Allen.

Spinoza, Benedict. 1927. *Ethics.* Translated by W. H. White and A. H. Stirling. Oxford: Clarendon.

Spivak, Gayatri C. 1988. *In Other Worlds: Essays in Cultural Politics.* New York: Routledge.

Sprague, Rosamon Kent, ed. 1972. *The Older Sophists.* Columbia: U of South Carolina P.

Stam, James H. 1980. "An Historical Perspective on 'Linguistic Relativity.'" In *Psychology of Language and Thought,* edited by R. W. Rieber, 239–62. New York: Plenum.

Stecker, Robert. 1986. "The End of an Institutional Definition of Art." *British Journal of Aesthetics* 26: 124–32.

———. 1990. "The Boundaries of Art." *British Journal of Aesthetics* 30: 266–72.

Stevens, Justice John Paul. 1992. *Concurring and Dissenting Opinion, Planned Parenthood of Southeastern Pennsylvania et al. v. Robert P. Casey et al.,* 505 U.S. 833, 911–22.

———. 2001. *Opinion of the Court, PGA Tour, Inc. v. Martin,* 532 U.S., slip opinion.

Stevenson, Charles L. 1944. *Ethics and Language.* New Haven: Yale UP.

Stiehm, Judith Hicks. 1984. "The Man Question." In *Women's Views of the Political World of Men,* edited by Judith Hicks Stiehm, 205–24. Dobbs Ferry, NY: Transnational.

Street, Brian V. 1984. *Literacy in Theory and Practice.* Cambridge: Cambridge UP.

Sullivan, Patricia, and Steven R. Goldzwig. 1995. "A Relational Approach to Moral Decision-Making: The Majority Opinion in *Planned Parenthood v. Casey.*" *Quarterly Journal of Speech* 81: 167–90.

Tabak, F. 1984. "Women and Authoritarian Regimes." In *Women's Views of the Political World of Men,* edited by Judith Hicks Stiehm, 99–120. Dobbs Ferry, NY: Transnational.

Tatarkiewicz, Wladyslaw. 1971. "What Is Art? The Problem of Definition Today." *British Journal of Aesthetics* 11: 134–53.

Thomas, Rosalind. 1989. *Oral Tradition and Written Record in Classical Athens.* Cambridge: Cambridge UP.

Thomma, Steven. 2001. "Reagan, Bush Have Plenty in Common." *Saint Paul Pioneer Press,* Feb. 11, 1A, 19A.

Thomson, J. C. 1973. "How Could Vietnam Happen? An Autopsy." In *At Issue: Politics in the World Arena,* edited by S. L. Spiegel, 270–80. New York: St. Martin's.

Tilghman, Benjamin R. 1984. *But Is It Art? The Value of Art and the Temptation of Theory.* New York: Blackwell.

Titsworth, B. S. 1999. "An Ideological Basis for Definition in Public Argument: A Case Study of the Individuals with Disabilities in Education Act." *Argumentation and Advocacy* 35: 171–84.

Tjaden, Patricia, and Nancy Thoennes. 1998. "Prevalence, Incidence, and Consequences of Violence Against Women: Findings from the National Violence Against Women Survey." In *National Institute of Justice/Centers for Disease Control and Prevention: Research in Brief.* Washington, DC: U.S. Department of Justice, Office of Justice Programs, National Institute of Justice.

"To Have and to Hold: The Marital Rape Exemption and the Fourteenth Amendment." 1986. *Harvard Law Review* 99: 1255–73.

Tollhurst, William. 1984. "Toward an Aesthetic Account of the Nature of Art." *British Journal of Aesthetics* 30: 261–69.

Tolstoy, Leo N. 1930. *"What Is Art?" and "Essays on Art."* Translated by Aylmer Maude. London: Oxford UP.

Totten, S. 1984. "Orwellian Language in the Nuclear Age." *Curriculum Review* 23: 43–46.

Toulmin, Stephen. 1958. *The Uses of Argument.* Cambridge: Cambridge UP.

———. 1970. "Reasons and Causes." In *Explanation in the Behavioural Sciences,* edited by Robert Borger and Frank Cioffi, 126. Cambridge: Cambridge UP.

———. 1988. "The Recovery of Practical Philosophy." *American Scholar* 57: 337–52.

Treloar, Carol. 1980. "The Politics of Rape: A Politician's Perspective." In *Rape Law Reform,* edited by Jocelynne A. Scutt, 191–98. Canberra: Australian Institute of Criminology.

Tribe, Laurence H. 1992. *Abortion: The Clash of Absolutes.* Rev. ed. New York: Norton.

Trigg, Robert. 1980. *Reality at Risk.* Totowa, NJ: Barne.

Tripp, James T. B. 1991. "Comments of the Environmental Defense Fund on National Wetlands Issues." In *Wetlands Conservation,* by U.S. Congress (1992), 194–208. Washington, DC: GPO.

Tronto, Joan C. 1987. "Political Science and Caring." *Women and Politics* 7: 85–98.

Turner, E. G. 1977. *Athenian Books in the Fifth and Fourth Centuries B.C.* 2nd ed. London: Lewis.

Tyler, S. A. 1969. *Cognitive Anthropology.* New York: Holt.

Tyner, Judith A. 1982. "Persuasive Cartography." *Journal of Geography* 81: 140–44.

Union of Concerned Scientists. 1986. *Empty Promise: The Growing Case Against Star Wars.* Boston: Beacon.

"U.S. Conducts Test of Nuclear Device." 1986. *New York Times,* Mar. 23, 2.

U.S. Congress. 1957. *The Nature of Radioactive Fallout and Its Effects on Man.* Joint Committee on Atomic Energy, 85th Cong., 1st sess. Washington, DC: GPO.

———. 1979. *Health Effects of Low-Level Radiation.* House Subcommittee on Oversight and Investigations of the Committee on Interstate and Foreign Commerce, and Senate Health and Scientific Research Subcommittee of the Labor and Human Resources Committee, and Senate Committee on the Judiciary. Diary of Gordon Dean, entry date May 27, 1953, 99th Cong., 1st sess. Washington, DC: GPO.

———. 1989. *Wetlands Conservation.* Hearings Before the Subcommittee on Fisheries and Wildlife Conservation and the Environment of the Committee on Merchant Marine and Fisheries, House of Representatives, May 17, 1989. Serial No. 101–16. Washington, DC: GPO.

———. 1992. *Wetlands Conservation.* Hearings Before the Subcommittee on Fisheries and Wildlife Conservation and the Environment of the Committee on Merchant Marine and Fisheries, House of Representatives, Oct. 16, 1991, and Nov. 21, 1991. Serial No. 102–50. Washington, DC: GPO.

U.S. Department of the Interior. 1990. *Wetlands: Meeting the President's Challenge.* Washington, DC: U.S. Fish and Wildlife Service.

"U.S. Policy Regarding Limitations on Nuclear Testing." 1986. *Department of State Bulletin* 86 (Oct.): 14–18.

Van Cleave, W. R., and S. T. Cohen. 1987. *Nuclear Weapons, Policies, and the Test Ban Issue.* New York: Praeger.

Vaughan, Diane. 1996. *The "Challenger" Launch Decision.* Chicago: U of Chicago P.

Veatch, Robert M. 1989. *Death, Dying, and the Biological Revolution.* Rev. ed. New Haven: Yale UP.

Veith, Frank J., et al. 1977. "Brain Death: A Status Report of Medical and Ethical Considerations." *Journal of the American Medical Association* 238: 1651–55.

Vervenne, Dirk, and Dani De Waele. 1985. "Some Remarks on the Construction of Definitions in the Day-to-Day Working of a Laboratory." In *Logic of Discovery and Logic of Discourse,* edited by Jaakko Hintikka and Fernand Vandamme, 123–43. New York: Plenum.

Waller, D. C., and J. T. Bruce. 1987. "SDI's Covert Reorientation." *Arms Control Today* 17 (June): 2–8.

Walsh, Edward J. 1988. *Democracy in the Shadows: Citizen Mobilization in the Wake of the Accident at Three Mile Island.* New York: Greenwood.

Walton, Douglas N. 1980. *Brain Death.* West Lafayette: Purdue UP.

———. 2001. "Persuasive Definitions and Public Policy Arguments." *Argumentation and Advocacy* 37: 117–32.

Weaver, Richard. [1953] 1985. *The Ethics of Rhetoric.* Davis, CA: Hermagoras.

———. 1970. *Language Is Sermonic.* Baton Rouge: Louisiana State UP.

Weitz, Morris. [1950] 1964. *Philosophy of the Arts.* New York: Russell.

———. 1956. "The Role of Theory in Aesthetics." *Journal of Aesthetics and Art Criticism* 15: 27–35.

———. 1967. "Analysis, Philosophical." In *The Encyclopedia of Philosophy*, edited by Paul Edwards, 1: 97–105. New York: Macmillan.

Wells, G. 1974. "Learning to Code Experience Through Language." *Journal of Child Language* 1: 243–69.

White, Justice Byron. 1986. *Opinion of the Court, Pope v. Illinois*, 481 U.S. 497–504.

Whorf, Benjamin Lee. 1956. *Language, Thought, and Reality.* Cambridge: MIT P.

Williams, David C. 1988. "Nuclear Criticism: In Pursuit of a 'Politically Enabling' Deconstructive Voice." *Journal of the American Forensic Association* 24: 193–205.

Wilshire, Bruce. 1968. *William James and Phenomenology: A Study of "The Principles of Psychology."* Bloomington: Indiana UP.

Wilson, P. 1986. "The U.S. Nuclear Test Program." 99th Cong., 2nd sess. *Congressional Record*, Apr. 30, vol. 132: S5048-S5050.

Winter, M. 1983. "Survivalism in the Schools." *Nuclear Times* (Jan.): 16–17.

Wittgenstein, Ludwig. [1921] 1974. *Tractatus Logico-Philosophicus*. Translated by D. F. Pears and B. F. McGuinness. London: Routledge.

———. 1958a. *The Blue and Brown Books.* New York: Harper.

———. 1958b. *Philosophical Investigations.* 3rd ed. Translated by G. E. M. Anscombe. New York: Macmillan.

Wood, Denis. 1992. *The Power of Maps.* New York: Guilford.

Yolton, John W. 2000. *Realism and Appearances.* Cambridge: Cambridge UP.

Youngner, Stuart J., Robert M. Arnold, and Renie Schapiro, eds. 1999. *The Definition of Death: Contemporary Controversies.* Baltimore: Johns Hopkins UP.

Zarefsky, David. 1986. *President Johnson's War on Poverty: Rhetoric and History.* Tuscaloosa: U of Alabama P.

———. 1990. *Lincoln, Douglas, and Slavery: In the Crucible of Public Debate.* Chicago: U of Chicago P.

———. 1998. "Definitions." In *Argument in a Time of Change: Definitions, Frameworks, and Critiques,* edited by James F. Klumpp, 1–11. Annandale: National Communication Association.

Ziff, Paul. 1953. "The Task of Defining a Work of Art." *Philosophical Review* 62: 58–78.

Ziman, John M. 1968. *Public Knowledge: An Essay Concerning the Social Dimension of Science.* Cambridge: Cambridge UP.

Index

Edward Schiappa holds the Paul W. Frenzel Chair of Liberal Arts at the University of Minnesota, where he is a professor and the director of graduate studies in the Department of Communication Studies. His work on classical and contemporary argumentation theory has appeared in many scholarly journals, and for a time he served as the editor of *Argumentation and Advocacy.* He is the author of *Protagoras and Logos: A Study in Greek Philosophy and Rhetoric* and *The Beginnings of Greek Rhetorical Theory* and the editor of *Warranting Assent: Case Studies in Argument Evaluation* and *Landmark Essays in Classical Greek Rhetoric.*